OFF THE BEATEN PATH®

Michigan

FIFTH EDITION

by
Jim DuFresne

The
Globe
Pequot
Press

Guilford, Connecticut

Illustrations on pages 6, 20, 28, 46, 53, 85, 88, 111, 120, 137, 147, 167, 178, and 196 by Steve Baldwin. Illustrations on pages 59, 79, and 206 by Carole Drong.
Cover and text design by Laura Augustine
Maps created by Equator Graphics © The Globe Pequot Press
Cover photo by Scott Shapiro/Index Stock

Library of Congress Cataloging-in-Publication Data

DuFresne, Jim.
      Michigan : off the beaten path / Jim DuFresne. —5th ed.
      p. cm. —(Off the beaten path series)
      Includes index.
      ISBN 0-7627-0269-9
      1. Michigan—Guidebooks. I. Title. II. Series.
  F564.3.D84   1999
  917.7404′43—dc21   99-21342
                                   CIP

Manufactured in the United States of America
Fifth Edition/Second Printing

To that wonderfully warm
and huggable person
I call Mom

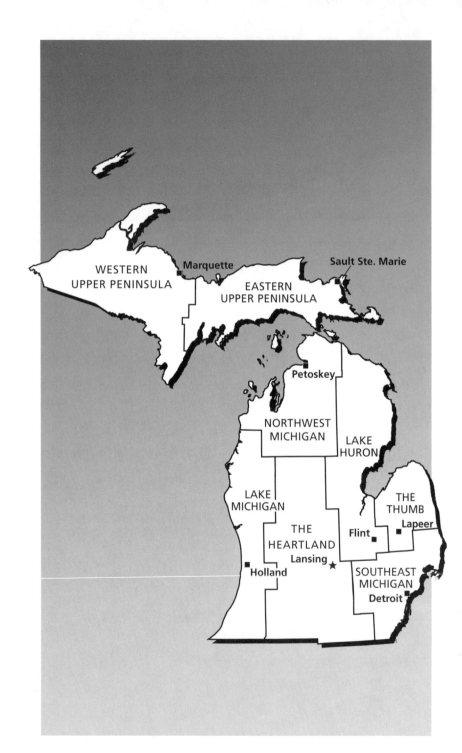

Contents

Introduction vi

Southeast Michigan 1

The Thumb 25

The Heartland 43

Lake Huron 71

Lake Michigan 99

Northwest Michigan 127

Eastern Upper Peninsula 157

Western Upper Peninsula 183

Indexes

  General 210

  Museums 213

  Parks and Natural Places 214

Introduction

Look at a map of the United States, spin a globe of the world, and the most prominent state is Michigan. It always stands out, regardless of the size of the map or how obscured the detail.

Michigan is set off from much of the country by water. Four of the five Great Lakes surround it and have turned its borders into 3,200 miles of lakeshore where you sit in the sand and look out on the watery horizon of the world's largest freshwater seas.

Michigan is inundated with water. It's not only outlined by blue, but its history was shaped by the Great Lakes, and today travelers search the state over for a bit of their own sand and surf. In Michigan, there is no short supply. Stand anywhere in the state and you are no more than 85 miles from the Great Lakes and only 6 miles from one of the 11,000 sparkling inland lakes or 36,000 miles of streams and rivers. Come winter, Michigan's water turns fluffy and white and gently lands all around, much to the delight of skiers.

Michigan is water, yet beaches and boating, swimming and sunbathing are only part of the state's attractions. To the adventurous traveler, to those who love to swing off the interstate highways onto the country roads that wander between the woods and the lakes, there are quaint villages to discover and shipwrecks to explore, art fairs and mushroom festivals to enjoy, wine-tasting tours to savor, a stretch of quiet trail to soothe the urban soul.

All you need is time, a good map of Michigan, and this book. The map can be obtained by writing the Michigan Travel Bureau at P.O. Box 30226, Lansing 48909, or by calling, toll-free, (800) 543–2937. The map will lead you away from the six-lane highways to the scenic country roads and then back again when you are ready to return home.

Michigan: Off the Beaten Path points out those half-hidden gems that travelers rejoice in discovering, from a lighthouse that has become a country inn to party-fishing boats that let novice anglers stalk and catch the Great Lakes' tastiest offering, the yellow perch. Because addresses, phone numbers, and hours of operation can change from summer to summer, the regional chapters and the appendix contain a list of tourist associations that can provide the most up-to-date information.

The same holds true for prices. Inflation, with its annual increases in everything from room rates and restaurant prices to entry fees at parks and museums, will quickly outdate anything listed. Therefore, only the prices for substantial items (rooms, meals, and major attractions) have been provided in this book to help readers judge whether a restaurant or hotel is affordable.

Most of all, more than this book and a map, you need time. Don't shortchange Michigan. Don't try to cover half the state in a weekend holiday. You will only be disappointed at the end of your trip. You could spend a summer exploring Michigan and never leave the shoreline. I have spent a lifetime here, yet my never-ending list of places to go and adventures to undertake only grows longer with each journey in the Great Lakes State.

Michigan Facts

Nickname: Great Lakes State

Capital: Lansing

Population: 9,295,297, eighth in the country

Area: 58,513 square miles, 23rd in the country

Admitted to Union: Michigan became the 26th state when it was admitted on January 26, 1837.

Major Cities: Detroit, population 1,027,974; Grand Rapids, 189,126; Warren, 144,868; Flint, 140,761; Lansing, 127,321; Ann Arbor, 109,592

Famous Residents: Henry Ford, Thomas Edison, Gen. George Custer, President Gerald Ford, Charles Lindbergh, Diana Ross, Stevie Wonder, the actor who played the Lone Ranger on the radio

National Park Units: Isle Royale National Park, Pictured Rocks National Lakeshore, Sleeping Bear Dunes National Lakeshore

Travel Information: The Michigan Travel Bureau, P.O. Box 30226, Lansing 48909; (800) 543–2937, will send you a free travel guide to Michigan along with a road map. The West Michigan Tourist Association, 1253 Front Avenue, Grand Rapids 49504; (800) 442–2084 or (616) 456–8557, covers accommodations, attractions, and visitor facilities in the western half of the Lower Peninsula. The Upper Peninsula Travel and Recreation Association, P.O. Box 400, Iron Mountain 49801; (800) 562–7134 or (906) 774–5480, covers the Upper Peninsula.

State Parks: For a guide to the Michigan State Parks system, contact the Michigan Department of Natural Resources, Parks & Recreation Division, Box 30257, Lansing 48909; (517) 373–9900.

INTRODUCTION

Major Newspapers: *Detroit Free Press, Detroit News, Grand Rapids Press, Flint Journal, Lansing State Journal*

Public Transportation: Michigan's major regional air center is Metro Airport, located in Romulus 15 miles southwest of Detroit. The main carrier is Northwest Airlines (800–225–2525), which uses Detroit as a major hub. Both Greyhound Bus Service (313–961–8011) and Amtrak (800–872–7245) maintain service throughout the state.

Climate: Michigan is split in the middle by the 45th Parallel; this northern position means that it has a very temperate, four-season climate. Summers reach the high 90s but rarely break triple digits. Winters can dip to minus 10 or 20 degrees at times in the northern half of the state but usually hover between 10 and 20 degrees in southern Michigan. Thanks to the Great Lakes, Michigan receives an abundance of snow, with some towns like Munising and Calumet totaling more than 250 inches by the end of March. Autumn colors are spectacular in the state, with trees beginning to change in late September in the Upper Peninsula and late October in Southern Michigan.

The prices and rates listed in this guidebook were confirmed at press time. We recommend, however, that you call establishments to obtain current information before traveling.

Maps provided are for reference only and should be used in conjunction with a road map. Distances suggested are approximate.

Southeast Michigan

Southeast Michigan, a region of seven counties, revolves around metropolitan Detroit, which sprawls into three of them. And Detroit revolves around automobiles. It's as simple as that.

Known best throughout the country as Motor City, Detroit carries several other titles, including Motown, after the recording company that produced such famous singers as Diana Ross and Stevie Wonder before it fled to Los Angeles from its studio on Woodward Avenue. The city is also home to the nation's oldest state fair (the Michigan State Fair dates to 1849) and the largest farmer's market.

Detroit and its neighboring suburbs wear many faces; some are good, some others are unjustly earned, but the least recognized one is that of a destination for travelers. Detroit is the sixth-largest city in the country, yet despite its size many tourists consider it very much "off the beaten path." Depart from the city and the rest of Southeast Michigan changes quickly, from the urban sprawl to the rolling hills and lakes of northern Oakland County, the blue water of St. Clair and Port Huron, and the culture and carefree college ways of Ann Arbor, the home of the University of Michigan.

Wayne County

Until the 1870s, Detroit was a commercial center for farmers, but at the end of that century the first automobiles appeared, as Ransom E. Olds and Henry Ford began tinkering with "horseless carriages." By 1903, Ford had organized the Ford Motor Company, and when he pioneered the assembly-line method of building cars and introduced the Model T, the vehicle for the common man, Detroit's place as the automobile capital of the world was established.

Cars are a way of life in Detroit. Michigan boasts of having the first mile of concrete rural highway (1909), the first traffic light (1915), and the first urban freeway free of those annoying stoplights (1942). The

Southeast Michigan

AUTHOR'S TOP TEN PICKS

Greenfield Village,
Dearborn; (313) 271–1620

Wright Museum of African
American History,
Detroit; (313) 494–5800

Motown Museum,
Detroit; (313) 875–2264

Ann Arbor Hands-On
Museum,
Ann Arbor;
(734) 995–KIDS

Eastern Market,
Detroit; (313) 202–1800

Belle Isle Aquarium,
Detroit; (313) 852–4141

River Raisin Battlefield
Visitor Center,
Monroe; (734) 243–7137

Ford Wyoming Drive-in,
Dearborn; (313) 846–6910

Lionel Train Company,
Mt. Clemens;
(810) 949–4100

People Mover,
Detroit; (313) 962–RAIL

best-known place to view this history of cars and their immense effect on the American way of life is **Greenfield Village and Henry Ford Museum** (313–271–1620), a 260-acre complex with one hundred historic buildings in Dearborn that has become the nation's largest indoor and outdoor museum.

Keep in mind that there are the museum and the village, each a separate attraction with a separate admission price and requiring at least a good part of a day to view. The Henry Ford Museum's main attraction is "The Automobile in American Life," an ode to the motor car culture that is a social history of twentieth-century America. Adjacent Greenfield Village features old buildings shipped in from all over the country, including Thomas Edison's laboratory from Menlo Park, New Jersey, Henry Ford's birthplace, and the Wright Brothers' cycle workshop.

The complex is located at 20900 Oakwood Boulevard and reached by following signs from Southfield Freeway. Admission is $12.50 each for the museum and the village, or $22.00 for a combination ticket good for two days. Serious history buffs purchase a two-day ticket.

For a more intimate view of the auto barons themselves, visit one of the many mansions that auto money built and historical societies have since preserved. **Fairlane**, the Henry Ford estate, is a fifty-six-room mansion located nearby on the University of Michigan–Dearborn campus. Built in 1915 at what was then an astronomical $1.8 million, the home is an extension of Ford's ingenuity wrapped up in his love for functionalism. It often hosted such dignitaries as Edison, President Herbert Hoover, and Charles Lindbergh. Tours begin underground among the massive turbines and generators that were designed by Ford and his friend Edison in the six-level powerhouse that made the estate self-sufficient in power, heat, light, even ice.

From the outside the house looks modest compared with other historic mansions. But inside you'll find such luxuries as a central vacuum cleaner, a sixty-five-extension phone system, a one-lane bowling alley, and a pool that has been covered and turned into a delightful restaurant

Fun Facts

that serves lunch. Guided tours lead you through the house and underground tunnels, show you where Edison used to sleep, and tell of April 7, 1947, when the Rogue River flooded and knocked out the powerhouse. That night, without heat, light, or phone service, Ford suffered a cerebral hemorrhage and died by candlelight.

To reach U of M–Dearborn, head west of Southfield Expressway on Michigan Avenue and then north on Greenfield Road, where signs point the way to the small campus. Guided tours of the national historic landmark are offered year-round. From April through December, Fairlane (313–593–5590) is also open daily with tours offered on the hour from 10:00 A.M. to 3:00 P.M. from Monday through Saturday and 1:00 to 4:30 P.M. Sunday. The rest of the year, there is only one tour per day. There is an admission fee.

Movie stars and fresh air . . . you do remember drive-in theaters, don't you? At the ***Ford Wyoming Drive-in*** in Dearborn, it's hard to forget them. Contrary to the popular belief that drive-ins are cinematic dinosaurs of the be-bop era, this motorized movieland in the hometown of Henry Ford is still packing them in.

Ford Wyoming is the largest drive-in complex in Michigan, with eight theaters—that's right, eight separate screens, each showing a different movie. On a good weekend there will be more than 2,000 cars and between 5,000 and 8,000 people watching a film.

Ford Wyoming Drive-in (313–846–6910 or 582–2200) is reached from I–94 by taking exit 210 and heading north on Wyoming Avenue. Some of the screens are entered from Wyoming Avenue and some from Ford Road.

To most people Detroit is Motor City, but to music lovers it will always be Motown, the birthplace of the famous record company that Berry Gordy, Jr., founded in 1958. Gordy started out with $800 and a small recording studio that was built in the back of his Grand Boulevard home. From Studio A emerged the distinct "Motown Sound" and such performers as Marvin Gaye, the Miracles, Gladys Knight and the Pips, the Supremes, The Jackson 5, and a very talented blind singer named Steveland Morris Hardaway, known now as Stevie Wonder. Eventually the famous Hitsville U.S.A. sign was hung on the front of the home, and Motown expanded into seven additional houses along the street before setting up its Woodward office.

TOP ANNUAL EVENTS

Montreux-Detroit Jazz Festival,
Downtown Detroit,
Labor Day weekend;
(313) 963–7622

International Freedom Festival,
Windsor and Detroit,
end of June;
(313) 923–8259

Michigan State Fair,
Detroit, August;
(313) 369–8250

Woodward Dream Cruise,
Birmingham, August;
(248) 433–3550

Ann Arbor Street Art Fairs,
Ann Arbor, July;
(800) 888–9487

Port Huron to Mackinac Island Yacht Race (Boat Night),
Port Huron, July;
(313) 822–1853

The company continued recording in Studio A until 1972, when it moved its operation to Los Angeles. What remains today at Hitsville U.S.A. is **Motown Museum,** a state historic site. The museum is two adjoining houses filled with gold record awards, old album covers, publicity photos, and even some old Temptations costumes that are viewed to the beat of Motown hits played continuously in every room. For most visitors the intriguing part is Studio A and its control booth, looking as it did thirty-five years ago, when Motown was a struggling recording company.

Motown Museum (313–875–2264) is located at 2648 West Grand Boulevard, 2 blocks west of the exit off the Lodge Freeway. The museum is open Sunday and Monday from noon to 5:00 P.M. and Tuesday through Saturday 10:00 A.M. to 5:00 P.M. There is a small admission fee.

Although Detroit has its mansions and its auto barons, it is known primarily as a blue-collar town, an assembly-line haven that has made it as ethnically diverse as any city in the country. Detroiters love their heritage, ethnic foods, music, and the traditions of an old way of life. The ethnic pride and the love of traditional foods can best be seen at the **Eastern Market**, a farmer's market that is said to be the largest of its kind (open to retailers rather than wholesalers) in the country. Two areas, one open-air, the other enclosed, and both decorated

Big Explosion

*I*n the spirit of international cooperation, Windsor and Detroit team up in late June for the Freedom Festival, which is highlighted with a fireworks display over the Detroit River. The fireworks are lit from a barge in the middle of the river and usually are watched by more than a million people oohing and aahing with every explosion. It is the largest fireworks show in North America.

If you're planning to attend, get there early, bring a lawn chair, and find a spot downtown within a few blocks of the river. Hart Plaza, naturally, is the prime spot to watch this brilliant performance.

with huge murals on the outside, are the heart of the market. On Tuesdays and Saturdays they overflow with shoppers, farmers, and vendors bartering for the freshest fruit, vegetables, flowers, meats, and cheeses to be found in the city. Everything from the farm is on sale here, from homemade bratwurst to live rabbits, and the market makes for an enjoyable stroll, even if you don't intend to buy anything.

Ringing the market are butcher shops, fish markets, and stores specializing in spices, nuts, and foods imported from around the world. The oldest shop is **R. Hirt Jr. Company** in a three-story red brick building that overlooks the market stalls. Rudolph Hirt, Jr., began his business in 1887 with a stall in the old Detroit Central Market, selling eggs, butter, and cheese from local farms. When land in Cadillac Square became too valuable to be used as a farmer's market, Hirt was one of the first to build a store in the new Eastern Market on land the city set aside in 1892.

The building still stands, and the old wooden cheese locker behind the counter is still used, although a much larger one has been built on

R. Hirt Jr. Company

the second floor. The second one was needed because 40 percent of Hirt's business is selling cheese: more than 250 kinds, from well-known Swiss cheese and French brie to the little-known Michigan Raw Milk Pinconning that is made in the Upper Peninsula. The shop also sells imported crackers and cookies, teas, jams, at least thirty kinds of mustard, olive oil, and other gastronomic items, all left stacked in their opened cases to make for leisurely and informal browsing. On the third floor, Hirt sells wicker baskets of all descriptions and sizes. You could purchase a basket on the third floor and then easily fill it with enough mouth-watering items on the first floor for a memorable gourmet dinner in the park.

To reach the Eastern Market, head downtown on I–75 and exit east on Mack Avenue. The market is 2 blocks east of the expressway, near Russell Avenue. R. Hirt Jr. is open Monday through Friday, 7:00 A.M. to 3:00 P.M., and Saturday, 7:00 A.M. to 2:00 P.M.

Restaurants also reflect the ethnically diverse, hard-working Detroiters who at nightfall put aside their jobs and enjoy themselves immensely with good food served in large portions at very reasonable prices.

Coney Island hot dogs and baseball are a summer tradition in the Motor City. Begin with the Detroit Tigers, an American League club that will move into its new stadium in 2000; after the ninth inning, head over to **Lafayette Coney Island**, Detroit's premier hot-dog place. Located where Lafayette and Michigan Avenues merge near Kennedy Square downtown, the porcelain white eatery with its male waiters is an institution in Detroit. The fare is Coney dogs (with loads of chopped onions, chili, and mustard), loose burgers (loose hamburger in a hot dog bun), and bean soup served on Formica counters and tables with paper napkins and truck-stop china. Yet arrive at midnight and you'll see patrons dressed in tuxedos enjoying a late-night hot dog after the symphony seated next to a couple of rabid baseball fans with a team pennant. Lafayette Coney Island (313–964–8198) is open twenty-four hours daily with hot dogs and loose burgers priced at around $2.00.

> **Fun Facts**
>
> *Lafayette Coney Island dates back to 1924 when Greek entrepreneur Bill Keros opened the restaurant, using the New York–style Coney Island stand concept. When his brother opened up American Coney Island right next door, they began slathering the hot dogs with chili to attract customers, inventing the Detroit version of a Coney Island. Today both restaurants are still battling it out side-by-side on Lafayette Avenue.*

A few blocks over at Monroe Street is lively **Greektown**, where a dozen restaurants, nightclubs, and Greek bakeries make it the liveliest spot in downtown Detroit. My favorite restaurant is the **New Hellas Cafe**, where flaming cheese and the cry of Opa! is a Detroit tradition. The best African-American cuisine in Detroit is at **Steve's Soul Food** (313–894–3464) at 8443 Grand River in west Detroit. Among its patrons are running back great Barry Sanders, who orders the smothered chicken between seasons, former Mayor Coleman Young, and singer Diana Ross, who once sent her chauffeur over for carry-out. Detroit's Polish community is centered around the city of Hamtramck, where Pope John Paul II once performed mass. At the **Polish Village Cafe** (313–874–5726) at Yehmans Street and Joseph Campau Avenue, you can dig into stuffed cabbage, pork goulash, and pierogi for less than $7.00.

It may not be "off the beaten path," but Detroit's Central Automated Transit System is definitely above the city streets. Better known as the **People Mover**, the mass transit project was opened in 1987 after several years of controversial delays and cost overruns. The 2.9-mile elevated track circles the downtown heart of Detroit. Its automated cars stop every three minutes at thirteen stations, each decorated with beautiful mosaics and other artwork. The ride costs only 50 cents and lasts fourteen minutes, but it gives an excellent overall view of the city from a superb vantage point. The best stretch comes when the cars wind around Cobo Hall and passengers see a panorama of the Detroit River and the skyline of Windsor, the Canadian city to the south. The People Mover (313–962–RAIL) operates from 7:00 A.M. to 11:00 P.M. Monday to Thursday, until midnight Friday and Saturday, and until 8:00 P.M. Sunday.

Motown move over. Long before there was Stevie Wonder or the Temptations, black musicians were picking up their horns to play on the steamers that in the mid-1800s were making regular runs to the Lake Erie resorts on Put-In-Bay.

By the early 1900s, Paradise Valley had emerged as a major force in the development of jazz talent, and then in 1922, the University of Michigan built the Graystone Ballroom along Woodward Avenue, and Detroit entered its golden era for jazz. Eventually Duke Ellington, Tommy Dorsey, Glenn Miller, Jimmie Lunceford, and many others played to capacity crowds before the ballroom was torn down in 1980 by its last owner—Motown.

Many of the furnishings that survived can now be seen in a replicated section of the ballroom at the **Graystone International Jazz Museum** along with posters, musical instruments, album covers, and other jazz memorabilia. The museum (313–963–3813) is located in suite 201 of

Detroit's Cool Jazz

*T*here's nothing like spending an evening in Detroit area nightclubs listening to jazz and blues. A list of clubs with the type of music they feature is found in **Metro Times**, a free entertainment newspaper. Some of the better-known clubs for local blues and jazz include Rinoceros at 265 Riopelle Street and the Soup Kitchen Saloon at 1585 Franklin Street in the Rivertown area. In Hamtramck there is the Attic Bar at 11667 Joseph Campau Avenue, a true blues bar where customers take over the piano when a band isn't around, and in Ann Arbor live jazz is found at Bird of Paradise, 207 South Ashley Street.

the Book Tower Building, 1249 Washington Boulevard. Hours are 11:00 A.M. to 4:00 P.M. Tuesday through Friday; there is a small admission fee.

The Detroit River, which connects Lake St. Clair with Lake Erie, was the avenue that the city's first residents—the French in 1701—used to arrive in Southeast Michigan. The river remains a focal point of activities for Detroiters, with several parks lining its banks and one—Belle Isle—located in the middle of it. Reached by a bridge at East Jefferson and Grand Boulevard, the island park features the **Belle Isle Aquarium** (313–852–4141), which opened to the public in 1904, making it one of the oldest freshwater aquariums in the country.

The center features thousands of fish in dozens of large tanks, everything from a school of piranhas and a 4-foot-long alligator gar to common bluegill, bass, and rainbow trout. One of the most popular tanks contains an electric eel, and when this fish is fed, at 10:30 A.M., 12:30 P.M., and 2:30 P.M. daily, it is an electrifying affair. The handlers drop a microphone into the tank so onlookers can hear the fish-made electric charges. The aquarium is open daily 10:00 A.M. to 5:00 P.M. There is a small admission fee.

Almost next door to the aquarium on the island is **Dossin Great Lakes Museum** (313–852–4051), which traces the sailing history of the Great Lakes in several rooms of displays and hands-on exhibits and a video room. A highlight of the museum is the preserved pilothouse from a Great Lakes freighter, which actually looks out on the Detroit River. The museum is open 10:00 A.M. to 5:00 P.M. Wednesday through Sunday. A small donation is requested at the door.

If the day is nice, you can spend an afternoon at Hart Plaza at the foot of Woodward Avenue overlooking the Detroit River and Windsor. For an even a better view of the waterfront, **Diamond Jack River Tours** (313–843–7676) offers two-hour cruises on the Detroit River that depart from Hart Plaza. The cruises are $10 per person.

Detroit's Cultural Center, clustered around Woodward Avenue and Kirby Street, is dominated by the **Detroit Institute of Arts** (313–833–7900). Thanks to auto baron wealth accumulated in the early 1900s, the DIA is considered one of the top art collections in the country. It is known for its Italian Renaissance, Dutch-Flemish and German Expressionist art, but the most-viewed work is probably Diego Rivera's mural, *Detroit Industry*, which fills a room and reflects the city's blue-collar work ethic. Hours are 11:00 A.M. to 4:00 P.M. Wednesday through Friday and until 5:00 P.M. on Saturday and Sunday. Adult admission is $4.00.

Within easy walking distance at East Warren Avenue and Brush Street is the equally impressive *Wright Museum of African American History* (313–494–5800), the largest such museum in the country. The main exhibit depicts the passage to and enslavement of Africans in America and includes a full-scale model of slaves chained up on an eighteenth-century ship that will leave you chilled. Hours are 9:30 A.M. to 5:00 P.M. Tuesday through Sunday. Adult admission is $5.00.

In 1975, the Michigan Department of Natural Resources opened *Maybury State Park* on a farm in the northwest corner of Wayne County. It was an unusual place to establish a state park, but Maybury is an unusual state park. The idea was to preserve a "living farm" close to the city so that residents, especially children, who have never experienced the sights, sounds, and—yes—smells of a working farm would have the opportunity to do so nearby. The area consists of several barns where visitors get a close, hanging-on-the-fence view of chickens, pigs, cows, goats, sheep, horses, and other typical farm animals. There is also a display of old farming equipment, but newer plows and harvesters are used by the staff that actually works the land. Kids not only get to feed the animals but also can view newborn chicks in the brooder room, modern tractors rumbling along, and huge draft horses pulling a plow through fields of corn, oats, beans, and other typical Michigan crops.

Also within the 1,000-acre state park are natural areas of meadows and forests with hiking trails and bike paths. A park concessionaire runs a horse stable with 8 miles of horse trails that during the winter are used by Nordic skiers, who can rent equipment at the park. But by far the most unusual aspect of Maybury is its Living Farm, which is open daily from 10:00 A.M. to 7:00 P.M. in the summer and 10:00 A.M. until 5:00 P.M. in the winter. Maybury State Park (248–349–8390) has an entrance on Eight Mile Road, 5 miles west of I–275. A vehicle fee is charged to enter the park.

In 1882 the Plymouth Iron Windmill Company began to manufacture and give away small BB guns to farmers to encourage them to purchase one of its windmills. Within four years, the northwest corner of Wayne County was well "windmilled," but the company kept producing the air rifles. Eventually Plymouth Iron Windmill Company became Daisey Manufacturing Company, and this small town was known as the "air rifle capital of the world" until the operations were moved to Arkansas in 1958.

You could learn about the start of Daisey air rifles and see a collection of the earliest models at the *Plymouth Historical Museum*. The museum also has many other exhibits, period rooms, and even a depiction of "downtown Plymouth" in the early 1900s, but it is the display of Daisey air rifles that brings back fond memories of tin cans in the backyard to so many of us.

To reach the Plymouth Historical Museum (734–455–8940) from I–275, get off at exit 28, head west on Ann Arbor Road, and then turn north on Main Street. Hours are 1:00 to 4:00 P.M. Wednesday, Thursday, and Saturday, and 2:00 to 5:00 P.M. Sunday. There is a small admission fee.

Monroe County

eneral George Armstrong Custer may have staged his ill-fated "last stand" at the Little Bighorn River in Montana, but he grew up in Monroe, Michigan. Custer was actually born in Rumley, Ohio, but spent most of his youth, until he entered a military academy at the age of sixteen, living with his half sister in this city along Lake Erie. Even after he became a noted brigadier general during the Civil War, Custer continued to return to Monroe, and in 1864 he married Elizabeth Bacon, his boyhood sweetheart, here.

Custer's intriguing life can be traced at the **Monroe County Historical Museum**, which features the largest collection of the general's personal artifacts in the country. The Custer exhibit room occupies a fourth of the museum floor and focuses on his youth in Monroe and his distinguished Civil War career rather than his well-known days on the western plains. There is an overcoat of buffalo hide that he wore during a winter campaign in 1868 and a buckskin suit that is impressive with its beadwork and porcupine quills. Custer was an avid outdoorsman and also a fine taxidermist. It comes as a surprise to many that Custer enjoyed mounting the game animals he hunted, and housed in the museum along with his favorite Remington buffalo rifle are many mounted game animals.

The museum also has displays on Monroe's early history, which dates back to French missionaries in 1634. But it is the life and tragic death of General Custer that most people find fascinating. The Monroe County Historical Museum (734–243–7137) is at 126 South Monroe Street in the heart of the city and is open Wednesday through Sunday from 10:00 A.M. to 5:00 P.M. During the summer through September, it is open daily. There is a small admission fee.

Unless you are a military buff, you might not realize that the Massacre of the River Raisin was among the largest battles in the War of 1812 and produced more American casualties than any other conflict. Now the city's newest museum, the **River Raisin Battlefield Visitor Center** is dedicated to what many historians believe became the turning point in the conflict with Great Britain.

After the disastrous opening months of the War of 1812 in which Mackinac Island, Chicago, and Detroit had fallen, two of them without even a shot fired, an elderly Revolutionary War veteran, General James Winchester, was sent to Michigan with almost 1,000 men. The large American force set up camp on an open field on the north side of the river. But in the pre-dawn darkness of January 22, almost 600 British regulars with six cannons and 800 Indians attacked. The fighting raged for twenty minutes and then turned into a panicked flight for Ohio for Winchester's army. Of the 400 Americans who ran, 220 were killed, another 147, including Winchester himself, were captured, and only 33 managed to escape to safety. The next day Indians returned to plunder the homes, scalp the wounded, and toss the bodies into burning homes. More than sixty unarmed Americans were killed, and a nation was horrified. Soon "Remember the Raisin!" became a battle cry that led U.S. troops to victory in the old Northwest.

Strange As It Sounds

The center of the University of Michigan campus is the Diag, a parklike opening that extends from State Street to South University Avenue. The bronze seal in the center was donated by the Class of 1953, and legend has it that any freshman who steps on it before taking his or her first exam at U of M will fail the test.

Nearby on the west side of State Street is the Michigan Union. It was on the steps of this imposing building that John F. Kennedy first announced his vision of the Peace Corps in 1960 while campaigning for the White House.

All this history has been carefully preserved and clearly presented at the battlefield visitor center. Its most impressive display is a fourteen-minute fiberoptic map presentation. On two wall-size maps, the story of the River Raisin is retold with the Americans, British, and Indians, as colorful lights, maneuvering and taking up positions in front of you. The visitor center (734–243–7137) is reached from I–75 by taking exit 14 and heading west on Elm Street. The center is open 10 A.M. to 5 P.M. daily from Memorial Day through Labor Day and on Saturday and Sunday the rest of the year. There is no admission charge.

Washtenaw County

Trendy Ann Arbor, the cultural capital of Southeast Michigan (and some say the entire state), is the site of the University of Michigan, the "Harvard of the West." The university dominates the city, its buildings and campus entwined in the town's landscape. It provides

Fun Facts

The University of Michigan was founded in 1837 when the state legislature set aside U of M's original forty-acre campus. Classes were held in the old Mason Hall in the fall of 1841 with a student body of seven and faculty of two.

many of Ann Arbor's top attractions, such as the *Kelsey Museum of Archaeology* (734–764–9304), a renowned collection of art and artifacts, including mummies, from Egyptian, Greek, Roman, and classical Mediterranean cultures. On Saturdays in the fall, Ann Arbor is U of M football; the largest stadium crowds in the country (112,000) gather to cheer on the Wolverines.

But there is another side to this college town, one that children will appreciate, and it begins at the *Ann Arbor Hands-On Museum*. This is no stuffy hall with an endless row of glass-enclosed displays. The entire museum is devoted to participatory exhibits—more than eighty on four floors—and the concept that kids learn by doing. Housed in the classic Central Fire House, the museum was dedicated on September 28, 1982, the one hundredth anniversary of the building. Inside, visitors try exhibits such as the sand pendular, a suspended funnel that you fill with sand and swing to make various patterns. There is also the bubble capsule, where participants step into a ring of soap film and slowly raise a cylinder bubble around them until it pops. Some exhibits use computers and deal with complex theories; others are as simple as the mystery boxes: A child sticks in a hand and attempts to guess what is touched. All the exhibits come with a printed explanation that is appreciated mostly by the parents.

The Ann Arbor Hands-On Museum (734–995–KIDS) is recommended for children eight years old and older. It is at Huron Street and Fifth Avenue, which can be reached by following Business US 23 (Main Street) from M 14 north of the city or from I–94 by exiting to US 23 and then to Washtenaw Avenue. Hours are Tuesday through Friday from 10:00 A.M. to 5:30 P.M., Saturday from 10:00 A.M. to 5:00 P.M., and Sunday from 1:00 to 5:00 P.M. There is an admission fee.

There are no mountains in Southeast Michigan, but that doesn't stop the region from being a mecca for mountain biking. In large part because of cycle-crazy Ann Arbor, the trails at *Pinckney Recreation Area* have been transformed into a playground for off-road cycling. It's estimated that more than 120,000 mountain bikers from Ohio, Indiana, and Illinois as well as Michigan visit the park annually to ride the challenging 17.5-mile Potawatomi Trail, the 5-mile Crooked Lake Trail, or the 2-mile Silver Lake Trail.

The trailhead for all trails is in the park's Silver Lake Day-Use Area reached from US 23 by taking exit 49 and heading west on North

Territorial Road to Dexter-Townhall Road. Head north on Dexter-Townhall Road past the park headquarters (734–426–4913) to the day-use area. In Ann Arbor bicycles can be rented at the Student Bike Shop (734– 662–6986) at 607 South Forest Street.

Oakland County

It's 4:00 P.M. in Birmingham and you're sipping tea from fine china in a setting that includes fresh-cut flowers, silver platters of cakes and other tempting edibles, a fire in a fireplace of imported Italian marble, and a tuxedo-clad piano player, er, excuse me, pianist.

Must be tea at the Townsend. The afternoon ritual, in all its elegance, takes place throughout the week in the **Townsend Hotel**, the most affluent hotel in this ritzy suburb of Detroit. Built in 1988, the hotel has eighty-seven rooms and fifty-two suites on three floors, and among its guests have been entertainers such as Madonna, Michael Jackson, Paul McCartney, and New Kids on the Block. (Remember them?) Just about anybody who plays in Detroit stays at the Townsend.

Have afternoon tea here, and who knows? Maybe you'll see Billy Idol stroll in. It has happened before. From Woodward Avenue in downtown Birmingham, turn west onto Townsend Street, and the hotel is reached in 3 blocks. There is one seating for afternoon tea at 3:00 P.M.

Big Leaguers in Motown

There is plenty of big league action in Southeast Michigan. The Detroit Pistons and the Detroit Vipers play basketball and hockey, respectively, at The Palace of Auburn Hills (tickets: 248–377–0100). The Detroit Red Wings play at Joe Louis Arena (313–396–7544) though it is almost impossible to get Red Wing tickets. The Detroit Lions play football in the Pontiac Silverdome (248–335–4151) but have decided to return to downtown Detroit. In 2000, the Detroit Tigers (313–962–4000) moved to a new stadium in downtown Detroit after playing for almost a century in venerable Tiger Stadium (formerly Briggs Stadium), where Babe Ruth and Ty Cobb use to swat home runs.

If you just want to see where the big leaguers play, The Palace (tours: 248–377–8278) offers tours Monday through Friday from 9:00 a.m. to 4:00 p.m. Tours include going behind the scenes to see the Palace broadcast center, the hands-on exhibits that it calls the "NBA Hall of Fame," and a look at the owner's suite, visitors' locker room, and the press lounge. Admission is $5.00 per adults and $3.00 for children.

Fun Facts

The country's first shopping mall, Northland, was built in Southfield in Oakland County in 1954.

Call the Townsend Hotel at (248) 642–7900 for reservations.

The urban sprawl of southeast Michigan runs its course to Pontiac, but from there the terrain changes quickly to the rolling hills, lakes, and woods of northern Oakland. A drive of less than an hour from the heart of Detroit can remove you from the city and bring you to the porch steps of a rustic cabin on a small pond in a wooded area where whitetail deer often pass by. ***Roston Cabin*** in Holly Recreation Area makes a weekend spent in the woods as comfortable and warm as sitting around the fireplace at night. The cabin is snug and tight but still rustic and secluded enough to make it seem like an adventure in the woods—even though the car is parked right outside.

Built by the Roston family as a weekend cottage in the early 1940s, the cabin was obtained by the park, which began renting it out in 1984. It's a classic cabin built with walls of logs, polished planked floors, and red-checkered curtains on the windows. There is electricity, and the kitchen features an electric stove and refrigerator as well as a table, benches, and a wood stove. The sleeping room is larger, with a set of bunks and an easy chair facing a fieldstone fireplace. Overlooking the cozy room is a loft, the warmest part of the cabin at night, with four more mattresses. Outside you'll find a vault toilet, woodshed, a hand pump for water, and a barbecue grill.

It's necessary to reserve the cabin in advance by calling the park headquarters, and, surprisingly, the most popular time to rent it is during the winter when families arrive to cross-country ski on the unplowed park roads around the lakes. The overnight rate for the cabin is $45, and reservations can be made by contacting Holly Recreation Area (248–634–8811). The recreation area is reached by taking Grange Hall Road (exit 101) east off I–75.

Many people exit I–75 at Grange Hall Road and head west to explore the historical town of Holly. Established in the early 1800s, Holly was a sleepy little hamlet until 1855, when the Detroit-Milwaukee Railroad reached the town, bringing immediate growth and prosperity with the twenty-five trains that passed through daily. Martha Street, near the tracks, was the site of the Holly Hotel, many saloons, and frequent brawls. In 1880 an uproar between local rowdies and a traveling circus left so many beaten and bruised that the street became known as ***Battle Alley***. The most famous moment in Battle Alley's history was on August 28, 1908, when Carry Nation, the notorious "Kansas Saloon Smasher," arrived in Holly at the request of the local Prohibition committee. The next day Nation, with umbrella in hand and her pro-temperance supporters a step behind her, invaded the saloons, smashing whiskey bottles, clubbing patrons, and preaching about the sins of "demon rum." Nation created the biggest flurry at the hotel, where she entered the "Dispensing Room" and attacked the painting of a nude over the bar.

Today the residents of Holly celebrate the occasion with a *Carry Nation Festival* the second weekend of September, highlighted by a reenactment of that special day in 1908 along with a parade, arts and crafts booths, and much food, entertainment, and, yes, a few swigs of the very stuff Nation campaigned against. Battle Alley and its hundred-year-old Victorian buildings have been restored as a string of twelve specialty shops that include antiques markets both along the alley and on nearby streets.

The *Holly Hotel*, which was built in 1891 and suffered through two devastating fires, the second in 1978, has since been completely restored, including the painting of the nude. It is now listed on the National Register of Historic Places but no longer provides lodging. Instead, the hotel is a fine restaurant, known for both its classic and its creative cuisine, all set in a Victorian tradition that reflects its birth during the railroad era. The main dining room, with its pedestal tables, soft glow of gas lamps, and red velvet wingback chairs, is the stage for such entrees as medallions of beef with morel mushroom sauce, fillet of beef Wellington, and sauteed Michigan rainbow trout. The hotel also provides gourmet picnic baskets that include not only appetizers, dinner, desserts, and wine but also linen, flatware, candles, and a map of good picnic spots in the area.

The Holly Hotel (248–634–5208) is open for lunch Monday through Saturday from 11:00 A.M. until 3:00 P.M. and for dinner Monday through Thursday from 5:00 to 10:00 P.M., Friday and Saturday from 5:00 to 11:00 P.M., and Sunday from noon to 8:00 P.M. Dinner prices range from $18 to $25, and reservations are recommended.

Michigan has more than its share of unusual bed-and-breakfasts. You can book a room in a lighthouse, on a two-masted schooner, at a farm, in a home that doubles as a microbrewery. Now you can also make reservations to spend a night at the country's first B&B train.

Coe Rail has renovated a pair of classic Pullman sleeper cars to offer people the opportunity to wake up on the rails. Owners claim their *Star Clipper Train* is the "first railroad to offer bed-and-breakfast service on rail."

If you don't have a night to spare, just drop by for dinner. Coe Rail has also re-created the romance of dining on the rail with prime rib, seafood, or such entrees as Duet au Poivre Pork in the train tradition of elegance with sparkling crystal, fine china, fresh-starched linens, and ever-changing scenery through the windows. Each evening features a three-hour rail excursion, with guests indulging in a five-course dinner while the train passes the new Depot Park in Wixom, the wooded West Bloomfield Bird Sanctuary, and Woodpecker Lake.

Star Clipper Bed and Breakfast (248–960–9440) is reached from I–96 by taking exit 159 and heading north on Wixom Road to Pontiac Trail. Continue north on Pontiac Trail into Walled Lake. Coe Rail Depot is on Pontiac Trail just past Maple Road. The Star Clipper departs Tuesday, Wednesday, Thursday, and Saturday at 7:00 P.M., Friday at 7:30 P.M., and Sunday at 5:00 P.M. year-round. A night on the train, which is offered only on Saturday, includes dinner and is $281.00 per couple. The dinner excursion only is $69.50.

Macomb County

I n the fall one of the favorite activities in Southeast Michigan is a trip to a cider mill. Parents pack the kids in the car and head out to the edge of the county where a river turns an old wooden water wheel. The wheel is the source of power for the mill, which crushes apples to extract the dark brown juice and refine it into cider, truly one of Michigan's culinary delights. After viewing the operation, visitors can purchase jugs of cider, cinnamon doughnuts, and sticky caramel apples and then retreat to a place along the river. Here they enjoy a feast in the midst of brilliant fall colors, in the warmth of an Indian summer, and with the fragrance of crushed apples floating by.

Cider mills ring the metropolitan Detroit area, but one of the oldest and most-colorful lies right on the border of Oakland and Macomb Counties west of Rochester on Avon Road (Twenty-Three Mile Road). *Yates Cider Mill* was built in 1863 along the banks of the Clinton River and began its long history as a grist mill. It has been a water-powered operation ever since, but in 1876 it began making cider, and today the water wheel still powers the apple elevator, grinders, and press as well as generating electricity for the lights inside. The mill can produce 300 gallons of cider per hour, all of which is needed in the fall to meet the demand of visitors who enjoy their treat around the huge red barn or across the street on the banks of the Clinton River. Yates Cider Mill (810–651–8300) is open daily from 9:00 A.M. until 7:00 P.M. from September through November, and from noon until 5:00 P.M. Saturday and Sunday from December until May.

You won't find much apple cider to sip, but an equally interesting mill in Macomb County is the focal point at **Wolcott Mill Metropark**. Built in 1847 on the North Branch of the Clinton River, Wolcott Mill was a grist and feed operation for more than a century, commercially milling as late as 1967. Today the mill's grain-grinding machinery is still turning for visitors while exhibits and interpreters provide a glimpse of a bygone era.

The 2,380-acre park also includes several other historical buildings, a short nature trail, and a farm learning center where children can have contact with barnyard animals. Wolcott Mill Metropark (810–749–5997) is southeast of Romeo, with the mill entrance off Kunstman Road just north of Twenty-Nine Mile Road. Building hours for the park are 10:00 A.M. to 5:00 P.M. Wednesday through Sunday with longer weekend hours during the summer and fall. There is a vehicle fee to enter the park.

Strange As It Sounds

The 1950s are alive and well at Eddie's Drive-in (810–469–2345), a landmark burger place at 36111 Jefferson Avenue in Harrison Township. It's a nightly show in the summer when hep cats and cool chicks show off their hot rods while waitresses on roller skates serve you shakes and fries to the be-bop music of that golden era. Eddie's is open from April to mid-October.

If there was ever a factory tour made for Christmas, it's the one offered at the **Lionel Train Company** near Mt. Clemens. The famous toy train company was founded in 1900 in New York City after Joshua Lionel Cowen combined his newly invented dry cell battery with a small electric motor and a model train. His original intention was to create a window display that would attract shoppers into the large department stores. But what the holiday shoppers wanted to buy was the train itself, and railroading with toy trains was born.

The most important dates to Michigan toy train lovers, however, are 1970, when Lionel moved its operations to the Mt. Clemens area, and February 1992, when it opened its Lionel Trains Visitor Center. The tours include cardboard engineer hats for children, a short film on the history of the company, and a visit to the center's layout room, which features a 560-square-foot stage complete with mountains, towns, tunnels, and 1,000 feet of track for eight Lionel trains and more than a hundred cars.

To reach the visitor center (810–949–4100, ext. 1211), head east on M 59 through Utica and then turn north on Romeo Plank Road and east on Twenty-Three Mile Road. The posted entrance to the Lionel Train Company is reached in 7 miles. Tours are offered at 10:00 A.M., 3:00 P.M., and 4:00 P.M. on Wednesday and Thursday, 10:00 A.M., 1:30 P.M., and 2:30 P.M. on Friday, and at 9:00 A.M., 10:00 A.M., 11:00 A.M., and noon on Saturday. There is no admission fee, but tours are by reservation only.

St. Clair County

This county is often referred to as the Bluewater region of Michigan because it is bounded by Lake St. Clair to the south, Lake Huron to the north, and the St. Clair River to the east. M 29 circles the north side of Lake St. Clair and then follows the river to Port Huron, passing small towns and many bait shops, marinas, and shoreline taverns advertising walleye and perch fish fries. The most charming town on the water is St. Clair, 15 miles south of Port Huron and a major shipbuilding center in the early 1900s. The city recently renovated its downtown section, centering it on **Palmer Park**, which residents claim has one of the longest boardwalks in the world facing freshwater. The favorite activity on the 1,500-foot riverwalk is watching the Great Lakes freighters that glide by exceptionally close, giving land-bound viewers a good look at the massive boats and their crews. The second-favorite activity is walleye fishing. The St. Clair River is renowned for this fish, and anglers can be seen throughout the summer tossing a line from the riverwalk, trying to entice the walleye with minnows or nightcrawlers.

Above the walkway is a wide, grassy bank filled with sunbathers, kids playing, and, in mid-June, the arts and crafts booths of the **St. Clair Art Fair,** a popular festival along the river. Call the St. Clair Art Association (810–329–9576) for the exact dates and times. The riverwalk ends to the north at the **St. Clair Inn** (800–482–8327), a historic hotel that was built in 1926 and today features outdoor dining in a courtyard overlooking the river.

Port Huron, a city of 30,000, is the site of the Bluewater Bridge, the international crossing between Michigan and Sarnia, Ontario. It is also recognized throughout the state as the start of the Port Huron–Mackinac Sailboat Race in late July. On the eve of the event, known as **Boat Night**, the downtown area of Water, Lapeer, and Quay Streets, which borders the docks on the Black River, becomes congested with block parties. Sailors, local people, and tourists mingle in a festival that spreads throughout the streets, the yacht clubs, and even onto the sailboats themselves.

On the quieter side is the historical aspect of Port Huron with its many stately homes, one of which has been renovated into *The Victorian Inn*. Located at 1229 Seventh Street in a neighborhood of nineteenth-century mansions, the home was built in 1896 by James Davidson, who owned a dry-goods company in town. Two families purchased the home in 1983 and established a fine restaurant on the main floor, a pub in the basement, and a place of lodging upstairs. Listed on the State Register of Historic Places, the home is an excellent example of nineteenth-century craftsmanship with its hand-carved oak woodwork, leaded-glass windows, and plasterwork and trim on the ceilings. Patrons enjoy their meals in one of three small rooms that make up the dining area, one with a massive fireplace. The menu changes every month but generally features entrees of beef, fish, and chicken and includes full explanations of every dish served. The dinners are excellent, and the dessert tray beyond the willpower of most people.

The restaurant (810–984–1437) is open Tuesday through Saturday from 11:30 A.M. until 1:30 P.M. for lunch and from 5:00 to 8:30 P.M. for dinner. Reservations are required. Evening entrees range from $18 to $32, while lodging upstairs is $85 to $125, depending on the room, for double occupancy.

A short walk from the Victorian Inn is the *Port Huron Museum of Arts and History* (810–982–0891) at 1115 Sixth Street. The museum combines an art gallery with collections of natural history and artifacts from Port Huron's past. Included are bones and displays of the prehistoric mammoths that roamed Michigan's Thumb 10,000 years ago, and memorabilia of Thomas Edison's boyhood home, which was located in the city. A popular attraction is the reconstructed

The Victorian Inn

Edison in Port Huron

*P*ort Huron's most famous resident was not its happiest one. Thomas Edison moved to the city with his family when he was seven years old but quit school after only three days when a teacher wrote that the future inventor was "addled." His mother taught him at home, and Edison, already fascinated with science and chemistry, turned the family basement into his personal laboratory.

To pay for the chemicals and equipment, he took a job selling candy and newspapers on the Grand Trunk Railroad's commute to Detroit and back. The Port Huron Depot that he worked out of is now the Bluewater Area Convention and Visitors Bureau (800–852–4242), and in its lobby are historical displays and artifacts from Edison's boyhood days.

But Edison left the town as a teen to seek telegraph work and eventually his fortune out east at Menlo Park, New Jersey. "I do not think that any living human being will ever see me there again," he wrote to his father when he was thirty years old and already a well-known inventor. "I don't want you to stay in that hole of a Port Huron, which contains the most despicable remnants of the human race that can be found on earth."

Historians said that over time, Edison softened his views on Port Huron and later in life did return several times, mostly to attend family funerals.

pilothouse of a Great Lakes freighter. All the furnishings were taken from various ships, and visitors can work the wheel, signal the alarm horn, and ring the engine bell. All around the pilothouse is a huge mural that gives the impression you are guiding the vessel into Lake Huron. The museum, housed in a 1904 Carnegie library, is open Wednesday through Sunday from 1:00 to 4:30 P.M. There is a small admission fee.

PLACES TO STAY IN SOUTHEAST MICHIGAN

ANN ARBOR
Comfort Inn,
2455 Carpenter Road,
(734) 973–6100

Weber's Inn,
3050 Jackson Road,
(734) 769–2500

AUBURN HILLS
Courtyard by Marriott,
1296 Opdyke Road,
(248) 373–1296

DEARBORN
Dearborn Inn,
20301 Oakwood Boulevard,
(313) 271–2700

Econo Lodge,
23730 Michigan Avenue,
(313) 565–7250

Super 8 Motel,
2101 South Telegraph Road,
(313) 274–0001

DETROIT
Shorecrest Motor Inn,
1361 East Jefferson Avenue,
(313) 568–3000

The Blanche House Inn,
506 Parkview Drive,
(313) 822–7090

Atheneum Suite Hotel,
1000 Brush Street,
(800) 772–2323

MOUNT CLEMENS
Comfort Inn,
1 North River Road,
(810) 949–9110

TROY
Drury Inn,
575 West Big Beaver Road,
(248) 528–3330

WARREN
Budgetel Inn,
30900 Van Dyke Road,
(800) 428–3438

Motel 6,
Thirteen Mile and Van
Dyke Roads,
(810) 826–9300

WOODHAVEN
Woodhaven Inn,
21700 West Road,
(734) 676–8000

**PLACES TO EAT IN
SOUTHEAST MICHIGAN**

ANN ARBOR
Gandy Dancer (seafood),
401 Depot Street,
(734) 769–0592

The Blue Nile (Ethiopian),
221 East Washington
Avenue,
(734) 998–4746

Arbor Brewing Co.
(brewpub),
114 East Washington
Avenue,
(734) 213–1393

Zingerman's Delicatessen,
422 Detroit Street,
(734) 663–0974

CLARKSTON
The Union (American),
54 South Main Street,
(248) 620–6100

DEARBORN
Big Fish (seafood),
700 Town Center Drive,
(313) 336–6350

DETROIT
Atwater Block Bewery
(brewpub),
237 Joseph Campau Avenue,
(313) 393–2337

New Hellas Cafe,
583 Monroe Street,
(313) 961–5544

Fishbone's Rhythm
Kitchen Cafe (Cajun),
400 Monroe Street,
(313) 965–4600

Jacoby's (German),
624 Brush Street,
(313) 962–7067

Roma Cafe (Italian),
3401 Riopelle Street,
(313) 824–1000

Dakota Inn Rathskeller
(German),
17324 John R Road,
(313) 867–9722

Tres Vite (American),
2203 Woodward Avenue,
(313) 964–4144

Traffic Jam (brewpub),
511 West Canield Street,
(313) 831–9470

Selected Southeast Michigan Tourism Bureaus

Ann Arbor Area Convention and Visitors Bureau,
120 West Huron Street, Ann Arbor 48104;
(800) 888–9487

Bluewater Area Tourist Bureau
(Port Huron and St. Clair),
520 Thomas Edison Parkway, Port Huron 48060;
(800) 852–4242

Metropolitan Detroit Convention and Visitors Bureau,
211 West Fort Street, Detroit 48226;
(313) 202–1800

Monroe County Tourism Bureau,
111 East First Street, Monroe 48161;
(800) 252–3011

Ypsilanti Area Visitors and Convention Bureau,
301 West Michigan Avenue, Ypsilanti 48197;
(734) 483–4444

Xochimilco (Mexican),
3409 Bagley Street,
(313) 843–0179

FARMINGTON
Bone Yard Bar-B-Que (ribs),
31006 Orchard Lake Road,
(248) 851–7000

FERNDALE
Howe's Bayou (Cajun),
22848 Woodward Avenue,
(248) 691–7145

NORTHVILLE
Geniti's Hole-in-the-Wall
(Italian),
108 East Main Street,
(248) 349–0522

OAK PARK
Bread Basket Deli,
26052 Greenfield Road,
(248) 968–0022

ROYAL OAK
BD's Mongolian Barbecue
(stirfry),
310 South Main Street,
(248) 398–7755

Inn Season Cafe
(vegetarian),
500 East Fourth Street,
(248) 547–7916

SOUTHFIELD
Sweet Lorraine's Cafe
(American),
29101 Greenfield Road,
(248) 559–5985

TROY
Charley's Crab (seafood),
5498 Crooks Road,
(248) 879–2060

WATERFORD
Mitch's (ribs),
4000 Cass-Elizabeth
Lake Road,
(248) 682–1616

Lion's Den (American),
4444 M 59,
(248) 674–2251

OTHER ATTRACTIONS

Meadowbrook Hall,
Rochester

Detroit Science Center,
Detroit

Cranbrook Institute of
Science, Bloomfield Hills

Detroit Zoo, Royal Oak

Holocaust Memorial
Center, West Bloomfield

Yankee Air Museum,
Belleville

Fox Theatre, Detroit

U of M Museum of Art,
Ann Arbor

U of M Exhibit Museum of
Natural History, Ann Arbor

Eddy Geology Center,
Chelsea

The Thumb

Within the mitten that is the Lower Peninsula of Michigan, there is a special area known as "the Thumb." The state's most recognized appendage is shaped by Saginaw Bay to the west and Lake Huron to the east. The bodies of water not only outline the peninsula but also have wrapped it in rural isolation, the Thumb's trademark and the reason it is called "the getaway close to home."

Home is likely to be one of three of the state's largest urban areas: Detroit, Flint, or Saginaw, all less than a two-hour drive from the four counties that compose the region. Yet the Thumb is a world away. In this place where interstate highways give way to country roads and indistinguishable suburbs turn into distinct villages, the bustle and heartbeat of the city is replaced by the rural charm of the country.

You don't have nightclubs in the Thumb or dominating skylines or symphony orchestras. But you have more than 90 miles of lakeshore to view, small museums to discover, and an easy way of life whose rural pace will soothe the soul and rest a weary urban mind.

Lumber companies opened up the Thumb in the early 1800s, but after the trees were gone and the loggers went north, the region slipped into the small-town realm of agriculture. Today the area is still predominantly a farm belt, and from its rich soil come corn, sugar beets, grains, beans, and the lush grass that supports vast dairy herds and livestock. Huron County produces more navy beans per acre than anyplace else in the world.

In recent years tourist dollars have become a significant part of the economy, but the region will never turn into one of the strips of motels and ice-cream stands that characterize much of the Lake Michigan shoreline, the heart of Michigan tourism. The Thumb lies on the other side of the state, away from the mainstream of summer traffic. And many travelers, who come for the fine beaches, country markets, and picturesque lighthouses, leave it cherishing that out-of-the-way character the most.

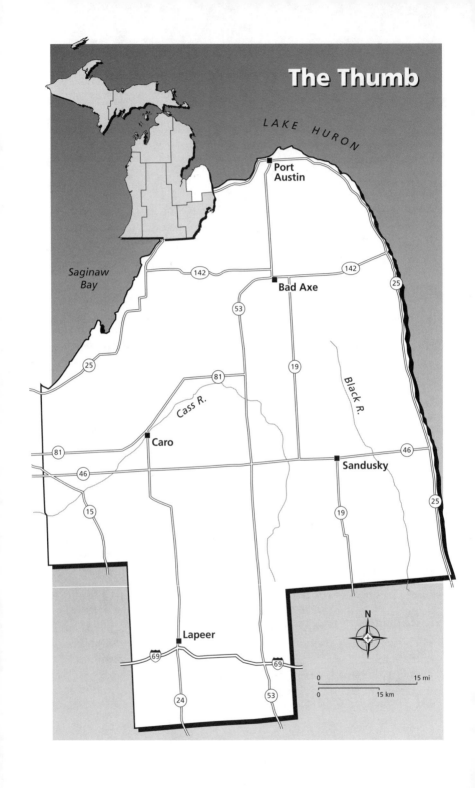

Lapeer County

Amisconception of the Thumb held by many Michigan natives is that the region is flat, without so much as a ripple between the shoreline of Saginaw Bay and the lapping waters of Lake Huron. A drive through Lapeer County dispels that notion immediately. The rolling hills that are the trademark of northern Oakland County continue north through the heart of the peninsula. In southern Lapeer County these hills have an enhancement that makes them unique in Michigan: the distinct white rail fences of horse country. Follow County Road 62 between M 24 and M 53 and dip south along the gravel cross-roads of Blood, Garder, or Barber, and you'll pass through one of the greatest concentrations of horse farms in the state. Come in late spring when the grass is green, a new coat of whitewash covers the fences, and the mares and foals are trotting through the fields—and this area could easily be mistaken for the bluegrass region of Kentucky.

The heart of Michigan's horse country is Metamora, a village of 500 that lies just east of M 24 and is crowned by the towering steeple of the Pilgrim Church (built in 1878). Settlers first began arriving in the area in 1838, but Metamora earned a spot on the map when it became a stop for a stagecoach route that turned into the Detroit–Bay City Railroad in 1872. Whether travelers were carried by horse or by rail, the resting place was the same: a large rambling carriage house built in 1850 on one corner of County Road 62 and Metamora Road.

Back then it was known as the Hoard House, after its proprietor, Lorenzo Hoard, who charged travelers, weary from a long day on the road, only 50 cents a room. Today it's called the *White Horse Inn*, and while it no longer has rooms for rent, it is still serving meals 143 years later, making it the oldest operating restaurant in the county. Half of the inn is the dining room, completely sealed off from the barnlike barroom and decorated in dark oak, leaded-glass windows, and red plaid carpeting. On Thursdays both halves are filled with customers, as the inn offers its weekly all-you-can-eat fish fry for $6.00 per person. The rest of its menu is equally tempting, especially its White Horse Wellington, a flaky pastry filled with tenderloin, mushrooms, and cheese. The inn also has a list of daily seafood specials such as Rainbow Trout a la Praline, boneless trout dusted with a seasoned flour and sautéed in butter with pecans.

The White Horse Inn (810–678–2150) is open for dinner Tuesday through Saturday 11:00 A.M. to 10:00 P.M., and Sunday 2:00 to 9:00 P.M. Menu prices range from $10 to $22 for dinners; reservations are recommended on the weekends.

North of Metamora along M 24 is Lapeer, a town of 6,270. Settlers began arriving in the area in 1828 and borrowed their village name from *la pierre*, the French translation of the Indian name for the Flint River, which lies nearby. Lapeer became the county seat in 1831, and eight years later the county courthouse was built on the town common.

Lapeer is still the center of government, and the **Lapeer County Courthouse** still stands at the corner of Court and Nepessing Streets. It is an impressive building featuring a Greek Revival style with four fluted Doric columns. It's topped by a three-tiered tower and a Roman dome and is noted as the "oldest courthouse still being used in Michigan today," even though the county has long since built a newer, all-brick building across the street. The old courthouse keeps its title because every summer, the judge, the jury, and a handful of history buffs move to the other side of

Lapeer County Courthouse

THE THUMB

Top Annual Events

Waterfront Jamboree,
Port Austin, June;
(517) 738–7600

Michigan Sugar Festival,
Sebewaing, June;
(517) 883–2150

Log Cabin Day,
Bad Axe, June;
(517) 269–9918

Caseville Walleye
Tournament,
Caseville, July;
(517) 856–3818

Fish Sandwich Festival,
Bay Port, August;
(517) 656–2121

the street to hear a few cases in the second-floor courtroom of this landmark structure.

The first floor is now the *Lapeer Historical Society Museum,* and for a small admission fee, visitors can wander through the turn-of-the-century judge's chambers or the first sheriff's office in the county. The Courthouse Museum is open from early June until November 15. Hours are 1:00 to 5:00 P.M. Tuesday through Friday.

More history and a lot of country charm can be found just up the road from Lapeer at the *Past Tense Country Store* (810–664– 5559). The store is only minutes from downtown Lapeer and can be reached by driving north on M 24 and then turning east on County Road 7 (Daley Road). The first intersection on Daley is Farnsworth Road, and visible to the south from this intersection is one of the most impressive houses in the region. The huge, twenty-three-room home was built by the Farnsworth family, who were part of the first wave of settlers to farm the county. There are several buildings on the old farm, including the original barn that Lucie Hiner renovated into the Past Tense Country Store in 1971.

The store is an intriguing place, worth browsing through even if you are not in a buying mood. It is part country store, part antiques shop, and part museum. Walk in on a chilly day and the rush of warm air from the wood-burning stove greets you. Then you'll notice the hundred-year-old German barrel piano and the classic red Texaco gasoline pump next to it. The store itself is four rooms, each stocked to the rafters with such items as handmade baskets, dried flowers, candles, knickknacks, and children's toys, including one of the most amazing teddy bear collections you'll ever see outside a museum. Upstairs are numerous pieces of antique furniture, while one room is devoted to Christmas, with an old sled in the middle and walls covered with ornaments.

Above every shelf of merchandise, Hiner draws you back into the rural history of Lapeer with small artifacts she has saved. Above the wall of hard candy, a requirement in every country store, are rows of cleaning products and cans of food, all from an era long gone. Some you'll recognize, like Oxydol, Quaker Oats, or Calumet Baking Powder, though the packaging hardly resembles the modern-day counterparts. Many you will not (Quick Arrow Soup Chips or Red Moon Early Peas), for they have long since vanished from supermarkets.

Hiner and her family live in the Farnsworth house and operate the store, which is open Monday through Saturday from 10:00 A.M. until 6:00 P.M. and Sunday from noon to 6:00 P.M.

Sanilac County

M 25, the state road that leads out of Port Huron, follows the shoreline of Sanilac County and continues along the entire coast of the Thumb, ending in Bay City. While the road does not offer a watery view at every bend, there are more than enough panoramas of Lake Huron and shoreline parks to make it one of the more scenic drives in the Lower Peninsula.

Heading north on M 25, the first town you reach in Sanilac County is Lexington, which was incorporated in 1855 and boomed at the turn of the century. Back then the bustling town of 2,400 was a common stop for Great Lakes shipping and boasted an organ factory, a brewery, a flour mill, and six saloons. In 1913 the great storm that swept across Lake Huron destroyed the town's docks and virtually isolated it. Lexington slipped into a standstill until the automobile and roads revived it in the 1940s, and today the town of almost 800 has worked harder than any other community in the Thumb to promote its future by preserving its past.

Lexington's streets are lined with turn-of-the-century homes and buildings, including four listed on the National Register of Historic Places. One of them is the **Charles H. Moore Public Library**, at Main and Huron Streets next to the village hall. The brick building was built in 1859 as the Devine Law Office but somehow passed into the hands of Moore, a local seaman who died in 1901, leaving the building to his three daughters. When a dispute erupted in 1903 as to where to put the town library, the daughters offered the former law office as a permanent site.

It has been the library ever since and today holds nearly 12,000 books, including a rare-book collection. Librarians will tell you that as many people wander through just to view the renovated interior as to check out a book. The wood trim and stained-glass windows have been fully restored inside, as has the graceful wooden banister that leads you past a picture of the "old seaman" to the upstairs. It's hard to imagine a more pleasant place to read than the sunlit room of the second floor, which features desks, tables, and office chairs that were originally used by the law firm.

The Moore Library (810–359–8267) is open Monday from 3:00 to 8:00

P.M., Wednesday and Friday from 10:00 A.M. to 5:00 P.M., and Saturday from 10:00 A.M. to 3:00 P.M.

Moore was also responsible for another building in Lexington that is now a National Historic Site. When the seaman built his home in the 1880s, he located it just a block from the lake where he plied his trade. The huge Queen Anne–style home at Simons and Washington Streets was constructed from white pine that loggers were shipping out of the port of Lexington. In 1901, Mary, the youngest daughter, used the house as a backdrop for her marriage to Albert E. Sleeper, a newly elected state senator. When Sleeper's political career led to his election as governor in 1917, the house became an important summer retreat for the couple, who were eager to escape the busy public life in Lansing.

Today the home is still used as a summer retreat as the ***Governor's Inn***, Lexington's first bed-and-breakfast. Guests spend summer evenings much the way the governor and his wife did—on the wraparound porch in wicker rockers (there are seven now instead of two), enjoying the cool breezes off Lake Huron. Reservations are recommended and can be made by writing the Governor's Inn, P.O. Box 471, Lexington 48450, or phoning (810) 359–5770.

From Lexington M 25 continues north along Lake Huron and in 11 miles reaches the next lakeside town, Port Sanilac. Like Lexington, Port Sanilac's early history and wealth can be seen in the old homes that border its streets. One is the Loop-Harrison House, a huge Victorian mansion just south of town on M 25 that now serves as the ***Sanilac County Historical Museum***. The home was built in 1872 by Dr. Joseph Loop, who arrived in Sanilac in 1854 and began a practice that covered a 40-mile radius. The home and its extensive furnishings passed down through three generations of the family until Captain Stanley Harrison,

Port Sanilac Lighthouse

*P*ort Sanilac's most distinctive landmark is its lighthouse, a red brick house and whitewashed tower overlooking the town harbor and the watery horizon of Lake Huron. Built in 1886, the 80-foot tower was originally a kerosene-fueled continuous white light. In 1889 it was changed to red, and in 1926 the lighthouse was wired for electricity and changed to a flashing light with a range of 12 to 15 miles. Although the lighthouse is not open to visitors, it's a photographer's delight thanks to its contrasting colors.

The Port Sanilac Lighthouse is on Lake Street, 1 block east of M 25.

grandson of the good doctor, donated it to the
Sanilac Historical Society in 1964.

The Historical Society has kept the home intact,
and visitors can wander through two floors of
rooms that have remained virtually the same
since the 1870s, right down to the original car-
pet, the cooking utensils in the kitchen, and the
doctor's instruments in his office. There are also
a dairy museum out back and a furnished 1882
pioneer log cabin. The museum (810–622–9946)
is open from Memorial Day through Labor Day from 11:00 A.M. to 4:30
P.M. Tuesday through Friday and noon to 4:30 P.M. on Saturday and Sunday. There is a small admission fee.

Closer to town on M 25 is another impressive home that has become
the **Raymond House Inn**, Port Sanilac's bed-and-breakfast. The home
was built in 1871 by Uri Raymond, one of the founding fathers of the
town, who established what is now Michigan's oldest continuously operating hardware store just up the street. The exterior of this Victorian-
style home makes it hard to miss with its red brick facade, high peaked
roofs, and white gingerbread trim. Inside, high ceilings, classic mold-
ings, winding staircases, and large rooms add to the inn's turn-of-the-
century charm.

Shirley Denison bought the house after three generations of Raymonds
had lived in it. Denison is a restorative artist from Washington, D.C., but
she spent her childhood summers in Port Sanilac, where her grandfa-
ther was a local boat and lumber baron. She was enchanted by the
antique furniture that filled the rooms, including the old-fashioned
parlor and the six bedrooms she rents out on the second floor. The inn
is open from April through December, with a rate of $95 for double
occupancy (private bath). Write to Denison at P.O. Box 438, Port Sanilac
48469, or call (810) 622–8800 for a reservation.

For dinner or what many say is the best fish fry in the Thumb, head
almost directly across the street to yet another century-old Victorian
home known as the **Bellaire Hotel**. Inside you'll find more arches, ceiling-high windows, and parquet floors. More important to the patrons,
however, are the dining rooms and what emerges from the kitchen.
Local people call them "porch dinners," for you sit in a glass-enclosed
room overlooking the gardens that surround the hotel. Diane Douros,
who has operated the Bellaire since she and her husband bought it in
1945, is best known for her perch and pickerel dinners. The meal is

complete only if it is topped off with a piece of her tart lemon meringue pie. The Bellaire (810–622–9981) is at 120 South Ridge Road, and its entrees are priced from $10 to $15.

The stretch of M 25 from Port Sanilac to Forestville is especially scenic and passes three roadside parks on high bluffs from which you can scramble to the Lake Huron shoreline below. For those who want to explore the center of the Thumb, the Bay City–Forestville Road, the only intersection in tiny Forestville, provides a good excuse to turn off M25. Head west, through the hamlets of Charleston and Minden, and look for the "Petroglyphs" sign at the corner of Bay City–Forestville and Germania Roads. *Sanilac Historical Site* is located just south on Germania and is marked by a large Department of Natural Resources sign. Situated in the wooded heart of the Thumb, the park features a large slab of stone with petroglyphs, Indian carvings that archaeologists believe to be between 300 and 1,000 years old and the only ones in the Lower Peninsula. The department has erected a large pavilion over the rock, which contains dozens of carvings. The most prominent one features a bowman with a single long line depicting his arm and arrow. A short trail leads from the parking lot a few hundred yards inland to the pavilion and then continues beyond as a 1.5-mile interpretive trail.

There is no entrance fee. From Memorial Day to Labor Day, the Michigan Bureau of History staffs the park from 11:30 A.M. to 4:30 P.M. Wednesday through Sunday with guides who help visitors recognize the carvings and lead guided walks.

Another reason to head inland in summer and fall is to pick berries—sweet, juicy, and back-breakingly close to the ground. Next to the town of Croswell is the *Croswell Berry Farm* (810–679–3273) at 33 Black River Road. This farm features strawberries in June and early July, then

Bark Shanty Point

*P*ort Sanilac dates back to the summer of 1830 when a group of lumbermen arrived to peel the bark from the hemlocks in the area for tanning leather. Their accommodations were in a hastily built shanty that was covered in bark. The crude shelter was left standing on the shore after the men departed in the fall, and it quickly became a landmark to sailors who referred to the spot as Bark Shanty Point. Eventually a settlement emerged, and in 1857 the residents decided that the name of a famous Wyandot Indian chief was a little more dignified for their community than Bark Shanty Point.

A John Deere Museum

*The Deckerville Historical
Museum is located on a
farm and includes a log
cabin, railroad depot,
windmill, and sawmill, but
its most noted collection is
its exhibit of John Deere
tractors. The museum has
more than twenty on dis-
play with all of them in
working order and some
dating to the 1930s.*

*The museum is a mile
north of Deckerville at
4208 Ruth Road and is
open Saturdays from May
through September from
9:00 a.m. to 5:00 p.m.
There is a small admission*

extends the picking season with blueberries, and finishes up the year with raspberries that are harvested as late as November. Hours are 8:00 A.M. to 4:00 P.M. daily.

One final reason to head inland to Croswell is to get some advice for keeping your marriage intact from a bridge that Dear Abby would appreciate. In the middle of this Sanilac County village is the **Be Good to Your Mother-in-Law Bridge**, which was first constructed in 1905 and has been rebuilt three times since then with David Weis, a local businessman, assisting in the effort.

Best known in town for offering sage advice to newlyweds, it was Weis who hung a sign at one end of the bridge that advises them to be good to their mothers-in-law and at the other end one that admonishes them to love one another. It's such good advice that the bridge has become something of a ritual with both newlyweds and long-time married couples, who are photographed under the black-and-white sign and then walk hand-in-hand across the structure.

They hold hands partly out of devotion to each other and partly to keep their balance. The 139-foot suspension footbridge is held up by four thick cables that make you bounce with each step across. The wooden slats sway, jiggle, and dip toward the Black River, coming within eight feet of its murky surface. Some people are even more nervous about crossing the 4-foot-wide swinging bridge than strolling up to the altar.

Small tree-lined parks are at each end of the bridge, while a short walk away on Wells Street is the **Croswell Museum**, a former railroad depot that features a horse-drawn hearse, local artifacts, and plenty of fading photographs of the town's beloved swinging bridge. The parks and bridge are open daily from dawn to dusk. The Croswell Museum is open Saturday and Sunday from 1:00 to 5:00 P.M.

Huron County

The country charm of M 25 continues into Huron County as it winds north toward Port Austin on the "Tip of the Thumb." Along the way it passes several museums, including two in Harbor Beach, a quiet rural town of 2,000 residents.

Murphy Museum preserves the birthplace of Governor Frank Murphy, best known for refusing to use the National Guard to end the 1937 Flint Sit-Down Strike at General Motors. By pushing for collective bargaining, Murphy, in effect, paved the way for the United Auto Workers and unionization of the auto industry. Murphy also served as mayor of Detroit, U.S. attorney general and a U.S. Supreme Court justice from 1940 to his death in 1949. The house is packed with historical artifacts relating to one of Michigan's most influential residents.

Murphy Museum (517–479–9554) is at 142 South Huron Street in downtown Harbor Beach and is open Memorial Day to Labor Day from 10:00 A.M. to 6:00 P.M. Wednesday through Sunday. There is a small admission charge. Just north of town on M 25 at the Harbor Beach harbor is the **Grice Museum**, which features a farmhouse from the late 1800s, a barn, and a rural school.

Another small museum along M 25 is at **Lighthouse County Park**, 15 miles north of Harbor Beach. The museum is on the first floor of the classic Pointe Aux Barques Lighthouse, which was built in 1857 and is still used by the U.S. Coast Guard. The lighthouse actually overlooks two parks; the county park around it features seventy-four campsites with electricity for recreational vehicles, a swimming beach, a boat launch, and a picnic area. Out in Lake Huron is an underwater park, the Thumb Area Bottomland Preserve, which the state set up in 1985 to protect the nine known shipwrecks that lie offshore. Relics gathered from the wrecks will be stored in the Lighthouse Museum, which is open weekends during the summer. There is no admission charge for the park (517–479–6393) or the museum.

The Fires of 1881

*W*hat began as small fires in the middle of a hot, dry summer turned into the Thumb's worst disaster when on September 5, 1881, a gale swept in from the southwest. The high winds turned the fires into an inferno that raged for three days and burned more than a million acres in Sanilac and Huron Counties alone.

The fire put a sudden end to the logging era in the region while killing 125 people and leaving thousands more destitute. Aid to victims was the first disaster relief effort by the new American Red Cross. Its prompt response quickly won the support of the country, which continues today.

Where Lighthouse Road loops back to M 25 is the Thumb's most impressive attraction, **Huron City**. The town was founded in the mid-1850s by lumberman Langdon Hubbard, who needed a port for his 29,000-acre tract of timberland, which included most of northern Huron County. It quickly became the largest town in the county, with several hundred residents and two sawmills that produced 80,000 feet of lumber a day. After the Great Fire of 1881 that swept across the Thumb devastated Hubbard's logging efforts, he sold his land to immigrant farmers (after opening a bank to lend them the money), and for a while Huron City hung on as a farming community.

By the early 1900s Huron City had withered away to a ghost town when it experienced a revival—a religious awakening, you might say. One of Hubbard's daughters had married William Lyon Phelps, a Yale professor and an ordained minister, and each summer the couple returned to Huron City and stayed at Seven Gables, the rambling Hubbard home. Eventually Dr. Phelps began preaching in the nearby church on Sunday. Local people soon discovered the magic of his oratory: simple solutions and relief from the problems of everyday life. The church, which originally held 250, was quickly enlarged to 1,000 in the 1920s as people throughout Michigan heard of the preacher and began finding their way to Huron City for his Sunday afternoon service.

Dr. Phelps died in 1937, but Huron City survived when the granddaughter of the founder preserved the community as a museum town. Twelve buildings are on the site, nine of them furnished and open to the public.

Grindstone Capital of the World

*W*here M 25 begins to curve around the top of the Thumb, you can take Pointe Aux Barques Road to Grindstone City. Amazingly, this tiny village was once the world's leading producer of natural-sandstone grinding wheels. Sandstone was first quarried in 1834 by Captain Aaron G. Peer, who shipped it to Detroit, where it was used to pave the intersection of Woodward and Jefferson Avenues. Two years later the first grindstone wheel was turned out, and for nearly a century Grindstone City grindstones were shipped all over the world. Today you can still see many of the huge grindstones, some 6 feet in diameter, on the beach and around the village's boat harbor.

They include a country store, a church, a lifesaving station, a settler's cabin, the old inn, a barn with antique farm equipment, and the Phelps Museum, which was built in honor of the minister in the early 1950s. Huron City (517–428–4123) is open July 1 through Labor Day from 10:00 A.M. to 5:00 P.M. Thursday through Monday. The admission fee is $10 for adults but includes an hour-long guided tour that tells the stories behind the buildings.

Where Lake Huron and Saginaw Bay meet is Port Austin, the town at the "Tip of the Thumb." M 25 winds through the center of Port Austin and near its two busiest spots in the summer, the city marina and, just east of the marina's breakwall, delightful *Bird Creek County Park*. This seven-acre park includes a beautiful sandy beach and a half-mile boardwalk where people fish during the day and gather nightly to watch the sunset over Saginaw Bay.

Travelers will find some antique accommodations in this New England–style town that boomed with lumber barons in the mid-1800s. One of them is the *Garfield Inn*, a huge red mansion on Lake Street that is named after a U.S. congressman who stayed in the home in the 1860s and once delivered a stirring speech from its balcony endorsing Civil War hero Ulysses Grant for president. That man was James Garfield, who later became the twentieth president of the United States. The inn, which became a restaurant, bar, and bed-and-breakfast in 1985, has been named a National Historic Site, and among its more striking features is the mahogany bar and the winding cherrywood staircase that leads to the ten bedrooms upstairs, seven of which are rented out.

The Garfield Inn (517–738–5254 or 800–373–5254) is open from the middle of April until January. Rooms based on double occupancy run from $75 to $85. The restaurant is open at 5:00 P.M. for dinner daily during the summer, on Friday and Saturday only during the winter.

In keeping with the restored atmosphere of the Port Austin inns, there is *The Bank 1884 Restaurant* for, unquestionably, the finest dining in town. Built in 1884 as the Winsorsnover Bank on the corner of Lake and State Streets, the red washed–brick building ceased being a place of financial business in 1957. In 1982 Anthony and Marilynne Berry began renovating the building, and two years later they opened its doors as a restaurant. The interior features stained glass over the classic stand-up bar, a teller's cage on the first floor, and walls of oversized photographs depicting early Huron County. The changing menu usually has shrimp scampi, prime rib, and En Papolote—walleye prepared with a crabmeat dressing and baked in parchment paper. During the summer The Bank 1884 is open from 5:00 to 10:30 P.M. Tuesday through Saturday and 2:00 to 8:00 P.M. on Sunday. During May and after Labor Day until mid-December, the restaurant is only open on weekends. Prices for entrees range from $14 to $22, and reservations (517–738–5353) are strongly recommended for the weekends.

West of Port Austin M 25 begins to follow the shoreline of Saginaw Bay and is especially scenic in its 19-mile stretch to Caseville. It passes many views of the bay and its islands, numerous roadside parks, and the finest beaches in the Thumb. One of the parks is **Port Crescent State Park**, popular with sunbathers and swimmers for the long stretches of sandy shoreline. The park also offers opportunities and facilities for camping, hiking, and fishing, and it contains the Thumb's only set of dunes, a unique place for beachcombers to explore. There is an entrance fee to Port Crescent State Park (517–738–8663) and a $15 charge to camp overnight.

Even more than for sand and sun, Saginaw Bay has always been known as an angler's destination for yellow perch. Visitors, especially families, can still enjoy good fishing even without a boat or knowledge of where to go by joining a perch party boat. The large charter boats hold between twenty and forty anglers and usually depart twice a day for half-day fishing trips. In Port Austin, **Miss Port Austin** (517–738–5271) offers party-boat charters that depart at 7:30 A.M. and 2:30 P.M. daily. The fee is $25 per angler. You need to bring your own pole; the boat provides the bait and takes you where the perch are biting. Perch fishing is easy, and on a good day you may need a bucket to bring home your catch.

To enjoy your perch without having to put a minnow on your hook, stay on M 25 as it curves southwest toward Bay Port. From the 1880s until the

One Bad Axe

*R*udolph Papst is credited by many with giving Bad Axe its name. While surveying for a new road across the heart of Huron County in 1861, he discovered a "bad axe" near his campsite one night and labeled the spot Bad Axe Corners on his map.

In 1872 county supervisors wanted the government moved from Port Austin to a more central location in the county and chose Bad Axe Corners, which in reality was little more than a junction in a dense forest. But five acres were quickly cleared, and in 1873 a courthouse was built. Since then Bad Axe has grown to be Huron County's largest city while its residents have resisted several attempts to give it a more dignified name.

late 1940s, this sleepy village was known as the "largest freshwater fishing port in the world," as tons of perch, whitefish, walleye, and herring were shipped as far away as New York City in refrigerated railroad cars. Today it honors its fishing past on the first Sunday in August with its annual **Bay Port Fish Sandwich Day**. The small festival includes arts and crafts, softball games, and lots of sandwiches—close to 8,000 are served during the event.

A small commercial fishery is still operating in Bay Port, a place to go for fresh walleye, perch, whitefish, and herring. From the center of town, head for the waterfront docks of the **Bay Port Fish Company** (517–656–2131) for the catch of the day or to watch fishermen work on the boats or nets in the evening. The company, which is open from 9:00 A.M. until 5:00 P.M. daily, also sells smoked fish.

In the heart of Huron County is Bad Axe, the county seat and a city of 4,000 residents. The town's most interesting attraction is **Pioneer Log Cabin Village**. This unique outdoor museum features a home, blacksmith shop, chapel, general store, barn, and one-room schoolhouse. All the buildings are log cabins that were built in Huron Cabin and moved to Bad Axe. The cabins are fully furnished to reflect the pioneer lifestyle of the nineteenth century and often are staffed during the summer by guides in period costumes.

The village is located in Bad Axe City Park on South Hanselman Street and is open Sunday from 2:00 to 5:00 P.M. May through September. There is no admission fee.

West of Bad Axe is Pigeon in the heart of Huron County's flat-as-a-pancake farm country. This is Michigan's largest agricultural area, and it's best viewed on a **Farm Tour**. The self-guided tours begin with a stop at the Village Qwick Stop on M 142 in Pigeon where you can pick up a map and self-guided tour tape. From there the tape directs you to fifteen stops that include an egg farm, hog farm, bean plant and cooperative elevator, and dairy farms. For more information about the tour or special events that many of the farms stage, call the Pigeon Chamber of Commerce at (517) 453–2733.

PLACES TO STAY IN MICHIGAN'S THUMB

BAD AXE
The Franklin Inn,
160 East Huron Street,
(517) 269-9951

CASEVILLE
Country Charm Farm
Bed & Breakfast,
5048 Conkey Road,
(517) 856-3110

Sand-N-Surf Motel,
6008 Port Austin Road,
(517) 856-4400

HARBOR BEACH
Wellock Inn,
404 South Huron Avenue,
(517) 479-3645

Train Station Motel,
2044 North M 25,
(517) 479-3215

LEXINGTON
Lex-on-the-Lake Lodges,
5795 Main Street,
(810) 539-7910

Governor's Inn,
7277 Simons Street,
(810) 359-5770

Lusky Lakefront Cottages,
8949 Lakeshore Drive,
(810) 327-6889

PORT AUSTIN
The Garfield Inn,
8544 Lake Street,
(517) 738-5254

Lakeside Motor Lodge,
168 West Spring Street,
(517) 738-8612

Krebs Cottages,
2966 Port Austin Road,
(517) 856-2876

Castaways Motel,
1404 Port Austin Road,
(517) 738-5254

PORT HOPE
Stafford House,
4489 Main Street,
(517) 428-4554

PORT SANILAC
Raymond House Inn,
111 South Ridge Street,
(810) 622-8800

Port Motel,
44 North Lake Street,
(810) 622-9613

PLACES TO EAT IN MICHIGAN'S THUMB

BAD AXE
The Franklin Inn
(American),
160 East Huron Street,
(517) 269-9951

CASEVILLE
Cozy Cafe (American),
6515 Main Street,
(517) 856-2266

Bay Window Restaurant
(American),
6750 Main Street,
(517) 856-2676

Country House
(American),
6567 Main Street,
(517) 856-2140

Selected Chambers of Commerce and Tourism Bureaus

Bad Axe Chamber of Commerce,
P.O. Box 87, Bad Axe 48413;
(517) 269-9918

Caseville Chamber of Commerce,
P.O. Box 122, Caseville 48725;
(800) 606-1347

Port Austin Chamber of Commerce,
P.O. Box 274, Port Austin, 48467;
(517) 738-7600

Huron County Visitors Bureau,
350 East Huron Street, Bad Axe 48413;
(800) 35-THUMB

HARBOR BEACH
Harbor Light Inn
(American),
1090 North
Lakeshore Road,
(517) 479–6005

Randolph's (Italian),
722 State Street,
(517) 479–3595

LEXINGTON
Stuben's (American),
5547 Main Street,
(517) 359–8500

METAMORA
The White Horse Inn,
1 East High Street,
(810) 678–2150

PORT AUSTIN
The Farm Restaurant
(American),
699 Port Crescent,
(517) 874–5700

Kornetti's Kitchen
(American),
42 West Spring Street,
(517) 738–5239

The Bank 1884
(fine dining),
Lake and State Streets,
(517) 738–5353

The Garfield Inn (fine dining),
8544 Lake Street,
(517) 738–5254

PORT HOPE
Stafford House,
4489 Main Street,
(517) 428–4554

PORT SANILAC
Bellaire Lodge (American),
120 South Ridge Street,
(810) 622–9981

Mary's Diner (American),
14 North Ridge Street,
(810) 622–9377

OTHER ATTRACTIONS

Sleeper State Park,
Caseville

Luckhard Museum,
Sebewaing

Pigeon Historical Museum,
Pigeon

The Heartland

y the 1830s "Michigan Fever" had become an epidemic. Scores of pioneer families from the East Coast floated through the Erie Canal, made their way to Detroit, and then took to the newly completed Detroit-Chicago Road, which cut across the southern half of the Lower Peninsula. They soon discovered the rolling prairies of Michigan, where the soil was very rich and the land very cheap—the federal government was selling it for only $1.25 an acre.

From this onrush of settlers between 1825 and 1855, some of the state's largest cities emerged: Kalamazoo, Lansing, Battle Creek, Jackson, and Grand Rapids, all in this central region. But the Heartland of Michigan, the only area without direct links to the Great Lakes, is still an agricultural breadbasket. It is faded red barns and rolling fields of oats, the birthplace of Kellogg's Corn Flakes, and the home of a village antiques dealer who scours area farms for the furniture and knick-knacks that fill her store.

The vibrant cities, each with a distinct downtown that never sleeps, are popular destinations for travelers who can zip from one to the next on interstate highways six lanes wide. But the unique nature of this region is found by rambling along its two-lane county roads, which take you past the horse-drawn carriages of Amish country, down main streets of small villages, and along roadside stands loaded with the summer's harvest. In these out-of-the-way places, you can sample the fruits of Michigan's Heartland.

Lenawee County

t the northern edge of Lenawee County are the famed Irish Hills, an area of green rolling hills with intermittent lakes and ponds. US 12 cuts through the middle of this popular area and has become an avenue of manufactured tourist attractions: miniature golf courses and Go Kart tracks, a dinosaur amusement park, another park called Stagecoach Stop U.S.A., motels, gift shops, and even an

AUTHOR'S TOP TEN PICKS

Van Andel Museum Center,
Grand Rapids;
(616) 456–3977

The Michigan Library
and Historical Center,
Lansing; (517) 373–3559

Gerald R. Ford Museum,
Grand Rapids;
(616) 451–9263

Kellogg's Cereal City USA,
Battle Creek; (616) 962–6230

Capital Tours,
Lansing; (517) 373–2353

Gilmore Classic Car Club of
America Museums,
Hickory Corners;
(616) 671–5089

Kalamazoo Aviation
History Museum,
Kalamazoo; (616) 382–6555

Antiquing in Allen,
Allen; (517) 869–2100

Hidden Lake Gardens,
Tipton; (517) 431–2060

Jerry's Diner Village,
Rockford; (616) 866–FOOD

international speedway that holds Indy car races. So overwhelming are these modern-day sights that it's easy to pass by one of the most interesting attractions and probably the only one that is free, **Walker Tavern**.

Located in Cambridge State Historic Park, the white clapboard tavern overlooks US 12, and rightfully so. The highway was originally an Indian trail and then became a stagecoach route known as the Detroit-Chicago Road. The stagecoach era lasted from 1835 to 1855, and on these rickety wagons, passengers traveled 50 miles a day with the hope of reaching Chicago in five days. The string of frontier taverns along the way was a crucial part of the system. They provided not only overnight accommodations (two or three travelers would share a bed for 25 cents a night) but also meals for the weary passengers who had just spent the day bouncing along the rough dirt road.

By the 1830s Walker Tavern had a reputation as a fine place to dine. Proprietor Sylvester Walker ran not only the inn but a small farm as well, while his wife, Lucy, performed miracles baking in the stone fireplace. A typical supper at Walker Tavern might include stewed chicken, biscuits, corn bread, and applesauce cake or pumpkin pie. The tavern still stands on its original site, and the pub, sitting room, and kitchen have been renovated. Next to the tavern is a reconstructed wheelwright shop, featuring the tools used to build and repair the fragile wooden wheels as well as the covered wagons and carriages of the era. Visitors begin the self-guided walking tour at the Interpretive Center with a film in its theater and an exhibit on the settling of Michigan.

Cambridge State Historical Park (517–467–4414) is at US 12 and M 50, 25 miles south of Jackson. The tavern complex is open from 10:00 A.M. to 5:00 P.M. daily from Memorial Day through Labor Day.

Also located in the Irish Hills is Lenawee County's other outstanding attraction, **Hidden Lake Gardens**. Glaciers were responsible for the rolling terrain of the gardens, and when the ice sheet finally melted away, it left a topography of prominent knolls, ridges, valleys, and funnel-like depressions. Harry A. Fee was responsible for preserving it. The

Adrian businessman fell in love with the scenic land formations and in 1926 purchased 226 acres, including its namesake lake. He began developing the landscape and supervising its early plantings before giving the gardens to Michigan State University in 1945. The visitor center was added in 1966, the plant conservatory four years later, and today Hidden Lake Gardens covers 670 acres with 6 miles of picturesque, winding, one-way roads, 5 miles of hiking trails to its remote corners, and more than 2,500 introduced species of plants.

Upon entering the gardens most people head for the visitor center, which includes an orientation and information area, a gift shop, and a walk-through exhibit concourse. Next door is the plant conservatory, where 8,000 square feet of glass houses plants from around the world. Along with the kumquats and vanilla plants in the tropical house and the old-man cacti in the arid dome, there is the 80-by-36-foot temperate house used to display unusual houseplants and seasonal flowers. From the conservatory visitors can follow a winding drive around Hidden Lake and then ascend through a unique forest carpeted in ivy

Walker Tavern

THE HEARTLAND

before topping out at Gobblers Knob with a view of the surrounding ridges and hardwood trees below. The network of one-way roads also leads visitors past a glacial pothole, through an oak upland forest, and around an open meadow, and ends, of course, at a picnic area.

The entrance to the gardens (517–431–2060) is located on M 50, 2 miles west of Tipton or 7 miles west of Tecumseh. The gardens, visitor center, and plant conservatory are open daily from 8:00 A.M. to dusk April through October and 8:00 A.M. to 4:00 P.M. November through March. There is a small per-person admission fee.

There are many mansions-turned-restaurants in Michigan, but few evoke an aura of gracious living and fine dining the way the **Hathaway House** does. A National Historic Site, the home was built by David Carpenter, who arrived in Blissfield in 1836 as a twenty-one-year-old with $25. Seventeen years later, Carpenter was a wealthy merchant, and he decided to build a home that would reflect his position as one of the county's most prominent residents. The eighteen-room Hathaway House resembles a southern mansion. Inside guests are seated in six distinctively decorated rooms that were previously the east and west parlors, the card room, and the library, among others. In this restaurant you can still run your hand along the original cherry banister of the sweeping staircase, be warmed during the winter by one of five fireplaces, and admire the classic woodwork.

Clare Irish Festival, Clare, March; (888) AT–CLARE

Alma Highland Festival and Games, Alma, May; (517) 463–5525

East Lansing Art Festival, May; (517) 337–1731

World's Longest Breakfast Table, Battle Creek, June; (800) 397–2240

U.S. National Hot Air Balloon Championship, Battle Creek, July; (616) 962–0592

Abbott's Magical Get-Together, Colon, August; (616) 432–3235

Riverfest, Lansing, September; (517) 483–4499

Michigan Wine and Harvest Festival, Kalamazoo and Paw Paw, September; (616) 381–2003

Historic Homes Tour, Marshall, September; (616) 781–5163

Celebration on the Grand, Grand Rapids, September; (616) 459–8287

Afterward you can drop in at the Main Street Stable. What used to be the carriage house in the back of Carpenter's mansion is now a lively little pub that still features a rustic interior of hand-hewn beams, wooden benches, and lanterns hanging from the ceiling.

The Hathaway House (517–486–2141) is reached from US 23 by taking exit 5 and heading 10 miles west on US 223. Hours are 11:30 A.M. to 9:00 P.M. Tuesday through Thursday, until 10:00 P.M. Friday and Saturday, and noon to 8:00 P.M. Sunday. Dinner entrees range from $15 to $22.

Hillsdale County

In 1827 a surveying crew from the Detroit-Chicago Road was working in the fertile prairie of the St. Joseph Valley when one crew member, Captain Moses Allen, fell in love with the area. His homestead led to a small hamlet of homes and shops known as Allen's Prairie, the first white settlement west of Tecumseh. This is the birthplace of Hillsdale County, but today **Allen** is better known as the "Antiques Capital of Michigan."

It began as a weekend flea market in the late 1960s and soon drew crowds of antiques hunters from several states to the junction of US 12 and M 49. Eventually some of the antiques dealers who rented the summer stalls began to set up permanent businesses in Allen. Today this quaint village of fewer than 300 residents supports more than a dozen antiques malls, each housing several dealers and other shops along a mile-long stretch of US 12, the town's main street. Some of the shops are located in red brick buildings near the intersection, others in old homes or weathered barns that are packed with furniture and other large antiques.

Fun Facts

Somerset Center's McCourtie Park, located in the northeast corner of Hillsdale County, was once the Prohibition-era playground of cement mogul William McCourtie and features seventeen sculpted cement bridges across a winding stream.

The largest shop is **Greentop Country Village** (517–869–2100), an antiques mall that consists of more than forty dealers displaying their wares in a dozen buildings. The best times to visit Allen are on the weekends of Memorial Day, Fourth of July, or Labor Day when the community holds open-air antiques festivals and even more dealers converge on the town and set up booths along the streets.

If you are heading south to Allen, swing through the picturesque village of Litchfield 14 miles to the north at the other end of M 49. Near the center of town is the Litchfield Town Hall, and featured in the huge storefront display windows is the **Litchfield Community Hand Tool Collection**. In one window are seventy-five tools from the turn of the century, in the other another sixty-three, all numbered to correspond to a list taped on the window and in surprisingly good condition. In the three smaller windows on the second floor, more tools are hung in display as the town's collection continues to grow and grow. Someday it might have to use all these tools to build a museum for them.

The **Tristate Corner** in Hillsdale County is hardly a major tourist attraction. But there is enough interest in this geographical oddity that the Hillsdale County Historical Association maintains a stone monument dedicated to where three states come together, the only such spot in the Midwest that doesn't involve a river.

The monument is actually in Michigan, but it explains exactly where the corner is (130 feet to the south) because when you actually reach this obscure spot, a farm field on a county dirt road, you want to make sure you're standing in all three states at the same time.

It's not as famous as Four Corners, the spot where Arizona, New Mexico, Colorado, and Utah come together, but on the other hand, as the locals say, it won't burn two weeks of your vacation to visit.

From Camden, in the southwest corner of Hillsdale County, head south on M 49 and then west on Territorial Road. In less than 3 miles turn south on Cope Road and look for the stone monument on the left-hand side of the road.

St. Joseph County

Michigan is known for many things, but to the average tourist, magicians and magic are not generally among them. Yet Harry Houdini died in Michigan, and the state has deep roots in the art of illusion and the related conjuring culture. One of the most famous American magicians in the 1920s, Harry Blackstone, toured the country with his act. At one time he passed through the village of Colon and then returned in 1926 and purchased property. Blackstone toured in the winter but spent his summers in Colon creating new illusions and rehearsing his show. One summer Australian magician Percy Abbott came to Colon to visit Blackstone and fell in love with a local girl and the quiet area. Abbott, eager to end his days of traveling, moved to Michigan and formed a partnership with Blackstone to begin a magic-apparatus manufacturing company.

The partnership went sour after only eight months, but the Australian magician went ahead with his plans and in 1933 set up *Abbott's Magic Manufacturing Company*. Today this sleepy farming village is the home of the world's largest magic company, an interesting stop even if you've never done a card trick. The walls inside are plastered with posters and photographs of magicians,

Langley Covered Bridge

The longest of Michigan's handful of remaining covered bridges is just north of Centreville along Covered Bridge Road. Built in 1887, the Langley Covered Bridge is 282 feet long and uses three spans to cross the St. Joseph River.

for all the famous performers, from Doug Henning to David Copperfield, have done business with this company. A display room in the factory, an all-black brick building, has cases and shelves filled with a portion of the 2,000 tricks and gadgets Abbott's Magic builds. And there is always a resident magician on hand to show you how they work.

A year after beginning his company, Abbott also instituted an open house for magicians as a sales incentive, and that quickly evolved into Colon's annual festival, Magical Get-Together. Every August more than a thousand amateur and professional magicians flood the village for a series of shows at the high school auditorium. Abbott's Magic Manufacturing Company (616–432–3235) is at 124 St. Joseph Street, 1 block off M 86, and is open from 9:00 A.M. until 5:00 P.M. Monday through Friday and until 4:00 P.M. on Saturday.

More magic memorabilia can be viewed at the ***Colon Community Museum***, which is housed in an 1893 church at 219 North Blackstone Road. Although many artifacts deal with the town's first pioneer families, one area is devoted to the personal items and photographs of Blackstone and Abbott. The museum is open Tuesday, Thursday, and Sunday from 2:00 to 4:30 P.M. There is no admission charge.

Jackson County

The Lower Peninsula lacks the waterfalls that grace the countryside in the Upper Peninsula, but in Jackson there are the ***Cascades.*** Billed as the largest constructed waterfalls in North America, the Cascades were a creation of "Captain" William Sparks, a well-known Jackson

More Magic in Marshall

If you need more conjuring, head to Marshall for the American Museum of Magic. Founded in 1978, the museum is located in a restored 1868 building, and its collection of almost a half-million pieces of memorabilia takes up three floors. There are props from all the great magicians of the nineteenth and twentieth centuries including the milk can escape apparatus that saved Houdini's career.

The American Museum of Magic (616–781–7674) is at 107 East Michigan Avenue in downtown Marshall. From Memorial Day through Labor Day, tours are offered at noon, 2:00 and 4:00 p.m. on Saturday, and 1:00 and 3:00 p.m. on Sunday. There is a small admission fee.

industrialist and philanthropist. They date to the early 1930s, when Sparks was developing a 450-acre park as a gift to the city and wanted it to showcase something different, something no other Michigan city had.

What he developed were the Cascades, a series of eighteen waterfalls with water dancing down the side of a hill from one to the next. Six fountains, varying in height and patterns, supply more than 3,000 gallons per

The Parlour

*L*ate one night, when The Parlour is humming with people, ice-cream dishes clanging, and waitresses hustling orders from the kitchen, a woman screams and no one takes notice. It's her first trip to the landmark ice-cream parlor, and a waitress has just placed in front of her the largest Black Cow she has ever seen. The fountain glass itself is 12 inches high, and still the rich mixture of root beer and ice cream is cascading over the top because at the Parlour, they put five scoops of vanilla—count 'em, five—in their Black Cow.

"Oh my goodness," said the woman in a near state of calorie shock. "All I asked for was a root beer float, and look what they brought me."

If you're a diehard ice-cream lover, then The Parlour is heaven on earth, or at the very least a parfait paradise. Operated by the Jackson Dairy, this hot fudge haven is basically four U-shaped lunch counters plus a handful of booths for those of us who like to pig out anonymously. Everybody else has to sit across from total strangers and indulge in five scoops of cherry ripple drowning in a sea of marshmallow syrup. Then again, maybe it's better they are strangers.

Or else, who cares? When you enter The Parlour, you have momentarily forgotten about your waistband if you ever thought about it to begin with. The most popular item is the Deluxe Pecan Combo: three scoops of ice cream smothered in hot fudge and hot caramel, sprinkled with pecans, and buried in real whipped cream. You don't eat this sundae, you attack it, using your spoon like a shovel to remove large portions from the sides before it avalanches onto your placemat.

There's also the Hot Fudge Ice Cream Cake, nicknamed "Awful, Awful." It's two thick slices of chocolate cake covered with four scoops of ice cream and drenched in hot fudge and whipped cream. But the greatest creation at The Parlour, the reason it was once voted the best ice cream shoppe in the state, is the Dare To Be Great Sundae— twenty-one scoops of ice cream, or roughly a half-gallon of assorted flavors, with four soup ladles of toppings and a mountain of nuts, and, of course, totally smothered in real whipped cream. It's served in a punch bowl for obvious reasons.

The Parlour (517–782–7141) is at Wildwood Avenue and Daniel Road in Jackson and reached from I–94 by taking exit 137. Head south on Lawrence and then east on Wildwood Avenue.

minute, while 1,200 colored lights turn the attraction into a nightly event of constantly changing light, color, and music. The total length of the falls is 500 feet, and energetic viewers climb the 129 steps that run along each side of the Cascades, dodging the spray along the way. Others prefer to sit in the amphitheater seats to watch the water and light show that takes place nightly from Memorial Day to Labor Day.

The Cascades (517–788–4320) can be reached from I–94 by taking exit 138 and heading south for 3 miles. Signs point the way to the falls. There is an admission fee.

Jackson is home for two U.S. astronauts, Brigadier General James S. McDevitt and Lieutenant Colonel Alfred M. Worden. The two men, and all other astronauts, are honored by the city at the *Michigan Space Center*, located on the Jackson Community College campus. The center is a gold geodesic dome with an 85-foot Mercury Redstone Rocket at its doorstep. More than a dozen other rockets and engines grace the grounds around it, and inside the center visitors can trace the history of spaceflight from the earliest rockets to the Challenger disaster. Exhibits include the Apollo 9 command module, Mercury and Gemini spaceships, and even the capsule used to carry the first astronauts, chimpanzees.

Fun Facts

The Republican Party was born on the corner of Second and Franklin Streets in Jackson. The hall where the founders had originally planned to meet on July 6, 1854, was too small for the 1,500 people who arrived to form a new political party. So the crowd walked eight blocks to an oak grove and met there "under the oaks."

Perhaps the most intriguing item in the museum is one of the smallest: Enclosed in a glass case is a slice from moon rock Number 15555. Around it are photos of astronauts picking it up and maps of its exact location on the moon, but it is the small grayish rock itself, the first piece of the moon most people ever examine, that commands most of the attention.

The Michigan Space Center (517–787–4425) can be reached from I–94 by taking exit 142 (US 127) south 6 miles to the M 50 exit. Turn left on McDevitt and go 1 mile to the first traffic light; turn left on Hague and follow it 2 miles to Jackson Community College. The center is open from May to Labor Day. Hours are 10:00 A.M. to 5:00 P.M. Monday through Saturday and noon to 5:00 P.M. on Sunday. Call the museum for the reduced hours September through April. There is an admission fee.

Ten miles southwest of Jackson is the Victorian town of Concord, the proper setting for the *Mann House*, a Michigan historical museum. The three-story house was built in 1883 by Daniel and Ellen Mann, two of the earliest settlers in the area. They raised two daughters, Jessie and Mary Ida, who continued to live in the house and maintained the original furnishings, most dating to the 1870s. The younger daughter died in 1969 but bequeathed the historic house and all its contents to the people of Michigan through the Michigan Historical Commission.

The house can be toured today, and its eight rooms are a well-preserved trip back to life in the 1880s. The table is set in the dining room; a chess game waits to be played in the parlor; toys, books, and knickknacks fill the children's rooms. As soon as you walk through the wrought-iron gate at the street, you enter an era gone by. The Mann House (517–524–8943) is at 205 Hanover Street in Concord

Michigan Space Center

and is open from 12:30 to 4:30 P.M. Wednesday through Sunday from Memorial Day to Labor Day. There is no admission fee.

Calhoun County

Homer is a small town in the southeast corner of the county, and its most impressive structure is a century-old gristmill on the banks of the Kalamazoo River. The U.S. government once wanted to turn the mill's black walnut beams into propellers for World War I airplanes. Another historic building in town, though considerably smaller, is a fun place to have breakfast on the Fourth of July: the *Homer Fire Museum*. The red brick structure with its arched windows and decorative cornice was built in 1876, five years after Homer was incorporated as a village. It has always been the classic fire hall on the main street, but in its early days it also served as a jail, town hall, and place for public meetings and local theater performances. It's the oldest building in town, and when Homer residents decided to replace it, they preserved the old fire hall by attaching the new fire station to it.

In 1983 it was set up as a museum, with suits and equipment donated by former firefighters. By far the most impressive item on display had always been there, a horse-pulled steam pumper built in 1887. Homer bought it from Union City in 1904 for $1,200 and placed it in the fire hall, where it has been ever since. The best time to see the displays is on the Fourth of July, when the town holds its annual Fire Hall Pancake Breakfast from 7:00 to 11:00 A.M. Almost 500 people enjoy the all-American morning meal in the new fire station on tables set up among the modern equipment. Then they wander into the old hall to see how fires were put out in days past. The museum does not have regular hours, but those who are passing through can go to the Homer City Offices (517–568–4311) next to the fire station, and an employee will open up the museum for you. There is no admission fee.

Battle Creek is best known as the Cereal Bowl of America, dating back to 1876 when Dr. John Harvey Kellogg joined the staff of the Battle Creek Sanitarium. Kellogg spent the next twenty-five years developing the sanitarium into an institution recognized around the world for its "health building and training" regimen of hydrotherapy, exercise, and vegetarian diet. Along the way he found a way to process grains into appetizing breakfast food for his sanitarium guests. Cornflakes and

Sojourner Truth

The Kimball House Museum is a restored 1886 Victorian home furnished with antiques and devoted to the history of Battle Creek. But by far the most interesting exhibit is dedicated to Sojourner Truth. This famous anti-slavery reformer was born into slavery in Hurley, New York, in 1797 but was freed when the state emancipated slaves in 1829. A mystic who believed she heard God's voice, Truth began to preach in the streets of New York City in 1829 and then along the Eastern Seaboard after embracing the abolitionist movement in 1843. She added women's rights to her causes a few years later, and in 1864 was received by President Abraham Lincoln at the White House.

Eventually Truth relocated to Battle Creek but continued to stump the country on speaking tours, advocating women's rights. Illiterate all her life, Truth was nevertheless a charismatic speaker who drew large crowds to her lectures and quickly became Battle Creek's first nationally known figure.

The second-floor exhibit at the Kimball House Museum features a handful of Truth's mementoes including her crude attempt to write her name. The museum is at 196 Capital Avenue, 3 blocks north of Michigan Avenue. Hours are 1:00 to 4:00 p.m. on Friday and the second and fourth Sunday of the month.

other cereals quickly revolutionized the eating habits of people everywhere, and by the early 1900s more than forty cereal manufacturers were based in Battle Creek, including Kellogg's.

The fascinating story behind the breakfast cereal industry is best told at *Kellogg's Cereal City USA*. Opened in the summer of 1998, the two-and-half story, 45,000-square-foot center contains 15,000 square feet of interactive displays along with theaters and galleries. A detailed replica of Kellogg's cereal production line demonstrates the process of manufacturing cereal. At the Marketplace gift shop, you can purchase Kellogg's apparel, and the Collectibles Cafe features novelty food made with cereal.

Tony the Tiger? Yeah, he's there too, and the kids think It's Grrrreat!

Kellogg's Cereal City USA (616–962–6230) is at 171 West Michigan Avenue. From I–94 take exit 103 and follow Michigan Avenue west into the downtown area. Hours are 10:00 A.M. to 4:00 P.M. Tuesday through Friday, 10:00 A.M. to 5:00 P.M. Saturday, and noon to 5:00 P.M. Sunday. Admission is $6.50 for adults and $4.50 for children.

Not every attraction in Battle Creek is wrapped around sugar frosted flakes. Just south of the city in a wooded area along Harper Creek is *Binder Park Zoo*, one of Michigan's most unusual displays of fauna and flora. Instead of a series of cages and animal houses in the middle of a city, Binder Park is a walk through the woods along boardwalks, brick walkways, and wood-chip trails, passing animal exhibits that have been designed around the existing flora and terrain.

There is the Northern Forest Boardwalk, where you can view timber wolves, great horned owls, and a Sitka deer; a Great Plains area, with bison, a prairie dog colony, and snowy owls; hungry trout that you can feed in Harper Creek; and a turtle log and viewing area in the pond. In other areas you will see giant tortoises, zebras, cheetahs, and even a bald eagle, but the most impressive section is Binder's zoo within a zoo. The newest addition to the park is Miller Children's Zoo, the largest animal-contact area in the state. Kids have a chance to feed and touch dozens of animals, including donkeys, rabbits, pygmy goats, draft horses, and pigs. Constructed around these contact stations are intriguing play areas. There's the Pig Pen, with models of pigs that children can play on; the dinosaur area, with a 100-foot-long brontosaurus and a fossil-find pit; a giant spider web to climb; and a farm area with a silo slide and cow climber.

Binder Park Zoo (616–979–1351) is reached from I–94 by taking exit 100 south along Beadle Lake Road and following the signs to the entrance. The zoo is open mid-April to mid-October from 9:00 A.M. to 5:00 P.M. Monday through Friday and until 6:00 P.M. on Saturday and 11:00 A.M. to 6:00 P.M. on Sunday. There is an admission fee.

Kalamazoo County

The *Kalamazoo Aviation History Museum* is dedicated to the aircraft of World War II and the role they played in the Allies' success. It's a "living museum" that not only displays many planes in its hangar at the southeast corner of the city's Municipal Airport but also

Strange As It Sounds

It looked so plain when the woman behind the counter handed it to me, wrapped in wax paper and placed in a brown paper bag. But there it is: a buttered turkey sandwich, slices of moist meat on a bun, topped with mayonnaise. It's the kind of sandwich you'd make after Thanksgiving dinner with the leftover rolls and that platter of turkey still sitting in the kitchen.

But here at a place they call Turkeyville, U.S.A., you don't have to wait until Uncle Harry and the kids go home. You can order one year-round because this simple sandwich— turkey, butter, mayonnaise on soft white bread—is the foundation of a multi-million-dollar company. Cornwell's Turkeyville, U.S.A. has been called "the oldest, best-known, and possibly largest all-turkey specialty restaurant in North America."

The Cornwells have done to the turkey what the Zehner family has done to the chicken in Frankenmuth: turned a meal into a tourist attraction. Today the restaurant is an entertainment complex serving an average of 1,000 people a day,

grossing more than $2 million annually, and feeding more than 400 busloads a summer—and pretty much does it all on the backs of 15,000, 30-pound toms a year. In 1985, when a photo of founders Wayne and Marjorie Cornwell was featured in People magazine with an item proclaiming their buttered bun "the world's best turkey sandwich," people around here knew the Cornwells had hit the big time.

After you've had your fill of turkey, you can wander into Cornwell's Ice Cream Parlour or browse Country Junction, a huge gift shop. Also on the grounds is the Antique Barn, St. Julian Wine Tasting shop, Turkey Barn, a play fort for the kids, and a gazebo with a band playing throughout the summer.

From I–94, take I–69 north to exit 42 and then head west on North Drive North, also known as Turkeyville Road. The restaurant is reached in a half-mile. Cornwell's Turkeyville, U.S.A. (616–781–4293) is open from 11:00 a.m. to 8:00 p.m. daily from April through October with reduced hours restores them to working condition. Visitors are treated to exhibits and historic films in the video room and to a close-up view of more than a dozen historic planes inside and more planes outside. They can even watch mechanics work on restoring the latest acquisitions.

The museum has twenty-two planes, of which fifteen are licensed to fly, and the high point of the day is when one is wheeled outside and taken on a short flight around the airport. The times of the flights are posted each day, and people have an opportunity to watch the planes perform and to talk to the pilots afterward. Planes include a Curtiss P-40 "Flying Tiger" and three Grumman cats—"Wildcat," "Hellcat," and "Bearcat," which led to the museum's nickname, the Air Zoo of Kalamazoo. For an even more personal experience, you can join a ride-along flight in a classic 1929 Ford Tri-Motor plane.

> **Fun Facts**
>
> *The city of Kalamazoo dates back to 1829 when Titus Bronson arrived and founded a settlement that was first called Bronson. The only known speech Abraham Lincoln gave in Michigan was in Kalamazoo.*

The Aviation History Museum (616–382–6555) is at 2101 East Milham Road and is open Monday through Saturday from 9:00 A.M. to 5:00 P.M. and from noon to 5:00 P.M. on Sunday. You can drive to the hangar or, if you have your own plane, fly in. Admission is $10 for adults.

Also on the edge of Kalamazoo is the ***Celery Flats Interpretive Center***. This is a truly unique facility that teaches the history of the efforts of Dutch immigrants to convert wetlands into one of the most productive celery-growing areas in the world. From the 1890s through the 1930s, fields of green-tipped celery covered Portage, Comstock, and Kalamazoo; the celery was touted as "fresh as dew from Kalamazoo."

The historic area offers an 1856 one-room schoolhouse, a 1931 grain elevator, and historical displays on celery, as well as an opportunity to rent canoes to explore the surrounding wetlands. Celery Flats (616–329–4518) is open May through August from noon to 5:00 P.M. on Friday and Sunday and 10:00 A.M. to 7:00 P.M. Saturday. In September the hours are noon to 5:00 P.M. Saturday and Sunday. From I–94 take exit 76A and head south 2.5 miles on South Westedge Avenue and then east a half-mile on Garden Lane.

Barry County

n 1962 Donald Gilmore, the son-in-law of Dr. W. E. Upjohn, founder of one of the nation's leading pharmaceutical firms, was restoring a 1920 Pierce-Arrow touring car in the driveway of his Gull Lake summer home. The project dragged on into the fall, and by the time it was finished, Gilmore had to erect a tent around the car and light a kerosene heater. This was no way to work on a classic car. So Gilmore purchased three farms north of his home and then scouted the countryside for old wooden barns, which he had dismantled and moved.

The wooden structures held his growing collection, and in 1966 Gilmore opened his barn doors to the public on ninety acres of rolling farmland. The Classic Car Club of America added its collection to what had become the Hickory Corners Museum in 1984, and today the **Gilmore-Classic Car Club of America Museums** form a complex of twenty-two barns displaying 120 vintage automobiles in mint condition. The car that attracts the most attention is a 1929 Duesenberg. Some visitors, however, are fascinated with Rolls Royces, and the museums contain fifteen of them, including eight in one barn, ranging from a 1910 Silver Ghost to a 1938 Phantom III.

There is also a 1927 Bugatti Grand Sport Roadster, the "Gnome-Mobile" from the Disney movie *Darby O'Gill and the Little People*, as well as other transportation displays, including a replica of the Wright Brothers' Kitty Hawk flier. Those intrigued by hood ornaments can view a collection of more than 800 that captures everything from a windblown angel to an archer taking aim at the road ahead. They come from as far away as the former Soviet Union and include leaded-glass ornaments from France.

The complex (616–671–5089) is located at M 43 and Hickory Road, 7 miles north of Richland. From I–94, take exit 80 and head north to M 43. The museums are open daily from 10:00 A.M. to 5:00 P.M. May through October. There is a small admission fee.

Nearby is the **Kellogg Dairy Center**. Founded in 1984 by Michigan State University, this experimental dairy is a working farm that combines research and teaching. It's also a popular spot for urban folks to visit and learn what it's like down on the farm. There is a visitor center with educational exhibits and a viewing area of the computerized milking parlor. There also is a self-guided tour through the farm that takes about an hour, or longer if you stop to pet and feed every calf.

The Kellogg Dairy Center (616–671–2507) is reached from I–94 by taking exit 85 and heading north 7 miles on Thirty-fifth Street. Turn east on M 89 and in 3 miles north on Fortieth Street to reach the posted entrance. Hours are 8:00 A.M. to sunset daily. There is no admission charge.

Ingham County

What was once a hardware store and then an ice-cream parlor in the heart of old Okemos was turned into a restaurant in 1982 by Jennifer Brooke and William White, whose extensive travels around the world gave them a love for ethnic food. Food, however, was only White's second love. His first was playing the tuba, something he had been doing since he was eleven years old.

Adorning the walls of *The Travelers Club International Restaurant and Tuba Museum* are more than two dozen tubas—over-the-shoulder baritones and alto horns— and memorabilia that White has collected over the years, including a photo of the Great Band Race staged in London in 1918, basically five guys running and playing instruments at the same time. White's most valuable piece is the only known double E-flat Helicon Tuba, which was made in 1915 and nicknamed "The Majestic Monster." His most unusual: the double Bell Euphonium; it has two horns. The Travelers Club International Restaurant (517–349–1701) is reached from I–96 by taking exit 110 and heading north on Okemos Road. Hours are 7:00 A.M. to 10:00 P.M. Monday through Thursday, until 11:00 P.M. on Friday and Saturday, and 9:00 A.M. to 10:00 P.M. on Sunday.

One of the best urban park developments in Michigan is Lansing's *River Trail*. The 6-mile-long park is a greenbelt that stretches on both sides of the Grand River from Kalamazoo Avenue just north of I–496 to North Street, 3 miles downstream. A riverwalk, made of long sections of boardwalk near or on the river, runs along the entire east side of the park, with bridges that lead to more walkways on the west side. Interesting attractions are throughout the park, and you could easily spend an entire day walking from one to the next.

Riverwalk in Lansing

Wilderness Capital

*W*hen Michigan was organized as a state in 1837, Detroit was its capital, as it had been in the territorial days. After much debate, the capital was moved to a more central location in 1847. Lansing did not exist then, and its first capitol, completed in 1848, was built in a wilderness. Among the towns that wanted to be Michigan's seat of government is Marshall, which went as far as to set aside land for the capitol and even build a "Governor's Mansion" in 1839.

At the south end is the **R. E. Olds Transportation Museum** (517–372–0422), dedicated to the history of transportation in Lansing, where at one time or another fifteen makes of automobile were manufactured. Almost twenty cars, from the first Oldsmobile, built in 1897, to an Indy 500 pace car, fill the old City Bus Garage along with old motoring apparel and other memorabilia. The museum is open Monday through Saturday from 10:00 A.M. to 5:00 P.M. and Sunday from noon to 5:00 P.M. There is an admission fee.

Right next door you'll find the **Impression 5 Museum** (517–485–8116), which is described as an "exploratorium" for children and their parents, stressing hands-on exhibits. The 240 exhibits on several floors range from a music room, filled with unusual instruments to be played, to a touch tunnel, where everything is explored using only your tactile sense. Impression 5 is open the same hours as the R. E. Olds Museum, and there is an admission fee.

Continuing north along the east side, you'll walk under Michigan Avenue and past views of the state capitol, around Sun Bowl Amphitheater and the city's Farmer's Market (open Tuesday, Thursday, and Saturday), and eventually reach the **Brenke River Sculpture and Fish Ladder**. The structure is a swirl of steps and stone benches leading down to the fish ladder that curves its way around scenic North Lansing Dam. Come mid-September you can watch salmon and steelhead trout leap from one water ledge of the ladder to the next on the way to their spawning grounds.

The park really comes alive during RiverFest, held Labor Day weekend, which includes, among other activities, a lighted boat parade and a fireworks display. On any clear evening there is a magnificent view of the capitol's lighted dome, shimmering over the Grand River.

For a closer look at Michigan's most famous government building, join a **State Capitol Tour** and be prepared for the building's stunning interior.

In 1992, a major renovation of the century-old capitol was completed at a cost of more then $45 million. When the building was originally dedicated on January 1, 1879, it was one of the first state capitols to emulate the dome and wings of the U.S. Capitol in Washington, D.C., and today it is considered by most as an outstanding example of Victorian craftsmanship. All tours begin in the Rotunda, where visitors stand on the floor of glass tiles imported from England and stare at the stars in the top of the dome 172 feet above. In between are portraits of governors on the second level and, on the main floor, flags carried by Michigan regiments during battles from as long ago as the Civil War. Tours also include a look into the restored state Senate and House of Representative chambers as well as other offices and rooms, each accompanied by bits and pieces of Michigan's history.

To reach the state capitol from I–96, follow I–496 through Lansing and take the Walnut exit. State capitol signs point the way to the building and parking nearby. Capitol Tour Guide Service (517–373–2353) offers the tours every half hour Monday through Friday from 9:00 A.M. to 4:00 P.M. and Saturday from 10:00 A.M. to 4:00 P.M. Visits by groups of more than ten must be scheduled in advance. There is no charge for tours.

Planet Walk

*F*or most children one of the most enjoyable aspects of the River Trail is the Planet Walk, a cleverly simple but thoroughly enjoyable trek through our solar system. It is also very enlightening. Most maps of our solar system have condensed the distances to fit the sun and nine orbiting planets on the same page. You learn the names of the planets, but distances in the universe, the 93 million miles from the sun to Earth or the 3.7 billion miles to Pluto, are simply too large for children to comprehend from textbooks.

That's the idea behind the Planet Walk. The one-way walk of 2 miles is strung out along River Front Park, beginning and ending at two of Lansing's most enjoyable attractions:

the Impression 5 Museum and Potter Park Zoo. In between it's a 45- to 60-minute walk from the sun to Pluto, a hike in which every step represents a million miles.

Not only are the distances properly scaled but so is the size and mass of the sun and each planet. The sun, located near the entrance to the Impression 5 Museum, is a 20-inch golden sphere looking like an over-inflated basketball.

From there it's a few quick steps to reach Mercury, the size of a pencil eraser. The first four planets are reached within a few hundred feet. But the rest are spread out, and it's probably three-quarters of a mile between Saturn and Uranus alone.

Almost as impressive as the state capitol is the **Michigan Library and Historical Center**, which opened in 1988. Nationally recognized for its architectural design, the 312,000-square-foot center houses the Michigan Historical Museum, the State Archives, and the Library of Michigan, the second-largest state library in the country.

Most people, however, visit the center to see the museum. The Michigan Historical Museum features twelve permanent galleries displaying facades of a lumber baron's mansion and the state's first territorial capitol, a walk-through copper mine tunnel, and an impressive woodland diorama. Other rooms feature a working sawmill, historic cars, a stake fort, and many other exhibits relating to the history of the Great Lakes State. To view the museum and the capitol is a full day for most families.

The Michigan Library and Historical Center (517–373–3559) is at 717 West Allegan Street, within easy walking distance of the capitol. Hours are 9:00 A.M. to 4:00 P.M. Monday through Friday, 10:00 A.M. to 4:00 P.M. Saturday, and 1:00 to 5:00 P.M. on Sunday. There is no admission charge.

The newest attraction in Lansing is really an old one. For the first time in more than two decades, tours resumed at the **General Motors Lansing Car Assembly Plant** in 1998. The plant produces the Oldsmobile Achieva, Buick Skylark, Pontiac Grand Am, and Chevrolet Cavalier, and its 7,000 employees turn out more than 400,000 cars per year, more than any other plant in the country.

You can tour either the body plant or the chassis plant or do both in one day and follow an automobile practically from the drawing board to the end of the assembly line where new vehicles roll off ready for the showroom. Start with the body shop in the morning where state-of-the-art robots turn raw metal into car bodies and then tour the chassis plant in the afternoon to see how the motors, seats, trim, and other features are added. Each tour takes ninety minutes.

The General Motors Lansing Car Assembly Plant (517–885–9676) is on Stanley Street just off Saginaw Highway on the west side of town. The tours are free and are offered three times at each plant Monday through Friday, but you must make reservations in advance.

Ionia County

When autumn arrives in Michigan and the leaves begin turning shades of red, yellow, and orange, many people instinctively head north to view the fall colors. But the southern portions of the state also enjoy their share of autumn brilliance, and one of the best drives is a 15-mile route that is lined by hardwood forests and rolling farm fields and crosses three covered bridges, including the oldest one in Michigan, **White's Covered Bridge**.

Nestled in a wooded area and spanning the Flat River, White's Covered Bridge was built in 1867 by J. N. Brazee for $1,700 and has faithfully served the public ever since. It is a classic covered bridge, its trusses hand-hewed and secured with wooden pegs and hand-cut square nails. The bridge is 14 feet wide and 116 feet long, and you can still drive a car across it; most travelers park on the other side and return on foot for a closer inspection. The bridge is reached by driving to the hamlet of Smyrna in Ionia County (5 miles southwest of Belding) and then heading south on White's Bridge Road.

Continue south on White's Bridge Road for 4 miles, and turn west (left) onto Potters Road for a short distance to Fallasburg Bridge Road, which will lead you over another covered bridge in Fallasburg County Park just inside Kent County. Brazee and his construction company also built the **Fallasburg Covered Bridge**. Its design is similar to White's bridge, and it was built with the same high standards that have allowed both these structures to exist for more than a century. Above both entrances to the Fallasburg Bridge is a stern warning: $5 FINE FOR RIDING OR DRIVING ON THIS BRIDGE FASTER THAN A WALK. The county park is a pleasant stretch of picnic tables and grills on the grassy slopes of the Flat River.

From the park, take Lincoln Lake Avenue south into the town of Lowell and head west on M 21 along the Grand River until you finally cross it into the town of Ada, where signs will point the way to the **Ada Covered Bridge.** The original bridge that crossed the Thornapple River was built in 1867 by Will Holmes but was destroyed by fire in 1980. The residents of Ada immediately opened their hearts (and their wallets), and the bridge was quickly rebuilt and restored. The Ada Bridge is open to pedestrian traffic only.

Kent County

The favorite son of Grand Rapids is Gerald R. Ford, a local congressman who eventually became the thirty-eighth president of the United States. In 1981 the **Gerald R. Ford Museum** opened, and today the center, dedicated to Ford's life and his days in office, is one of the city's top attractions. More than two million visitors have passed

The Roadside Table

*F*or those who like obscure historical sites, Ionia County has one of the best in the state. Located at Morrison Lake Road and Grand River Avenue, south of the town of Saranac, is the place known simply as The Roadside Table. It was at this very spot that in 1929 county engineer Allen Williams used a stack of leftover guardrail planks to build a table, the first public picnic table ever placed on a highway right-of-way. Today, of course, there are roadside tables and rest areas in all fifty states, and the only sights more common on our nation's highways are billboards and McDonald's restaurants. Along the road, the site is marked only by a small white historical site sign, but a green state historic site plaque detailing the story has been erected next to the tables. The state still maintains the tables and garbage barrels, even though most of the traffic now flows along I–94 to the south.

through the center, which features two floors of exhibits and displays that underwent a $5.3 million makeover in 1997.

The museum still features a full-scale reproduction of the Oval Office as it appeared in Ford's administration but now has several new galleries that feature hands-on and computerized exhibits. Among them is a TelePrompTer that allows you to give a Ford speech, videos of President Richard Nixon resigning, and a holographic device that puts you into ten rooms of the White House, including the famous Lincoln Bedroom.

The Gerald R. Ford Museum (616–451–9263) is at 303 Pearl Street NW on the west bank of the Grand River, and is reached by exiting US 131 at Pearl Street. Hours are 9:00 A.M. to 5:00 P.M. daily. There is a small admission fee.

Long before the Presidential Seal was stamped on this portion of Kent County, Grand Rapids was known as the City of Furniture. In 1853 it was a small frontier town surrounded by forests with a seemingly endless supply of lumber and situated on the banks of the Grand River, which provided power for the mills. In this setting William "Deacon" Haldane opened a cabinet shop and soon was building not only cupboards but also cradles, coffins, and tables and chairs. By the end of the decade, there were several shops, and soon "Grand Rapids–Made Furniture" became the standard of excellence.

As impressive as the Ford Museum is, it now has a rival practically next door. In 1995 the **Van Andel Museum Center** opened to the public, replacing the old Grand Rapids Public Museum. The $40 million structure is on the Grand River, and overlooking the water is its centerpiece, a glass pavilion housing a working 1928 carousel with hand-carved horses and a Wurlitzer organ. Rides are 50 cents, and it's debatable who has more fun—children or their parents.

Other exhibits in the three-story building include a replica of a Union Depot waiting room, a 76-foot finback whale suspended from the ceiling, an entire street from Grand Rapids in the 1890s, a high-tech planetarium, and many interactive and hands-on exhibits that focus on natural science and the unique western Michigan environment.

The Van Andel Museum Center (616–456–3977) is at 272 Pearl, just east of the Pearl exit off US 131. Hours are 9:00 A.M. to 5:00 P.M. daily. There is an admission fee of $5.00 for adults and $2.00 for children.

When the state began stocking salmon in the Great Lakes in the 1960s, the fish would spawn up the Grand River but had problems getting beyond the Sixth Street Dam in Grand Rapids. The solution was the **Fish Ladder Sculpture**, a unique sculptured viewing area designed by local artist Joseph Kinnebrew. Located at 606 Front Street NW, just on the north side of I–196, the ladder is a series of seven small ledges on the west bank of the river that let the salmon easily leap around the dam. The rest of the sculpture is a platform above the ladder that provides a close view of the large fish as they jump completely out of the water from one ledge to the next.

The first salmon begin arriving in early September, and the run is over in October. Local people say the third week of September is when you'll see the major portion of the spawning run. Spectators won't be the only ones there, however, as the river will be filled with anglers trying to interest the fish in a lure, a spectacle in itself.

Fred Meijer, founder of the chain of Meijer's stores, is also responsible for **Frederik Meijer Gardens**, the largest tropical conservatory in the state. Meijer funded the project after members of West Michigan Horticultural Society pointed out to him that their side of the state had no large public gardens.

Fun Facts

Grand Rapids entered the national furniture market with exhibits at the Philadelphia Centennial Exposition in 1876. Today the city still accounts for 40 percent of the business/office furniture market.

Opened in 1995, the one-hundred-acre complex features plants from around the world, waterfalls, streams, and more than sixty bronze sculptures by Marshall Fredericks and other renowned artists. Along with the main conservatory are smaller garden areas including Arid Gardens, Victorian Garden, and Gardener's Corner where specialty plants are sold. Winding through the complex is the "magnificent mile," a system of barrier-free nature trails and boardwalks that overlook wetlands, ponds, and meadows.

The gardens (616–957–1580) are northeast of Grand Rapids. From I–96 take exit 38 and head north on East Beltline Road and then east on Bradford Street to reach the gardens. Hours are 9:00 A.M. to 5:00 P.M. daily, until 9:00 P.M. on Wednesday, and noon to 5:00 P.M. on Sunday. Admission is $4.00 for adults.

Just 15 miles north of Grand Rapids is the small town of Rockford, which dates back to the 1840s when a dam and sawmill were built along the Rogue River. Soon a railroad line passed through Rockford, and the town became a trading center with warehouses, a train depot, mills, and

Jerry's Diner Village

I'm drawn into the large parking lot off US 131 by the warm glow of a huge neon sign that says "Rosie's." But when I step out, it's Elvis that greets me. "All Shook Up" is crackling over the speakers attached to the streamlined diner of shiny stainless steel and glass brick.

I step through the door and am hit by an aroma of french fries, mom's homemade apple pie, and meatloaf, and then slip into a half-moon booth and order a hot roast beef sandwich that comes with an ice-cream scoop of potatoes smothered in a sea of gravy.

To those of us who love road food, this is our temple—a cathedral with spin-around stools and a lunch counter wiped every five minutes by a waitress in bobby socks and tennis shoes. What isn't pink tile or stainless steel here is red vinyl.

You've heard of Disneyland in California? Now there's Dinerland in Rockford, a wild combination of fine art, tacky souvenirs and miniature golf,

road food and gourmet dining, and not one but three authentic diners salvaged and saved by artist Jerry Berta.

The main diner is Rosie's, which Berta saved and moved 700 miles from New Jersey to Rockford in 1989. Built in 1946 by the Paramount Dining Car Company, the classic diner was used in several movies and more than one hundred commercials but was made famous by actress Nancy Walker when she cleaned up spills in it with "the quicker picker-upper," Bounty paper towels. In 1991, Berta opened it up as a restaurant because so many people were stopping in at his Diner Store wanting to buy hamburgers or milkshakes instead of his art.

The diners are 15 miles north of Grand Rapids. From US 131 take exit 101 and head east a quarter-mile. Rosie's (616–866–FOOD) is open from 6:00 a.m. to 9:00 p.m. Sunday through Thursday and until 10:00 p.m. Friday and Saturday.

a bean-processing plant built along the river. What connected them on land was an unnamed alley that eventually became known as Squires Street. In 1970, the bean plant was renovated into the Old Mill, a cider mill and restaurant. This led to more historical buildings being bought and turned into a strip of specialized shops and stores.

Today **Squires Street Square** is the heart of Rockford, a charming 3-block section of more than forty shops and restaurants. You'll find stores in old warehouses, barns, a former shoe factory, a carriage house, even in railroad cars. The Rockford Historical Museum occupies the Power House, which sits on the banks of the Rogue River and at one time was a generator plant for a local factory. All the businesses are within walking distance of each other, and most are open Monday through Saturday. Rockford can be reached from US 131 by taking exit 97 and following Ten Mile Road east a short way.

Hot Dog Hall of Fame (No Kidding!)

To travelers passing through Rockford, The Corner Bar appears from the outside to be just that, a small-town tavern on the corner of Main Street and Northland. Once you step inside, though, you soon realize that this pub, decorated in brass nameplates, sports memorabilia, and newspaper clippings, is packed with history and hot-dog legends. For starters, The Corner Bar is the oldest brick building in Rockford. Built in 1873, it survived several fires, including the "Great Main Street Fire" of 1896, and today is exceeded in age only by a wood-frame house behind the railroad depot.

At one time the building was a dry-goods store, then a hardware store, and finally, at the turn of the century, its most enduring business moved in. It became a saloon noted for its hot dogs. People came from all around to enjoy hot dogs served in steamed buns and topped with special sauce, a good heaping of relish, and chopped onions. Among the patrons one night in 1967 were several members of the Detroit Lions football team who amazed their waitress when they challenged each other to eat twelve hot dogs apiece. By the following year owner Donald R. Berg had turned that twelve-dog challenge into The Hot Dog Hall of Fame, Michigan's most unusual hall of fame, where twelve hot dogs at $1.13 apiece can immortalize your appetite with a brass nameplate on the wall. The present record of forty-two and a half hot dogs was set in 1982. The bar (616–866–9866) is open from 10:00 a.m. to midnight Monday through Wednesday, 10:00 a.m. to 1:00 a.m. Thursday through Saturday, and noon to 8:00 p.m. on Sunday.

Mecosta County

ig Rapids may be the county seat of Mecosta County, but in recent years the city has also become known as the "Tubing Capital" of Michigan. Owners of **Sawmill Canoe Livery**, which began renting out large truck tubes in 1979, say the portion of the Muskegon River that runs through Big Rapids from their livery to Highbanks Park is the most tubed waterway in the state, with more than 30,000 people floating down every summer. It's easy to see why on a hot day. Tubing is a lazy and carefree way to beat the heat; you simply place the tube in the water, sit in it, and float. No skills or paddling are needed.

The run takes about two hours, and tubers often take small coolers (larger ones require their own tube) and plenty of suntan lotion with them. For a small fee the livery provides the tube and transportation back from Highbanks Park, and on a hot August day, there will be hundreds floating along the Muskegon at every bend. Sawmill Canoe Livery (231–796–6408) is at 230 Baldwin Street and rents tubes from May to September.

PLACES TO STAY IN MICHIGAN'S HEARTLAND

BATTLE CREEK
Battle Creek Inn,
5050 Beckley Road,
(800) 232–3405

Hampton Inn,
1150 Riverside Drive,
(616) 979–5577

COLDWATER
Chicago Pike Inn,
215 East Chicago Street,
(800) 471–0501

EAST LANSING
Marriott East Lansing,
300 M.A.C. Avenue,
(517) 337–4440

Kellogg Hotel,
on the Michigan State
campus,
(517) 432–4000

GRAND RAPIDS
Amway Grand Plaza Hotel,
187 Monroe Street,
(800) 253–3590

Country Inn & Suites,
5399 Twenty-eighth Street,
(800) 456–4000

Days Inn Airport,
5500 Twenty-eighth Street,
(800) 325–2525

Peaches Bed & Breakfast,
29 Gay Street SE,
(616) 454–8000

JONESVILLE
Munro House Bed &
Breakfast,
202 Maumee Street,
(800) 320–3792

Horse & Carriage Bed &
Breakfast,
7020 Brown Road,
(517) 849–2732

KALAMAZOO
Kelly Inn,
3800 East Cork Street,
(616) 381–1900

Red Roof Inn,
3701 East Cork Street,
(616) 382–6350

Stuart Avenue Inn,
229 Stuart Avenue,
(616) 342–0230

Hall House Bed & Breakfast,
106 Thompson Street,
(616) 343–2500

LANSING
Governor's Inn,
6133 South Pennsylvania
Avenue,
(517) 393–5500

Red Roof Inn,
3615 Dunckel Road,
(517) 332–2575

Sheraton Lansing Hotel,
925 South Creyts Road,
(517) 323–7100

MARSHALL
McCarthy's Bear Creek Inn,
15230 C Drive North,
(616) 781–8383

National House Inn,
102 South Parkview
Avenue,
(616) 781–7274

MENDON
Mendon Country Inn,
440 West Main Street,
(616)496–8132

STANTON
Clifford Lake Hotel,
561 West Clifford Lake
Drive,
(517) 831–5151

**PLACES TO EAT IN
MICHIGAN'S HEARTLAND**

ADA
Thornapple Village Inn
(fine dining),
445 Thornapple Village
Drive,
(616) 676–1233

BATTLE CREEK
Arcadia Brewing Company
(brewpub),
103 West Michigan Avenue,
(616) 963–9690

Pancake House (breakfast),
185 Capital Avenue,
(616) 946–6790

Mexicali Restaurant (Mexican),
595 Columbia Avenue,
(616) 963–8188

EAST LANSING
Beggar's Banquet (American),
218 Abbott Road,
(517) 351–4573

El Azteco (Mexican),
225 Ann Street,
(517) 351–9111

GRAND RAPIDS
Cygnus (Mediterranean),
Amway Grand Plaza,
(616) 776–6425

Schnitzelbank (German),
342 Jefferson Avenue,
(616) 459–9527

Gibson's Restaurant (American),
1033 Lake Drive SE,
(616) 744–8535

Yen Ching (Chinese),
57 Monroe Center,
(616) 235–6969

JACKSON
Otello's (Italian),
151 West Michigan Avenue,
(517) 782–2411

The Parlour (ice cream),
1401 Daniel Road,
(517) 782–7141

Selected Chambers of Commerce and Tourism Bureaus

Greater Battle Creek Visitor and Convention Bureau,
34 West Jackson Street, Suite 4-B, Battle Creek 49017;
(800) 397–2240

Grand Rapids/Kent County
Convention & Visitors Bureau,
140 Monroe Center NW, Suite 300, Grand Rapids 49503;
(800) 678–9859

Jackson Convention and Tourist Bureau,
6007 Ann Arbor Road, Jackson 49201;
(800) 245–5282

Kalamazoo County Convention and Visitors Bureau,
128 North Kalamazoo Mall, Kalamazoo 49007;
(616) 381–4003

Greater Lansing Convention and Visitors Bureau,
P.O. Box 1506, Lansing 48901;
(800) 968–8474

KALAMAZOO

Club Car Restaurant
(American),
6225 West D Avenue,
(616) 342–0807

Theo & Stacy's (Greek),
5225 Portage Road,
(616) 345–3000

François Seafood & Steak-
house (fine dining),
116 Portage Road,
(616) 381–4958

LANSING

The Blue Coyote Brewing
Company (brewpub),
113 Père Marquette Street,
(517) 485–BLUE

Clara's Lansing station
(fine dining),
637 East Michigan Avenue,
(517) 372–7120

The Dancing Goat Coffee-
house (espresso),
301 South
Washington Square,
(517) 487–5120

MARSHALL

Schuler's (American),
115 South Eagle Street,
(616) 781–0600

ROCKFORD

Rosie's Diner (American),
4500 Fourteen-
Mile Road NE,
(616) 866–3663

OTHER ATTRACTIONS

Kingman Museum of
Natural History,
Battle Creek

Leila Arboretum,
Battle Creek

Honolulu House,
Marshall

Kalamazoo Valley Museum,
Kalamazoo

Kellogg Bird Sanctuary,
Augusta

Potter Park Zoo,
Lansing

Michigan State University
Museum,
East Lansing

The Kresge Art Museum,
East Lansing

Michigan's Women's
Historical Center &
Hall of Fame,
Lansing

Grand Rapids Children's
Museum

Grand Rapids Art Museum

John Ball Zoological
Gardens,
Grand Rapids

Lake Huron

The Lake Huron shoreline, the eastern side of Michigan, is a region that has gone full circle in its history and its appearance. The first inhabitants of the area were Indians who traveled lightly through the woods and lived off the land but rarely disfigured it. When Europeans arrived, they were awed by what was perceived as an endless forest, woods so thick with towering white pines that the sun rarely reached the forest floor.

All that changed in the mid-1800s. Lumbering companies that had exhausted the forests in Maine were looking for pine to cut for new settlements on the Great Plains, which were desperate for wood in their treeless region. Michigan met those needs as the greatest lumber-producing state in the nation between 1850 and 1910, with an estimated 700 logging camps and more than 2,000 mills. Massive log drives filled the Saginaw and Au Sable Rivers, which were avenues to the sawmill towns on Lake Huron. In mill towns like Saginaw and Bay City, sawmills lined the riverbanks, and huge mansions lined the streets as more wealth was made off Michigan's white pine than by miners in the Klondike Gold Rush.

By the turn of the century, all that was left were the stumps. The lumbering era had devastated the region, turning it into treeless areas that were wastelands of soil erosion. The Huron National Forest was established in 1909 along the Au Sable River, the first of many such preserves, in an effort to repair and manage the land. Lake Huron entered a new era in which terms such as reforestation, conservation, and renewable resources replaced the lumber lingo of log drives, river rats, and clearcuts.

Almost a century later the northeastern portion of the Lower Peninsula is once again a forested region. The trees are of a different generation and often a different species, but the effect on visitors is the same as when the first Europeans wandered through. To walk quietly among the towering pines in a forest padded by needles while listening to the

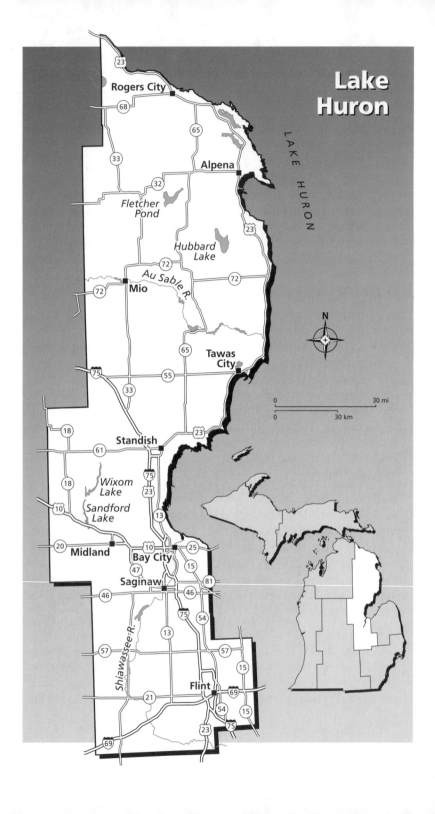

gentle rustling of a coldwater trout stream is as much an attraction in this part of the state as sandy beaches or a cottage on the lake.

Shiawassee County

I n the early 1900s a young writer was tracking a grizzly bear he had shot in British Columbia when suddenly the wounded animal appeared and trapped the man on a narrow mountain ledge. As the author would write later, "Sudden death seemed the hunter's inevitable fate. Then the huge bruin turned away, leaving the hunter unharmed. But not unchanged—the man packed away his guns and never hunted for sport again."

Instead James Oliver Curwood used the experience in his best-selling novel *The Grizzly King*, which was published in 1916. In 1989, when the book served as the basis of the movie *The Bear,* Owosso's favorite son—and one of its best-kept secrets—was finally exposed to the rest of the country. Curwood was born in the Shiawassee County town of Owosso in 1878 and returned with his family in 1891. After attending the University of Michigan for two years and working on a newspaper in Detroit, Curwood resigned to pursue literary work entirely in 1907.

He wrote thirty-three novels, most of them fast-paced tales set predominantly in northwest Canada, or "God's country," as the author called it. They were best-sellers worldwide and, between royalties and movie deals, made Curwood a millionaire and allowed him to build **Curwood Castle** along the banks of the Shiawassee River in Owosso in 1922. Built solely as a writing studio, the castle features a great room on the first floor, where the author entertained guests; a twisting staircase leads to his work area upstairs. Today the castle is a museum devoted to the author, featuring memorabilia from Curwood's life, including his original writing desk, which is used in the reception center.

The castle, a replica of a French chateau, is part of the city's historical area, which also includes the first cabin built in Owosso. The museum (517–725–0597) is at 224 Curwood Castle Drive, which is reached from

M 52 south of the Shiawassee River. The castle is open from 1:00 to 5:00 P.M. daily except Monday. There is a small admission fee.

At the turn of the century, Durand was what Detroit's Metro Airport or Chicago's O'Hare is today—the transportation hub of the Midwest. The first railroad, the Detroit-Milwaukee Line, arrived at the small town in 1865 because of Durand's central location, and by 1907 there were seven lines, promoting the construction of **Union Station**, a massive depot 239 feet long and costing $60,000 to build. It burned down two years later but was quickly rebuilt by Grand Trunk Railroad as the age of railroading and the town of Durand entered their golden eras. Almost half of the town's population of 2,500 worked for Grand Trunk, and more people changed trains in Durand than there were residents living there!

Union Station (517–288–3561), often called the "most photographed depot in the country," was designated the Michigan Railroad History Museum and Information Center. Visitors can wander through the station and view a gallery of railroading artifacts, including hand cars, engine lights, rolltop desks, and other furnishings of a 1900-era depot.

Durand can be reached from I–69 by heading south at exit 116. Union Station is on the south side of Main Street and is open Tuesday through Saturday from 1:00 to 5:00 P.M.

Genesee County

The heart of Genesee County is Flint, Michigan's fourth-largest city and the home of the Buick Division of General Motors. For an intriguing look inside an auto factory, join a tour of the *GM Truck & Bus Assembly Plant*. This historic plant was built in 1947 and produced the first Corvairs and later Chevrolet Suburbans and vans and even military vehicles used in Operation Desert Storm. The facility covers fifty-six acres and employs up to 3,500 workers who build thirty-four cars per hour.

Tours last ninety minutes and include considerable walking. The GM Truck & Bus Assembly Plant (810–236–4978) is reached from I–75 by taking exit 116A and heading east on Bristol Road for a mile. Turn north on Van Slyke Road and enter the plant at Gate 6A. The free tours are offered Monday through Friday at 9:00 A.M., but you must make reservations.

The automobile industry and cars are a major part of Flint's livelihood, and both have been well preserved in the city's *Sloan Museum*. The most dramatic chapter in Flint's history is the Great Sit-Down Strike of 1937, which is retold in the museum's permanent 10,000-square-foot exhibit entitled "Flint and the American Dream." The forty-four-day ordeal ended when General Motors agreed to sign its first contract with the United Auto Workers. It was a bitter struggle that led to the unionization of all American autoworkers and changed the course of history in Michigan, if not the entire country.

Sloan Museum, however, is probably best known for its classic car collection. More than sixty cars are on display in two buildings and range from the oldest production-model Chevrolet in existence and a 1910 Buick "Bug" raced by Louis Chevrolet to prototypes vehicles that never made it into production.

The museum (810–760–1169) is in the Flint Cultural Central and is reached from I–475 by taking exit 8A. Head east on Longway Boulevard and follow the signs to the Cultural Central at 1221 East Kearsley Street. Hours are 10:00 A.M. to 5:00 P.M. Monday through Friday and noon to 5:00 P.M. Saturday and Sunday. There is an admission fee.

Flint also has many interesting non-automotive attractions, including its delightful *Children's Museum*. Described by its staff as a "touchable discovery center," the museum was proposed in 1980, and after six years of collecting donated materials, the center opened in 1986. Unlike other hands-on museums in Ann Arbor and Lansing, the exhibits here are not complex demonstrations in science or physics. They're simply everyday items that children can touch, ride, climb, and make believe with.

The television studio is probably the most popular area. The news desk, weather map, and talk show set were actually used by Saginaw's WNEM-TV from 1981 to 1987 and then donated to the museum. The set is compete with real television cameras, control board, and monitors so children can not only give you the straight scoop on current events or weather but watch themselves doing it as well.

If they'd rather play doctor, there are a hospital room with an elevated bed, patient gowns, doctors' coats, bandages, crutches, an instrument to

---

Top Annual Events

Kirtland's Warbler Festival,
Mio, May;
(800) 800–6133

Mushroom Festival,
Lewiston, May;
(517) 786–2293

Bavarian Festival,
Frankenmuth, June;
(517) 652–8155

Brown Trout Festival,
Alpena, July;
(800) 425–7362

Chesaning Showboat Festival,
Chesaning, July;
(800) 844–3056

Nautical City Festival,
Rogers City, July;
(517) 734–4656

Great Lakes Lighthouse Festival,
Alpena, October;
(800) 425–7362

Perchville USA,
Tawas City, February;
(800) 55–TAWAS

Fun Facts

The largest planetarium in Michigan is the Longway Planetarium (810–760–1181) in Flint, which features a 60-foot domed screen.

---

check your blood pressure, and another to check your reflexes. Kids can also try their hands in the judge's chambers, appear on stage in costumes, or jump into a role as a bus driver, firefighter, or captain of a full-size boat, where even the life jackets are provided for a safe cruise on the imaginary Seven Seas.

The museum (810–767–5437) is located at 1602 West Third Avenue. Take I–75 to I–475 and then exit 8A to head west on Robert T. Longway Road, which turns into Fifth Avenue. Turn south on Grand Traverse Street and then west on Third Avenue. The center is open year-round from 10:00 A.M. to 5:00 P.M. Monday through Saturday and noon to 5:00 P.M. on Sunday. There is a small admission fee.

There's more fun for the kids just north of Flint at **Penny Whistle Place**, the unique contemporary play park administered by the Genesee County Parks and Recreation Commission. Forget about teeter-totters, swings, and monkey bars. Park officials describe Penny Whistle Place as "a colorful, imaginative play area designed to encourage creative, unstructured play."

That's for sure. Modeled after highly successful parks such as Children's Village in Toronto, Michigan's first futuristic play area features Punch Bag Forest, where you run through an area of swinging, suspended punching bags, taking your best shots at them. There are also the Buick Bounce, a version of a moonwalk; the Cable Glide, which sends you flying across the park; and Together Toys, best described as giant Legos. Kids love the Net Climb, where they scramble across on all fours to reach a platform high above the park, and the Ball Crawl, in which they swim or sink through hundreds of thousands of colorful plastic balls. This playground abounds with unique attractions.

From I–75, follow I–475 and then get off at Saginaw Street (exit 13). Head north to Stanley Road, then east to Bray Road, where you head south to the entrance. Penny Whistle Place (800–648–PARK) is open from June through mid-August daily from 10:00 A.M. to 6:00 P.M. Monday through Saturday and noon to 6:00 P.M. Sunday. Admission is $3.50 for children two years and older but only $1.50 for adults.

Saginaw County

The only Michigan county without a natural lake, Saginaw County still has plenty of water, as the Saginaw, Tittabawassee, Bad,

Cass, Shiawassee, and Flint Rivers make it the largest river basin in the state, with 160 miles of waterway. It was these natural avenues and the vast forests bordering them that allowed the area to boom with loggers and sawmills in the mid-1800s. By the early 1900s the trees and loggers were gone, but reminders of the immense wealth they produced are seen throughout the county in magnificent Victorian-era homes, especially along the Boulevard in Chesaning, a major lumbering center on the Shiawassee River in the southwest corner of the county.

The Boulevard (part of M 57) and its historic homes were developed into the *Old Home Shoppes,* seven of the houses that are now gift and antique shops. At the beginning and the heart of it is the *Chesaning Heritage House*, one of the finest restaurants in Saginaw County. The house was built in 1908 by George Nanson as a monument to his family's lumbering business. Nanson's father, Robert, was born in England but arrived in 1852 in Chesaning, where he began as a farmer but ended up building a sawmill and, true to the American dream, became one of the wealthiest people in the lumber town. The Georgian Revival–style house reflects all this with stately Ionic columns outside and its grand rotunda opening between the first and second floors.

The house changed hands a few times and was even vacant for ten years before Howard and Bonnie Ebenhoeh purchased it and opened the restaurant in 1980. Dining is a leisurely affair in one of seven rooms on the first or second floor. Four of the rooms have fireplaces that are lit during the winter; another room is the original sun porch, now a glass-enclosed terrace that holds a half-dozen tables. The Heritage House prides itself on its preparation of Michigan beef, and one of its specialties

Chesaning Showboat

*I*n 1937, after local businessman Harley Peet provided a $400 loan, the city of Chesaning launched its first "Showboat." At the time it was little more than a local talent show performed on the Shiawassee River with residents sitting in borrowed bleachers. Today the six-day event, called the Chesaning Showboat Festival, is one of the top entertainment venues in the state. Each evening show still arrives on the showboat to a packed house but is now headlined by a nationally known entertainer. Artists appearing there have ranged from Steve Allen and Donny and Marie Osmond to Roy Clark and Louise Mandrell. It's normally standing-room-only for the shows, which attract more than 40,000 visitors before the showboat takes its final trip back up the river. For dates and ticket information, call the Chesaning Chamber of Commerce at (800) 844-3056.

is baked tenderloin for two, which arrives with a crown of mushrooms. The dessert tray is also deliciously tempting and always includes an ice-cream sundae pie.

The Heritage House (517–845–7700) is open Monday through Thursday from 11:00 A.M. to 9:00 P.M., Friday and Saturday 11:00 A.M. to 10:00 P.M., and Sunday noon to 9:00 P.M. Dinners range from $12 to $25. Behind the restaurant, the original carriage house has been turned into an antiques and gift shop with two floors of furniture, crafts, and dolls, and a 1908 horse carriage on display upstairs.

Practically across the street from the Heritage House is the **Bonnymill Inn.** The country inn is along the railroad tracks and overlooks a grain elevator.

But what did you expect?

The Bonnymill was originally the Chesaning Farmers Coop Elevator, built in the 1920s to replace one that had just burned down. For more than half a century, it stored the corn and soybeans of local farmers and loaded the grain into railroad cars until it was closed down in the fall of 1987.

Then it was renovated into a delightful inn that features twenty-nine guest rooms, including eleven suites featuring king-size beds, fireplaces, and in-room Jacuzzis; some even have wet bars. The center of the inn is a large atrium that includes a winding oak staircase, a spacious lounge complete with a piano and fireplace, and an eating area where a hot breakfast buffet is served in the morning and tea in the afternoon. Outside is a long rambling porch that owners claim is "the biggest porch in mainland Michigan." (The longest porch in the state is at the Grand Hotel on Mackinac Island.)

Shopping at Birch Run

In the early 1980s, Birch Run was a sleepy little village at the Frankenmuth exit of I–75. Today it's the discount shopping capital of Michigan, thanks to Prime Outlets at Birch Run (517–624–4868). The 170 stores form the largest manufacturer's mall in the state and include everything from Ann Taylor to Anne Klein and Eddie Bauer to Bugle Boy. The mall is right off I–75, exit 136, and most shops are open from 10:00 a.m. to 9:00 p.m. Monday through Saturday and 11:00 a.m. to 6:00 p.m. Sunday. This place can be unbearably crowded on the weekends with travelers dropping in for a little shopping on their way up north. The best time to shop is the middle of the week from 3:00 to 6:00 p.m.

Rooms at the Bonnymill Inn (517–845–7780) range from $65 to $145 per couple. Special midweek packages include a voucher for dinner at the Heritage House.

Generally recognized as Michigan's number one attraction is the German town of Frankenmuth. "Little Bavaria" is famous for home-style chicken dinners served at one of two huge restaurants, *Zehnder's* and the *Bavarian Inn*, which face each other on Main Street. The restaurants were founded by the Zehnder brothers, whose family arrived in Frankenmuth from Bavaria in 1846. Each restaurant is a sprawling complex of a dozen German-themed dining rooms, gift shops, bakeries, and candy shops. More than 700 tons of chicken are served annually in the restaurants along with buttery noodles, savory dressing, giblet gravy, salads, and homemade breads in an all-you-can-eat affair.

Chicken dinners are $15 per person at the restaurants, which stop seating at 9:30 P.M. Sunday through Friday and 9:00 P.M. on Saturday. The Bavarian Inn (517–652–9941) is at 713 South Main Street, and Zehnder's (517–652–9925) is across the street.

What could be better with a chicken dinner than a mug of dark German beer? Frankenmuth is the home of the state's oldest brewery, *Frankenmuth Brewery*, which is located near the corner of Tuscola and Main Streets. It began making beer in 1862 as the Cass River Brewery and then became Geyer Brewing in 1874. The company was temporarily shut down in 1976 before reopening the following year under its present name with a German brewmaster arriving to direct the operation. A state historic site, Frankenmuth Brewery (517–652–6183) offers tours of its plant year-round. Visitors meet in the Hospitality Center for a brief history of the company, a video of the beer-making operation, and a tour of the facility from brew kettles to bottling. They end up back at the Hospitality Center to sample the finished product. The tours are offered daily from April through December from 11:00 A.M. to 5:00 P.M. on the hour. There is a $2.50 per-person charge.

Frankenmuth Brewery

You can enjoy a stein of the local brew in almost every restaurant and bar in town, but the most intriguing place is the *Tiffany Biergarten* just north of Zehnder's Restaurant on South Main Street. The lumbermen's saloon is located on the first floor of the Hotel Goetz, which was built in 1895, when Frankenmuth was one of the leading logging communities in the Saginaw Valley. The tavern picks up its name from its eighteen Tiffany chandeliers, made in the 1930s. It is also adorned by a beautiful wooden bar, the original tin ceiling, the inlaid tile floor, and leaded stained glass. Tiffany Biergarten is open from noon to 1:00 A.M. on Friday and Saturday, when there is live entertainment, and from noon to midnight the rest of the week.

Christmas in July? Only in Frankenmuth, where *Bronner's Christmas Wonderland* is home of the world's largest year-round display of holiday ornaments, decorations, trimmings, and gifts. More than 50,000

Shiawassee National Wildlife Refuge

When the fall migration peaks in late October or early November, more than 25,000 Canada geese and 30,000 ducks are often at the Shiawassee National Wildlife Refuge. The sight of so many birds gathered at one time is nothing short of spectacular, making this one of the great wildlife sightings in Michigan.

One of two federal wildlife refuges in Michigan, Shiawassee encompasses 9,042 acres on the doorstep of Saginaw and includes the confluence of four major rivers, the Flint, Cass, Shiawassee, and Tittabawassee. When combined with the Shiawassee River State Game Area, which borders it to the west, this goose management area exceeds 20,000 acres and is larger than any state park in the Lower Peninsula.

The Ferguson Bayou Trail, a 5-mile loop from the Curtis Road parking area, is the best trail to see birds any time of the year but especially during the fall migration. The trail is a network of gravel roads, two-tracks, and paths along the dikes that leads to an observation tower in the heart of the refuge. Most visitors walk to the tower, but the easiest way to explore the park is on a hybrid or mountain bike.

From the tower in the fall, small flocks of geese can be seen arriving by late afternoon. By evening it's practically pandemonium with hundreds of birds coming and going. Stick around for the sunset and your day will end with the most memorable sight at the refuge: flights of geese silhouetted against a red-orange sky.

The Shiawassee National Wildlife Refuge is 7 miles south of M 46 in Saginaw and reached from M 13 by turning west on Curtis Road. Within a mile is the refuge headquarters (517–777–5930) where trail maps and bird checklists are available. The Ferguson Bayou Trail is 3 miles beyond the headquarters near the end of Curtis Road.

items are stocked in the 200,000-square-foot building that houses the store's showroom, warehouse, and offices. The business can be traced back to 1945, when Wally Bronner operated Bronner's Displays and Signs out of his parents' home and was approached by Bay City officials to decorate the city streets for the upcoming holiday.

Bronner created and built lamppost panels for the city, leading to more requests by other towns and eventually to his present business providing Christmas decorations to businesses, communities, and private homes. The store is an amazing trip into the spirit of the holiday, especially its religious aspect. Inside you will find more than 500 kinds of nativity scenes, figures from 1 inch tall to life-size; 260 Christmas trees decorated in such themes as sports and wildlife; and more than 6,000 ornaments from around the world. There are music boxes, every model of Hummel figurine ever produced, and, in the store's Nutcracker Suite, 200 styles of wooden characters imported from Austria, Switzerland, and Germany.

You can't miss the store—outside it is surrounded by fifteen acres of painted snowflakes, twinkling lights, and the same kind of lamppost Bronner designed more than forty-five years ago for Bay City. Bronner's Christmas Wonderland (517–652–9931) is at the south end of town just off Main Street (M 83). It is open from June through December 24

Père Marquette Rail-Trail

*D*eparting from the Tridge is the Père Marquette Rail-Trail, a perfectly paved path without so much as a ripple, much less a hill. Originally a line for the Flint and Père Marquette Railroad, the rail-trail extends from Midland to Clare, with the 22-mile stretch to Coleman already paved.

It's open to a variety of non-motorized users, including runners, walkers, and cyclists. But in the first 3 miles, from the Tridge to Dublin Road, the most popular form of transportation is in-line skates. The Père Marquette is well designed for that. At the street crossings are locator maps, benches, and, most important, large red posts to stop skaters from flying across the intersections.

This stretch is also very scenic. From the Tridge you skirt the Tittabawassee River for more than a mile, passing fishing docks, the historic Upper Bridge, and one of the original cement mile markers that told railroad engineers how far it was to Saginaw. The trail also passes the H. H. Dow Museum, which has installed interpretive displays along the way.

For more information call the Midland County Parks and Recreation Commission at (517) 832–6870.

from 9:00 A.M. to 9:00 P.M. Monday through Saturday, and noon to 7:00 P.M. Sunday. From December 26 through May, hours are 9:00 A.M. to 5:30 P.M. Monday through Thursday and Saturday, 9:00 A.M. to 9:00 P.M. Friday, and noon to 5:30 P.M. Sunday.

In Saginaw, near the Anderson Water Slide, an American creation, is the city's *Japanese Cultural Center and Tea House*. The house was actually built by Japanese artisans, who used no nails, only intricate traditional hand tools. Today the center is the only facility in the country where visitors can observe the classic formal tea ceremony.

The house is open from noon to 4:00 P.M. Tuesday through Saturday. The symbolic tea ritual is performed and interpreted on the second Sunday of each month beginning at 2:00 P.M. There is a small fee. The house (517–759–1648) and its tranquil gardens are located in Saginaw's Celebration Square, just north of M 46 at South Washington Boulevard and Ezra Rust Drive.

Midland County

To most people the city of Midland is Dow Chemical Corporation, the place where Herbert Dow founded the company in 1897 that today gives us everything from Ziploc sandwich bags and Saran Wrap to much of the aspirin used in the country. The *H.H. Dow Museum* tells the story of the young chemist and features replicas of the gristmill and brine well that he built to launch his famous company as well as the 1890 lab where he perfected his bromine-extracting process. The *Dow Visitors Center* features more than 500 products that are made in Midland, along with exhibits on the company's history. You can also tour the huge chemical facility that includes close-up views of such areas as the Saran Wrap plant.

The H.H. Dow Museum (517–832–5319) is reached from downtown Midland by heading west on Main Street for 1.2 miles and then turning north on Cook Road. Hours are 10:00 A.M. to 4:00 P.M. Wednesday through Saturday and 1:00 to 5:00 P.M. on Sunday. There is a small admission fee. The Dow Visitors Center (517–636–8658) is reached from Business US 10 by turning south on Bayliss Street. The center is at Bayliss and Lyon Road and is open from 8:00 A.M. to 5:00 P.M. Monday through Friday.

Another interesting museum is the *Hall of Ideas* in the Midland Center of the Arts. The science, history, and art museum reopened in 1994 after a $3 million facelift and is four floors of hands-on displays and exhibits. Staff members estimate that 340 topics are covered in the new exhibits and that a person who pushed every button, viewed every screen, and took part in every interactive display would spend more than twenty hours in the hall.

A 500-pound life-size mastodon skeleton greets visitors, and from there the topics range from how an Olympic skater does a triple axle to viewing a replica of Midland's famed Frolic Theater (complete with the aroma of popcorn). The hall (517–832–0881) is at Eastman Avenue and West Street and is open daily from 10:00 A.M. to 6:00 P.M. There is a small admission fee.

Midland is also a city of parks, with 2,700 acres in seventy-four parks scattered throughout the community. The most famous of these is **Dow Gardens**, a hundred acres of streams, waterfalls, small bridges, and beautifully manicured landscaping next to Discovery Square, home of the Midland Center for the Arts.

What began as Herbert Dow's back yard in 1899 was eventually extended and shaped in the 1970s by his son, Alden Dow, a noted architect and a student of Frank Lloyd Wright. It was the younger Dow who installed the "jungle walk" through a thicket, the sensory trail and various waterfalls.

The gardens (517–631–3677) are just northwest of downtown Midland off Business US 10 (Eastman Road), next to the **Midland Center for the Arts.** Hours are 10:00 A.M. to sunset daily. There is a small admission fee.

Another intriguing park is Chippewassee, site of the **Tridge**, the only three-way footbridge in the world, city officials proudly claim. The unusual bridge was built in 1981 over the confluence of the Tittabawassee and Chippewa Rivers, and its wooden spans connect three shorelines. In the middle they form a hub where benches overlook the merging currents of two rivers. The Tridge and the nearby riverfront area form the center of activity in downtown Midland. The Midland Music Society hosts free outdoor concerts in the park Thursdays at noon in June and July, which have unofficially become known as "Brown Bag-It Days," as office workers stream to the area to enjoy their lunch break.

Also located near the Tridge is the Midland Farmer's Market and its 4-H Club petting zoo for children (open Sundays in July from 1:00 to 4:00 P.M.) as well as a city-operated canoe livery for a leisurely paddle up the river of your choice. The canoes can be rented Saturday and Sunday from 10:00 A.M. to 7:00 P.M. in April and May and during the week from

Sugar Beets

Bay and Saginaw Counties are the heart of Michigan's sugar beet industry and the home of Pioneer Sugar. The state's first sugar beet factory opened in Bay City in 1889 after Dr. Robert Kedzie of Michigan Agricultural College (now Michigan State University) encouraged local farmers to grow the crop the year before. Within a few short years Saginaw Valley became the sugar bowl of Michigan.

2:00 to 7:00 P.M. June through September. The zoo is free, but there is a rental fee for the canoes.

Bay County

The shoreline of Saginaw Bay was the final destination for much of the lumber from the valley, with thirty-two sawmills clustered on the waterfront of Bay City. The city flourished on money from timber and shipbuilding, and a drive down Center Avenue shows where much of it went. The lumber barons seemed infatuated with building the most elaborate homes they could afford, and the restored mansions in this historic district overwhelm visitors. In the middle of this Victorian-era street is the **Historical Museum of Bay County** (517–893–5733), which spins the story of Bay City's golden era through three-dimensional exhibits. The museum is open from 10:00 A.M. to 5:00 P.M. Monday through Friday and noon to 4:00 P.M. Saturday and Sunday. There is no admission charge, but donations are welcomed.

More impressive than the grand homes, however, is the **Bay City City Hall**. Built in 1894, the Romanesque-style stone building dominates the city skyline with its 125-foot clock tower at the southeast corner. It was listed in the National Register of Historic Places, and in 1976 the building underwent major renovation that preserved the original woodwork and distinctive metal pillars in the huge lobby. Visitors are welcome to stroll throughout the massive structure and view the 31-foot Chmielewska Tapestry that hangs in the council chambers. Woven with hand-dyed yarns of 500 colors by a young artist from Poland, the tapestry depicts the historic buildings of the community. A climb of sixty-eight steps up the clock tower brings you to a most impressive view of Bay City, the Saginaw River, and the surrounding countryside.

The City Hall (517–894–8147) is located downtown at 301 Washington Avenue and is open from 8:00 A.M. to 5:00 P.M. Monday through Friday. Inquire at the Personnel Office in Room 308 for a trip up to the clock tower. There is no admission fee.

The newest attraction in Bay City is the **Delta College Planetarium and Learning Center**. Opened in 1997 with funding from NASA, the center is a striking red-domed building that looks like a spaceship in the middle of Bay City. The planetarium uses state-of-the-art equipment to take visitors on simulated outer-space journeys, while the exhibit hall features displays on astronomy and space travel.

The center is at Center Avenue and Water Street and stages two to six shows daily. Call the planetarium (517–667–2260) for the times. There is a small admission fee.

Iosco County

erhaps the most famous river of the logging era was the Au Sable, which begins west of Grayling and ends at Lake Huron between the towns of Oscoda and Au Sable. In the 1890s it was assumed that forests were meant to be cut, and "driving the Au Sable" was a group of men known as "river rats" and "bank beavers," who floated logs down the Au Sable to sawmills on Lake Huron. A century later it's "downstaters," "flatlanders," and "fudgies" driving the river. Now, however, they're following the Lumbermen's Monument Auto Tour, an especially popular fall trip in Iosco County when tourists come to admire the color of the leaves rather than the size of the trunks.

Many begin the 68-mile loop at the Tawas Area Chamber of Commerce (800–55–TAWAS), where they pick up a free copy of the Lumbermen's Monument Auto Tour brochure. From Tawas City you head west on M 55 for a mile, then turn north (right) onto Wilber Road to reach Monument Road, which ends at River Road. A half-mile to the east (right) is the entrance to the *Lumbermen's Monument*.

The impressive bronze statue of three loggers was erected in 1931 and is now surrounded by trees very much like those they made a living cutting down. Even more impressive to many is the nearby interpretive area and museum, which give a good account of the logging

Bay City City Hall

Paddlewheel Tours

The best way to enjoy the fall colors in Iosco County is aboard the River Queen, a full-size paddlewheel river boat that began operating on the Au Sable River in 1966. The River Queen departs from a dock on the Au Sable River 6 miles west of Oscoda and offers its two-hour tours daily at noon and 3:00 p.m. from late June through late August and then at 1:00 p.m. through late September.

The tours most in demand are the weekend color tours from late September through mid-October at 10:30 a.m., 1:00 p.m., and 3:30 p.m. These are relaxing cruises along the Au Sable in which passengers enjoy the spectacular fall colors, beautiful scenery, and possibly even a few wildlife sightings such as bald eagles. Most trips are $6.75 per adult, but the color tours are $8.00. Reservations are a must in the fall and can be made by calling the River Queen

era with displays and hands-on exhibits. They put the logger into perspective, a man viewed by many today as a colorful, Paul Bunyan–like character who ate apple pie and fry cakes for breakfast. In reality he provided cheap labor. In the middle of the winter, he made $2.00 for a twelve-hour day spent pulling a saw while cold water sloshed in his boots. Little wonder that by the time most loggers turned thirty-five years old, they were too worn out or too sick to continue their trade.

The auto tour continues west along River Road and in 1.5 miles comes to **Canoe Race Monument**. The stone monument, topped off by a pair of paddles, was originally built as a memorial to Jerry Curley, who died practicing for the annual Au Sable River Canoe Marathon. Today it stands in honor of all racers who attempt the annual 150-mile event from Grayling to Oscoda, often cited as the toughest canoe race in the country. From the monument site there is another fine overview of the Au Sable River Valley, and for those who keep one eye on the sky, bald eagles can often be seen in this area.

Still heading west on River Road, you reach **Iargo Springs** in another mile. Iargo is the Chippewa Indian word for "many waters," and this was a favorite spot for members of the tribe traveling along the Saginaw-Mackinac Trail. It's almost 300 steps and eight rest stops down to the springs but well worth the exertion of the climb back up. The area below is pleasant and tranquil as the springs gurgle out of the moss-laden bluffs into the Au Sable River under a canopy of towering pine trees.

Alcona County

At Harrisville, US 23 swings away from Lake Huron and remains inland well into Alpena County. Taking its place along the water in northern Alcona County is Lakeshore Drive, the route to two interesting attractions. The first is **Cedar Brook Trout Farm,** reached 2.5 miles north of Harrisville immediately after turning off US 23. Because of the almost perfect conditions for raising rainbow and brook trout, Cedar Brook was established in the early 1950s as the first licensed trout farm in Michigan. The key to the farm's success is the cold-water springs that flow from the nearby sandy bluffs. The water is funneled into the thirteen ponds and rearing tanks, and its year-round constant temperature (47 degrees) and high level of oxygen are ideal for trout. The constant flow allows owner Jerry Kahn to manage without pumps. He begins with eggs and raises the trout from frylings to rainbows that will measure well over 16 inches.

The bulk of Kahn's business is shipping thousands of trout in a tank truck to individuals and sportsmen's organizations for stocking their own lakes and rivers. He also lets travelers stop by and catch their own in two ponds, one stocked with rainbows, the other with brook trout. The water in the ponds is cold and clear, and below the surface you can easily see hundreds of fish swimming around. Throw some feed in the ponds (available from a coin-operated dispenser), and dozens of large fish rise to the surface in a feeding frenzy. Anglers are provided with cane poles, tackle, bait, and a warning that catching the trout is not as easy as it looks. No fishing license is needed.

Cedar Brook (517–724–5241), one of the few farms in the state that raises brook trout, is open for anglers daily from 9:00 A.M. until 6:00 P.M. from Memorial Day to Labor Day. The cost depends on the size of trout caught, but for $3.00 or $4.00 and a little fishing luck, you can depart with a hefty rainbow.

From the trout farm Lakeshore Drive continues north and in less than a half-mile passes the marked side road to **Sturgeon Point Lifesaving Station** and the preserved lighthouse, built in 1869. The last lightkeeper left in 1941, but the U.S. Coast Guard continues to maintain the light. In 1982 the Alcona County Historical Society began renovating the attached lightkeeper's house and soon opened it to the public. The structure is a classic Michigan lighthouse, but the unique feature is that you can climb to the top of the tower (eighty-five steps) and not only be greeted by a panorama of Lake Huron but still view a working prism as well. Amazingly, all that is needed to throw a light miles out on the Great Lake is this huge work of cut glass and an electric light no larger than your smallest finger.

Lighthouse at Sturgeon Point Lifesaving Station

The lightkeeper's house is now a museum, with the five rooms downstairs furnished as a turn-of-the-century residence for those who maintained the attached tower. The four rooms upstairs are also open, and each showcases a different aspect of the county's history: shipwrecks, fishermen, the original lightkeepers, and, perhaps the most interesting, the ice-collecting industry that boomed in the area during the winter so iceboxes could be kept cold in the summer.

The lighthouse is operated by a volunteer staff that tries to keep it open year-round Monday through Thursday from 10:00 A.M. until 4:00 P.M. and Saturday and Sunday from noon to 4:00 P.M. There is no admission, but donations are accepted to maintain the lighthouse.

Alpena County

umbering turned Alpena from a handful of hardy settlers in 1850 into a booming town of 9,000 in 1884, and when the white pine ran out, the community sustained itself by becoming "Cement City," utilizing its huge supply of limestone. From the cement factories emerged Besser Manufacturing Company, the world leader in concrete block-making equipment. Today Alpena is a manufacturing center that can boast the largest population (12,000) and the only enclosed shopping mall in northeast Michigan. The residents of this modern community also value their past and have begun restoring the historic downtown area as Old Town Alpena.

The original shopping area is clustered around North Second Street and features small and specialized shops that could have been found here as early as the 1920s. One of the most unusual stores is **The Country Cupboard**. This antiques and general store is located in the old Sepull's Pharmacy, a landmark in Alpena from its opening in 1920 until Hutton Sepull retired in 1986. Outside, its aluminum facing looks plain, but inside it has the character of an old-time pharmacy, which catches unsuspecting visitors by surprise. There are the tin ceiling and the wraparound balcony on the second floor and the traveling ladders that lead up to the ceiling-high shelves stocked with old medicine containers, apothecary bottles, and boxes of tonic. On the ground floor the walls are lined with hundreds of wooden drawers, each holding some herb, tin of pills, or other merchandise left from pharmacy days.

When the store went on the market, Rita and Al Hess couldn't think of a better place to relocate their antiques business down the street. They filled the shop with collectibles, baskets, stained glass, and country gifts but kept the old pharmacy atmosphere intact and even began to restore much of the original woodwork. They still sell several of Sepull's more unusual or popular products, including Iceland moss (an herb for folk medicine) and the custom-blended Wellington tobacco.

The Country Cupboard (517–356–6020) is located at 102 North Second

Negwegon State Park

*T*he only development Negwegon State Park has ever experienced since the state picked up the tract in 1962 is the construction of a parking area and a 10-mile trail system. What has never been improved is Sand Hill Road. This sandy, deeply rutted county road provides the only access to Negwegon and, in effect, has made it the most remote state park in the Lower Peninsula. Four-wheel-drive vehicles are recommended, and during extended dry spells, spinning tires in shifting mounds of sugary sand is not an uncommon occurrence.

After an agonizing 2.5-mile drive along the Alcona County road, most first-time visitors are stunned to arrive at a huge park sign and a wide, graveled entrance drive in the middle of nowhere. From the parking area at the end, they head into the woods and suddenly emerge at a crescent-moon bay framed by towering red pines on one side and the turquoise waters of Lake Huron on the other. In between is a sweeping shoreline of golden sand unmarred by beach blankets and beer coolers.

Paradise.

This is as far as most people get in the 1,775-acre park. If you can tear yourself away from the beach, Negwegon's trail system offers some interesting hikes. Departing south from the parking lot is the Potawatomi Trail, a 3.3-mile loop that hugs Lake Huron for more than a mile. To the north is the Algonquin Trail, which in 2 miles reaches the spectacular views at the tip of South Point.

To reach the park from US 23, head east on Black River Road and north on Sand Hill Road. Follow the two-track for 2.5 miles to the park entrance. It is best to first stop at Harrisville State Park (517–724–5126) on US 23 for a map and current road conditions before trying to reach Negwegon.

Lone Gold Mine

Alcona County is the site of the only gold mine to operate in the Lower Peninsula. Prospectors went to the vicinity of Harrisville looking for silver or copper after hearing reports of Indians finding large quantities of the minerals in the area. What the miners found in 1912 wasn't copper or silver but gold nuggets. To avoid a gold rush, they kept the discovery secret for several months until a stock company was formed and a mine shaft sunk. Tons of Alcona black dirt was processed for gold, but the venture ended in disaster when the steam-operated equipment blew up.

Street and is open year-round Monday through Friday 10:00 A.M. to 5:30 P.M., Saturday until 5:00 P.M., and Sunday noon to 4:00 P.M.

Another Old Town favorite is the **John A. Lau Saloon**. The restaurant dates to the 1880s when it was a rough-and-tumble waterhole for lumberjacks with a reputation that reached far into the woods. Part of the reason is that Lau always had three bartenders on staff, one who could speak German, one French, and the other Polish, so any logger, no matter where he came from, could order a beer-and-whiskey.

The restaurant still maintains that lumberman's decor with its thick plank floors, tin ceiling, crosscut saws on the walls, and historic photos of the original saloon. Dinners range from $10 to $20. The John A. Lau Saloon (517–354–6898) is at 414 North Second Avenue.

Alpena's **Jesse Besser Museum** is the only accredited museum in northern Michigan and boasts one of the finest collections of Great Lakes Indian artifacts in the country.

The museum also features a sky theater planetarium and a small historic village outside. Hours are 10:00 A.M. to 5:00 P.M. during the week and noon to 5:00 P.M. on the weekends. The museum (517–356–2202) is a block east of US 23 at 491 Johnson Street. There is a small admission charge.

Presque Isle County

*J*esse Besser, founder of the massive concrete block corporation, was also a humanitarian, and in Alpena the Besser Museum is named after him. But Besser also was responsible for leaving something in Presque Isle County—a small tract of land on Lake Huron whose towering white pines somehow escaped the swinging axes of lumbermen.

The industrial genius, realizing the rarity of the uncut pines and the beauty of the undeveloped Lake Huron shoreline, gave the area to the people of Michigan in 1966. Today it is the **Besser Natural Area**, managed by the Department of Natural Resources. The remote preserve, reached from US 23 by taking County Road 405 to the south end of

Grand Lake, offers a small niche of beauty and a little history in a quiet setting. Looping through the Besser Natural Area is a sandy 1-mile foot trail, which takes you past a small lagoon that once was part of Lake Huron. Look carefully at the bottom of the lagoon (you need polarizing sunglasses on sunny days) and you'll spot the hull of an old ship. The vessel served the community of Bell, which was located here in the 1880s and consisted of one hundred residents, several homes, a sawmill, a saloon, a store, and a school.

The most noticeable remains of Bell are the rock pier along Lake Huron, a towering stone chimney, and the collapsed walls of a building whose steel safe and icebox counter indicate it might have been the saloon. Toward the end of the walk, you pass through some of the oldest and largest white pines remaining in a state once covered with the trees. There is no fee to enter the preserve, nor is there a visitor center or any other facility. Descriptive brochures that coincide with the footpath are available from a small box near the trailhead.

Visitors who exit US 23 for the east side of Grand Lake, the state's nineteenth-largest lake, with more than 5,000 acres of water, usually want to view lighthouses. They take in the beautifully renovated **Old Presque Isle Lighthouse** near the end of County Road 405 (Grand Lake Road). Built in 1840, this squat, stone lighthouse is open to the public and features an interesting museum crammed with artifacts and exhibits. The lighthouse is open daily from 9:00 A.M. to 7:00 P.M. through October 15. There is a small admission charge. Just a mile north of it is **New Presque Isle Lighthouse Park** with nature trails, picnic area, and a small museum of its own. Built in 1870, the New Presque Isle Lighthouse is one of the tallest on the Great Lakes, standing 109 feet tall.

The **Fireside Inn** is yet another reason to come to this part of the country, especially for anyone whose idea of a vacation in northern Michigan is renting a quaint log cabin on the edge of a lake. The Fireside Inn began its long history as a resort when the original lodge was built in 1908, and the first few authentic log cabins soon began to appear around it. Little has changed about the

Strange As It Sounds

Though it sounds like a tacky roadside attraction, Dinosaur Gardens is actually an interesting, even eerie place to visit. The forty-acre park was the creation of the late Paul Domke, a self-taught artist and sculptor. In the 1930s Domke built twenty-seven life-size dinosaurs from concrete, wire, and deer hair within the tangled branches of a cedar swamp forest. A winding path leads through the dark woods where a dino lies waiting for you around every bend.

Eeek!

Dinosaur Gardens (517–471–5477) is right on US 23, 10 miles south of Alpena. It's open mid-May through mid-October from 10:00 a.m. to 4:00 p.m. daily. There is a small admission fee.

Scenic Lake Huron Drive

The 56-mile stretch of US 23 between Mackinaw City and Rogers City is one of the most scenic drives in the Lower Peninsula, featuring a dozen parks and scenic turnouts overlooking Lake Huron.

Many of them are clustered around Rogers City. Five miles north of the town is Forty Mile Point Lighthouse Park. The small but delightful park is crowned by the towering lighthouse and includes a picnic area and beach. On the north side of Rogers City is Seagull Point Park, a mix of Lake Huron shoreline, low dunes, and woods that are best-enjoyed in the fall by walking a 2-mile interpretive trail.

lodge or the dining room inside with its rustic wooden beams, plank floor, and large windows looking over Grand Lake. They still ring a dinner bell to signal supper time and serve only one entree family-style; afterward guests still wander out to the rambling porch, an immense sitting area 215 feet long, to claim a favorite wicker chair or rocker.

You can rent one of the cabins with a wood interior and stone fireplace or just a room (shared bath) in the lodge itself. Daily rates range from $30 to $40 per adult for the large cabins with three or four bedrooms. Or you can stop in just for dinner, a delightful experience in itself. Dinner prices range from $5.00 to $7.00, depending on what is being served that night, and you should call ahead if possible. The Fireside Inn (517–595–6369) is located off County Road 405 at the end of the spur, Fireside Highway.

Presque Isle County is home to another unique inn, **Nettie Bay Lodge**. Located 14 miles west of Rogers City, the lodge is on the shores of Lake Nettie and surrounded by 2,000 private acres. Originally developed as a hunting and fishing camp, Nettie Bay Lodge has since become known as a wildlife-viewing destination, offering not only accommodations but also the use of photography and observation blinds that overlook marshes and other prime spots to sight wildlife.

Because of the area's diverse habitat, it is not unusual to sight one

Limestone Capital of the World

*T*he world's largest limestone quarry is operated on the edge of Rogers City by Michigan Limestone. Millions of tons are removed annually and loaded into Great Lakes freighters to be used in the production of steel, cement, chemicals, and construction materials. There are two viewing points of the quarry operations. The Quarry View is an observation deck off Business US 23 where you can look into the 6,000-acre open-pit quarry. From the Harbor View off Calcite Road southeast of town, you can watch freighters entering the harbor and leaving after being loaded.

hundred different birds in a single weekend. Loons nest on a small island right in front of the lodge, bald eagles and ospreys often feed in the shallow waters of the lake, flocks of wild turkeys can be spotted in the woods. Several times in May the Nettie Bay School of Birding is held at the lodge and includes two nights' lodging, some meals, and bird identification workshops and field trips with professional ornithologists.

Posen, a village of 350 residents, is the agricultural heart of Presque Isle County with its farmers ranking third in the state as producers of packed and graded table potatoes. The best time to visit the community is during the Posen Potato Festival held the first weekend after Labor Day.

Nettie Bay Lodge (517–734–4688) is west of Hawks on County Road 638 and offers eight cottages and two rooms in the lodge. The birding school is $195 per person.

Montmorency County

One of the most popular attractions in Montmorency County isn't a museum or a scenic overlook but a 700-pound elk. Almost 1,500 elk thrive on state forest land between Gaylord and Hillman, making it the largest herd east of the Mississippi River. A unique way to view the animals is an ***Elk Viewing Sleigh Ride Dinner*** arranged through the Best Western Thunder Bay Resort in Hillman. The popular wildlife-viewing adventure began in 1993 when Jack and Jan Matthias started offering sleigh rides to their 1940-vintage hunting cabin. But the high point for most guests was not the gourmet dinner at the cabin but seeing an elk along the way, including bulls whose antlers often exceeded a span of 4 feet.

The Matthiases eventually built a larger cabin to accommodate more people but still cook the five-course meal—crown roast of pork, pear and apple crepes, and homemade soup, among other dishes—over a 1915 wood-burning stove. If you anticipate joining a sleigh ride, bundle up and grab one of the blankets that are provided. The ride through the snowy woods is a forty-five-minute trip each way.

The sleigh ride is offered each winter from Christmas through the third week of March. A two-night weekend package including accommodations at the Thunder Bay Resort, breakfasts, and the sleigh ride is $198 per person, while the one-night package is $133 each. When there is available space, you can also book just the dinner and sleigh at $69 per person. For more information or reservations, call the Best Western Thunder Bay Resort at (800) 729–9375.

In the rugged hills that surround the village of Lewiston is **LakeView Hills Country Inn**, occupying one of the hilltops at an elevation of 1,442 feet. Even after a steep drive to reach the resort, the inn still looms above you. It is an impressive log and natural wood lodge with a fieldstone chimney and large windows on all four floors. Surrounded by trees and buried in deep snow during the winter, its most impressive feature remains the 165-foot-long porch. The veranda encircles the inn, passes every room, and features a variety of rocking chairs and swings from which guests can look down on the hills or gaze upon East Twin Lake and the village of Lewiston on its north shore.

Ocqueoc Falls

Located 11 miles inland from Rogers City along M 68 is Ocqueoc Falls, one of only two waterfalls in the Lower Peninsula. This cascade is a series of ledges that drops 6 feet in the Ocqueoc River. Ocqueoc is not the thundering waterfall that you experience throughout the Upper Peninsula, but it's still a beautiful spot, especially in the fall. The day-use area includes picnic tables and foot trails that follow the east bank of the river, while on the south side of M 68 is a rustic state forest campground.

Inside, the natural wood interior is accented by beams across the ceiling, polished oak floors, and a sweeping wooden banister leading to the rooms upstairs. Each of the fourteen bedrooms is furnished in antiques and has a different theme related to the history of Lewiston. The most popular room by far is on the fourth floor: the inn's observatory. The cubbyhole has large windows on every wall, a pair of rocking chairs, and binoculars to enjoy the view of more than 30 miles.

The inn is located just south of Lewiston, overlooking East Twin Lake. From Business I–75 in Grayling, head east on M 72 for 23 miles and then north on County Road 485 for 21 miles to Fleming Road, where the inn is situated to the west. Room rates range from $98 to $125 per night and include a full breakfast. For reservations write to LakeView Hills Country Inn at P.O. Box 365, Lewiston 49756, call (800) 524–2455, or check out its Web site at www.lakeviewhills.net.

Oscoda County

The state bird of Michigan is the robin, but many argue that it should be the Kirtland's warbler. This small bird, the size of a sparrow, with a distinctive yellow breast, is an endangered species that breeds only in the jack pines of Michigan. It spends its winters in obscurity in the Bahamas and then migrates to areas between Mio and Grayling, arriving in mid-May and departing by early July. Only in these preserved nesting areas do birders and wildlife watchers have the opportunity to observe this rare bird, with fewer than 300 breeding pairs remaining.

The nesting areas are closed to the public, but you can join a ***Kirtland's Warbler Tour,*** which is sponsored by the U.S. Forest Service. The tour, which lasts from an hour and a half to two hours, includes a movie and a discussion by a Forest Service naturalist and then a short trip to the nesting area. The guided group hikes through the jack pines, usually covering 1 to 2 miles, until the warblers are spotted. Seeing a Kirtland's warbler is not guaranteed, but most tours do, especially in late May through June.

This tour is famous among birders, who come from all over the country for their only glimpse of the warbler, but it is also an interesting spot for anybody intrigued by Michigan's wildlife. The Forest Service office (517–826–3252), north of Mio on M 33, offers the tours Wednesday through Sunday at 7:00 A.M. and also Saturday and Sunday at 11:00 A.M. There is a $5.00 per-person fee.

PLACES TO STAY IN MICHIGAN'S LAKE HURON REGION

ALPENA
Days Inn,
1496 M 32 West,
(800) 582–9050

AUGRES
Pinewood Lodge,
510 West US 23,
(517) 876–4060

BAY CITY
Americ Inn,
3915 Three Mile Road,
(517) 671–0071

Clements Inn Bed-and-Breakfast,
1712 Center Road,
(517) 894–4600

CHESANING
Bonnymill Inn,
710 Broad Boulevard,
(517) 845–7780

FLINT
Walli's Motor Lodge,
4184 Pierson Road,
(517) 789–0400

Red Roof Inn,
G–3219 Miller Road,
(810) 733–1660

FRANKENMUTH
Bavarian Inn Lodge,
1 Covered Bridge Lane,
(517) 652–7200

Frankenmuth Motel,
1218 Weiss Street,
(517) 652–6171

Drury Inn,
260 South Main Street,
(517) 652–2800

HARRISVILLE
Stratton's Springport Inn,
629 US 23 South,
(517) 724–6308

HAWKS
Nettie Bay Lodge,
9011 West Highway 638,
(517) 734–4688

LEWISTON
LakeView Hills
Country Inn,
One Lakeview Hills Drive,
(800) 524–2455

Garland Resort,
County Road 489,
(800) 968–0042

MIDLAND
Sleep Inn,
2100 West Wackerly Street,
(517) 837–1010

Valley Plaza Resort,
5217 Bay City Road,
(517) 496–0100

ROGERS CITY
Manitou Shores Resort,
7995 US 23,
(517) 734–7233

Driftwood Motel,
540 West Third Street,
(517) 734–4777

SAGINAW
Motel 6,
6361 Dixie Highway,
(517) 777–2582

Hampton Inn,
2222 Tittabawassee Road,
(517) 792–7666

TAWAS CITY
Harbor View Motel,
1008 US 23,
(517) 362–3971

Paradise Beach Resort,
1029 Lake Street,
(800) 472–6512

**PLACES TO EAT IN
MICHIGAN'S LAKE
HURON REGION**

ALPENA
John A. Lau Saloon
(American),
414 North Second Avenue,
(517) 354–6898

Lud's Hamburgers
(American),
1223 State Avenue,
(517) 356–0339

The Owl Cafe (American),
121 West Chisholm Street,
(517) 356–6915

BAY CITY
Krzysiak's House (Polish),
1605 Michigan Avenue,
(517) 894–5531

White's Restaurant
(American),
305 North Euclid Avenue,
(517) 686–0700

FLINT
Bill Thomas' Halo Burger
(hamburgers),
800 South Saginaw Street,
(810) 238–4607

Makuch's Red Rooster
Restaurant (American),
3302 Davison Road,
(810) 742–310

Walli's (smorgasbord),
4160 West Pierson Road,
(810) 789–9167

FRANKENMUTH
Main Street Tavern
(German),
310 South Main Street,
(517) 652–5551

Riverview Cafe
(American),
445 South Main Street,
(517) 652–8844

Zehnder's (German and
chicken),
730 South Main Street,
(517) 652–9925

Selected Tourism Bureaus

Alpena Area Convention and Visitors Bureau,
235 West Chosholm Street; Alpena 49707;
(800) 425–7362

Flint Area Convention and Visitors Bureau,
519 South Saginaw Street, Flint 48502;
(800) 25–FLINT

Frankenmuth Convention and Visitors Bureau,
635 South Main Street, Frankenmuth 48734;
(800) FUN–TOWN

Oscoda Area Convention and Visitors Bureau,
4440 North US 23, Oscoda 48750;
(800) 235–4625

Rogers City Visitors Bureau,
540 West Third Street, Rogers City 49779;
(517) 734–2535

Saginaw Visitors Bureau,
6191 Sheridan Road, Saginaw 48601;
(800) 444–9979

Tawas City Tourist Bureau,
P.O. Box 10, Tawas City 48764;
(800) 55–TAWAS

Bavarian Inn (German and chicken),
713 South Main Street,
(517) 652–9941

MIDLAND
Pi's (Chinese),
1815 North Saginaw Road,
(517) 832–5848

The Sweet Onion
(American),
1415 South Saginaw Road,
(517) 631–2062

OSCODA
The Pack House (seafood),
5014 US 23,
(517) 739–0454

ROGERS CITY
Chi Chi's (Mexican
and American),
409 US 23,
(517) 734–4454

SAGINAW
El Farolito (Mexican),
115 North Hamilton,
(517) 799–8959

Montague Inn (American),
1581 South
Washington Avenue,
(517) 752–3939

Levi's Saloon (American),
6415 State Street,
(517) 790–3538

TAWAS CITY
Pier 23 Restaurant
(American),
821 US 23,
(517) 362–8856

OTHER ATTRACTIONS

Crossroads Village and
Huckleberry Railroad, Flint

Junction Valley Railroad,
Bridgeport

Chippewa Nature Center,
Midland

Saginaw Historical
Museum

Saginaw Children's Zoo

Lake Michigan

The Lake Michigan shoreline may be the Lower Peninsula's western edge, but many will argue that its heart lies in Chicago. The shoreline is now connected to the city by an Interstate highway, but that has only cemented what was already a long and enduring relationship between the Windy City and this watery edge of Michigan.

It began with the Great Chicago Fire of 1871, which left the city smoldering in ashes. Chicago was rebuilt with Michigan white pine, and the mill towns along the Great Lake, communities like Muskegon and Saugatuck, worked around the clock to supply the lumber. Maybe it was during these excursions to the sawmills that Chicagoans discovered that this region of Michigan possessed more than towering trees and two-by-fours.

They discovered the sand, the surf, and the incredibly beautiful sunsets of the Lake Michigan shoreline. By the 1880s, the tourist boom was on, and it was being fed by vacationers from cities outside Michigan, places like St. Louis, and South Bend, Indiana, but most of all from Chicago. They arrived by steamships, trains, and eventually automobiles. They caused luxurious resorts and lakeside cottages to mushroom, beginning in New Buffalo on the edge of the Indiana-Michigan border and continuing right up the coast: St. Joseph, South Haven, Saugatuck, Grand Haven, and Muskegon.

They call it the "Michigan Riviera," and even Richard Daley, Chicago's famed political boss and mayor, had a summer home on the strip. With the completion of I–94, the two regions were linked by a four-lane belt of concrete. Many Chicagoans, eager to escape the city heat, were less than two hours from the cool breezes of their favorite resort.

The Lake Michigan shoreline is still the heart of Michigan tourism. This incredibly beautiful region is characterized by great dunes and watery sunsets, but it's also known for its bustling resorts, streets full of quaint shops, and attractive beachfront hotels. The region lies on the western edge of Michigan, but Chicago's influence is unmistakably clear.

Just go to the beach and look at the license plates of the cars, listen to the

baseball games the radios are tuned to, or see what city's newspaper someone is snoozing under. You're in Chicago's playland.

Berrien County

Y ou barely cross the state border from Indiana before the first lakeshore communities appear on the horizon with their hotels and motels clustered near the water. Many are new, each with features little different from the one next door. But if you search a little, you can find an old inn from another era unique in its appearance and half-hidden in a quiet neighborhood near the lake. If you search harder, you might even find **The Inn at Union Pier**.

Union Pier is a cluster of well-shaded streets and nineteenth-century summer homes about 10 miles north of the border. Locate Berrien Street and you'll pass the inn, three nautical buildings painted light blue with white railings. The inn began in 1918 as a single building called the Karonsky Resort, but business was so good that by 1929 two more structures had been added. An easy journey from Chicago (today it is only ninety minutes by car), the inn thrived in the golden age of the Lake Michigan resorts but by the 1960s was abandoned and closed up. In 1983, Bill and Madeleine Reinke purchased the place, gutted it, and after two years of renovation, opened for business.

From the outside the inn's most striking feature is the wraparound porch on one of the smaller lodges and the matching balcony above it, the ideal place to unwind after a day on the beach. Walkway decks connect the buildings; one has a large hot tub, and tables for breakfast outdoors are on another. Most of the rooms are furnished in light pine and include a Swedish ceramic wood stove. The heart of the main lodge is a spacious common area with a grand piano, overstuffed chairs and sofas, and lots to read. Guests begin each day with a full breakfast of local fruit and fresh baked goods on the deck and then head across the street to the beach, check out one of the inn's bicycles, or take to nearby roads for a winery tour or antiques excursion.

The Inn at Union Pier (616–469–4700) has sixteen rooms priced for double occupancy from $125 to $195 per night, including breakfast. Write ahead for reservations to P.O. Box 222, Union Pier 49129.

In downtown Three Oaks, in the southwest corner of Berrien County, is the *Three Oaks Spokes Bicycle Museum*, where twenty-two bicycles are displayed on the walls, ranging from the Companion, a side-by-side two-seater, to an 1860 Velocipede, one of the earliest bicycles ever made, featuring two wheels, handlebars, and a seat—but no rubber tires, inflated inner tubes, or anything resembling a spring or wire spoke. Thus its nickname: the Boneshaker.

The museum is much more than old bicycles and exhibits. What it really showcases is the southwest corner of the state, a pedaler's paradise called Michiana. Promoting recreational cycling in Michiana was the aim of the Three Oaks Spokes Bicycle Club when it was formed in 1974. The club developed the *Backroads Bikeway,* a selection of 12 tours throughout the region that have been posted with color-coded bike route signs. The tours range from 8 miles to more than 50, and wind past sand dunes, wineries, cider mills, and one of the last stands of virgin hardwoods left in southern Michigan.

The developed bike routes brought an increasing number of cyclists passing through town and prompted the club to move its museum from a cramped storefront on Main Street to the historical Michigan Central Railroad Depot in 1994. The century-old depot, featuring tin ceilings, beveled, leaded glass windows and handcrafted copper light fixtures, was called "the finest depot between Niles and Chicago" in its heyday. Along with two exhibit rooms displaying the twenty-two classic bicycles, the museum also serves as a information center, promoting Michiana tourist attractions as well as cycling events and trails throughout the state. You can even rent a bike here.

The Bicycle Museum (616–756–3361) is located at 1 Oak Street, 16 miles west of Niles on US 12 or 71 miles southwest of Kalamazoo. It is open daily year-round from 9:00 A.M. until 5:00 P.M., and there is no admission charge.

The Lake Michigan dunes, the most spectacular natural feature of the region, begin in Indiana and hug the shoreline almost to the Straits of

LAKE MICHIGAN

TOP ANNUAL EVENTS

Trillium Festival,
Muskegon, May;
(231) 798–3517

Tulip Time Festival,
Holland, May;
(616) 394–0000

National Asparagus
Festival, Hart, June;
(231) 873–2247

Manistee National Forest
Festival, Manistee, July;
(616) 723–2575

National Blueberry
Festival, South Haven,
August; (616) 637–5252

Jazz Celebration,
Saugatuck, September;
(616) 857–2287

Apple Cider Century,
Three Oaks, September;
(616) 756–3361

Goose Festival,
Fennville, October;
(616) 561–5550

Mackinac. The largest preserve of dunes in Berrien County is at **Warren Dunes State Park**, located on the lake 12 miles north of the state border. The park has more than 2 miles of fine sandy beaches and dunes that rise 240 feet above Lake Michigan. The dunes are a popular place in the summer for sunbathers and swimmers during the day and campers at night. What many people don't realize is that Warren Dunes is the only state park that permits hang gliding, and is considered by most gliders to be one of the best places in the Midwest, if not the country, for soaring.

Gliders are drawn to the park because of Tower Hill, which looms over the beach parking lot. They trudge up the hill carrying their gliders and then soar into the winds from the top, flying over the sandy park or even above Lake Michigan. When the sport enjoyed its heyday in the mid-1970s, there would be almost a hundred gliders on Tower Hill on a windy weekend, with as many as twenty in the air at one time. The park rangers were so burdened with accidents caused by unqualified fliers that they instituted a certification system and stricter regulations for gliders.

What makes the park so attractive for these soaring adventurers, especially those just learning the sport, are the smooth winds that come off the lake and the soft and relatively forgiving sand below. Gliding takes place year-round, but the best time to watch it is a weekend in the fall or spring with a wind out of the north-northwest. Arrive then and you'll see a half-dozen or so colorful gliders. Or, better yet, sign up for a one-day lesson from one of the glider instructors who set up school in the park. For an up-to-date list of the instructors, call Warren Dunes State Park (616–426–4013).

Lake Michigan does more than provide water for the beaches or a view from the top of sand dunes. It also tempers the winter storms that roll in from the Great Plains and moderates the sweltering summer heat felt elsewhere in the Midwest. These effects, combined with the light soil of the region, have turned the lakeshore strip into a cornucopia of orchards, berry farms, and especially vineyards. Michigan is the third-leading wine-producing state in the country after California and New York. Paw Paw in Van Buren County is the unofficial center for the state's winemakers, with the largest vineyards, St. Julian Wine Company and Warner Vineyards, located right off I–94.

Smaller wineries are also found throughout the region, including a frequent winner in national competition, **Tabor Hill Winery**, in the center of Berrien County. The winery began when two Chicago salesmen who sold steel but loved wine brought a selection of hybrid grapevines back from France in 1968. They chose their vineyard site in the rolling hills of the county, hoping the conditions there were similar enough to those in France to bring success. They were. The transplanted vines thrived, and the winery produced its first bottle in 1970. Seven years later a bottle of its 1974 Baco won a gold medal in the American Wine Competition, and since then both the vineyard and Leonard Olson, steel-salesman-turned-winemaker, have won numerous awards. The winery remains small, producing 40,000 gallons (or about 15,000 cases) of wine annually in almost two dozen types of whites, reds, and blends.

Fun Facts

Bear Cave near Buchanan is one of the few caverns in Michigan. Formed in rare "tura rock," the cave is estimated to be 25,000 years old. In 1875, bank robbers hid their loot in the cave, an event that inspired the movie The Great Train Robbery, *in which the cave was featured.*

Bear Cave (616–695–3050) is 6 miles north of Buchanan on Red Bud Trail. Tours of the cave are available during the summer.

The best way to view Tabor Hill is on a walking tour that begins where workers bottle the wine and then heads out into the rows of trellised vines for a history of the grapes. You also descend into the wine cellar for a look at the huge vats and hand-carved oak casks that age the wine, and then finish the tour in the tasting room for some tips on how to "judge" wine. The twenty-five-minute tour ends with everybody sampling some of Tabor Hill's finest wines.

The winery also includes an excellent restaurant with tables that overlook the rolling vineyard and a huge deck outside. A favorite activity of many, especially during fall, is to pack a picnic lunch and enjoy it on the open deck with a bottle of Tabor Hill wine.

Tabor Hill (616–422–1161 or 800–283–3363) is on Mount Tabor Road and can be reached from I–94 by taking exit 16 and heading north on Red Arrow Highway to Bridgman. From Bridgman head east along Shawnee Road and keep an eye out for the signs. This vineyard is definitely off by itself. The free tours go from noon to 4:30 P.M. every day in summer and weekends only in the winter.

Nuclear energy and nature might seem like strange bedfellows, but they are the reasons to visit the Cook Nuclear Plant in Bridgman. A tour begins at the **Cook Energy Information Center**, an on-site interpretive center with enough atom-splitting displays and hands-on exhibits to keep most families entertained for the afternoon. There are also several video theaters that explain the "nuclear process" as well as observation decks overlooking Lake Michigan.

To demonstrate how clean and compatible nuclear power can be, the Cook Energy Information Center built the Nipissing Dune Trails, a three-loop system in ten acres of wooded dunes bordering the nuclear plant complex.

The entire system makes for an enjoyable 3-mile hike on which hand-hewn steps and thick ropes help with the steepest climbs and more than two dozen interpretive stops point out the surrounding habitat.

The Cook Energy Information Center (800–548–2555) is just north of Bridgman with an entrance on Red Arrow Highway. From I–94, take exit 23 and head south on Red Arrow Highway for 3 miles. The center is open Tuesday through Sunday from 10:00 A.M. to 5:00 P.M. There is no admission charge.

In between the sand dunes, the orchards, and the wineries of Berrien County is a lot of history. Niles, the community of four flags, was the first settlement in the Lower Peninsula and claimed one of the first museums in the country when a private one opened here in 1842. Eventually it became the **Fort St. Joseph Museum**, and today it houses more than

Strange As It Sounds

*T*ree-Mendus Fruit is like many U-pick fruit farms in western Michigan. The Eau Claire farm has 250 acres of apple orchards to pick, hayrides, a petting area with goats, chickens, and rabbits for children, a country store and gift shop featuring baked goods, jugs of cider, and apple and cherry products, and a picnic area.

But in some ways Tree-Mendus Fruit is the only farm of its kind. Take its International Cherry Pit Spitting Championship held annually on the first

Saturday in July. In 1998 the farm celebrated the event's twenty-fifth anniversary with the champion spitting a cherry pit 72 feet, 11 inches, a record effort at the farm.

Tree-Mendus Fruit (616–682–7101) is 2 miles north of Eau Claire and east of M 140 on East Eureka Road. The farm is open July through October from 10:00 a.m. to 6:00 p.m daily except Tuesday through Labor Day, and Friday through Monday in the fall.

10,000 historical items on two floors. Much of the museum's collection relates to its namesake fort, for which the French built the stockade in 1691. The British took it over in 1761, and the Spanish captured it twenty years later. In 1783, the Americans arrived and raised the fourth and final flag over Fort St. Joseph.

The museum's most noted displays, however, are devoted to the Sioux Indians of the Great Plains, not to the residents of Fort St. Joseph. Many of the Indian artifacts were obtained by Captain Horace Baxter Quimby, whose daughter moved to Niles. While the U.S. Army captain was based in the Dakota Territory in 1881 and 1882, he became friendly with Sitting Bull, the most famous Sioux chief. Among the gifts Quimby received from Sitting Bull were thirteen pictographs of the chief's greatest battles. The set of pictures is one of only three known collections of the Sioux chief.

The museum (616–683–4702) is right behind the Niles City Hall at 508 East Main Street. Niles can be reached from US 12, 23 miles east of I–94 or 33 miles west of US 131. Hours are 10:00 A.M. to 4:00 P.M. Wednesday to Saturday.

More history can be seen at Berrien Springs' *1839 Courthouse*. The building, which at various times was a militia drill hall, a college, and even a church, was repurchased by the county in 1967 and restored as the nineteenth-century courtroom where law was interpreted and justice dispensed in Michigan's early years of statehood. The classic Greek Revival–style structure is the centerpiece of the Berrien County Courthouse Square, a complex of five buildings that is listed on the National Register of Historic Places. It gives visitors a glimpse of the machinery of old-fashioned government.

You can climb the wooden stairs to the second-floor courtroom where former Michigan Supreme Court Justice Epaphroditus Ransom presided over the first session in April 1839. Little in the building has changed since then. The wooden floors still creak as you approach the bench, and floor-to-ceiling windows still illuminate the courtroom furnishings of pewlike benches, wood-burning stoves, and the curved railing that separated the participants from the gallery.

The historic complex (616–471–1202) is located in Berrien Springs at US 31 and Union Street. Berrien Springs is 11 miles southeast of exit 27 off I–94. Hours for the buildings are 9:00 A.M. to 4:00 P.M. Tuesday through Friday and 1:00 to 5:00 P.M. Saturday and Sunday.

Van Buren County

South Haven has a long and colorful history spiced with Great Lakes vessels and shipbuilding, and much of it is explained at the *Lake Michigan Maritime Museum*, which is dedicated to the boats that were built and used on the Great Lakes. Founded in 1976, the museum includes a 600-foot outdoor boardwalk around a historical fishtug and a vessel used in the U.S. Life Saving Service. Inside the museum hall the exhibits range from collections of small vessel motors and tools used by local shipbuilders to personal belongings of Great Lakes mariners.

Lake Michigan Maritime Museum (616–637–8078) is on Dyckman Avenue where it crosses the Black River and is reached from I–196 by taking exit 20 and heading west on Phoenix Street. Turn north on Broadway Street and then west on Dyckman Street. Hours are 10:00 A.M. to 5:00 P.M. Tuesday through Saturday and noon to 5:00 P.M. on Sunday. There is a small admission fee.

The good life on the lakes can also be enjoyed at dinner time aboard the *Idler* at the *Magnolia Grille,* a restaurant floating in the Black River downtown in Old Harbor Village. The Idler was built in Clinton, Iowa, in 1897 for Lafayette Lamb, a lumber baron who used the 120-foot house-boat for his own personal enjoyment on the Mississippi. He never installed an engine in the Idler because he didn't want to be disturbed by the vibrations, so the vessel was always pushed up and down the river by a small tug.

The Idler appeared at the 1904 World's Fair in St. Louis, but in 1910 it burned to the waterline. It was immediately rebuilt and eventually captured the fancy of actor Vincent Price's father. He owned it for fifty-eight years, and in a letter now framed and hanging in the restaurant, Price said that what his father liked most about the riverboat was playing the piano on board. Eventually the boat was purchased, and it was brought to South Haven in 1979. Today it has been beautifully restored, and top-side is the Bayou Beach Club, an open-air bar with sweeping views of the town and the Black River from every table. In the Magnolia Grille, located below, you can dine on white linen in either the original dining quarters or one of four staterooms. Each accommodates a party of six for a private gastronomic evening. The menu lists more than twenty entrees priced from $12 to $22, and every day six new entrees are featured. Many local people know the restaurant best for its Cajun dishes—blackened fish and steak, barbecued shrimp, and Louisiana steak salad—and its sinfully rich cheesecakes.

Magnolia Grille (616–637–8435) is open daily from 11:00 A.M. until 10:00 P.M. Monday through Thursday, until 11:00 P.M. Friday and Saturday, and on Sunday until 8:00 P.M. Reservations are accepted, and dress is casual on the riverboat.

Sport-fishing fans throughout Michigan head for the streams, inland lakes, and Great Lakes to fill their creels with a variety of catch. If they are passing through Van Buren County on M 43, they should also head for the *Wolf Lake State Fish Hatchery*, one of the main reasons fishing is so good in Michigan. The hatchery dates to 1928 and by 1935 was the largest in the world. Construction of the present facility began in 1980, and three years and $7.2 million later, the technological upgrading had made Wolf Lake the finest complex in the country for producing both warm-water and cold-water species. No other hatchery in Michigan raises as many species as Wolf Lake, which hatches steelhead, brown trout, Chinook salmon, and grayling along with the warm-water species of tiger musky, northern pike, walleye, bass, and bluegill.

Hatchery tours should begin at the interpretive center, which will fascinate anybody who dabbles in sport fishing. In the lobby is a wall with plaques of Michigan's record fish—sort of a fishing hall of fame—plus displays of trout fishing on the state's renowned Au Sable River. Off to one side is the "Michigan Room," a walk-through exhibit area that

Caruso's Candy Kitchen

*S*ince the Roaring Twenties, vacationing families have been stepping up to the Italian marble soda fountain bar at Caruso's Candy Kitchen in Dowagiac to sip a creamy soda or indulge in an ice-cream concoction served in a tall glass sundae dish. They're still doing it today because little has changed at this venerable ice-cream parlor.

Founded in 1822 by Antonio Caruso, who had just sailed to the U.S. from Italy with his wife, Caruso's still features pedestal stools, a wavy mirror behind the counter, lime green Hamilton Beach malt mixers, and high wooden booths. This is where you come for a real milkshake, made with hand-dipped ice cream in a metal malt glass. The specialty of the shop is the Green River: lime phosphate syrup on the bottom of a sundae dish, two scoops of vanilla ice cream, and topped off with crushed cherries, pineapple, mixed nuts, and real whipped cream. It is based on the green, white, and red flag of Italy and was Antonia Caruso's way of saluting his native country.

Caruso's (616–782–6001) is in downtown Dowagiac at 130 South Front Street and is open Monday through Saturday.

begins with an interesting series of habitat dioramas, cross sections of every type of water you might drop a line into, from trout streams to the Great Lakes. Each diorama shows the species that will be found, the habitat they like, and the lure of a frustrated angler trying to land the lunkers that lie below. There are also exhibits on fish anatomy, slide presentations of Michigan's commercial fisheries, and an area devoted to sport-fishing gear, including a delightful display of more than a hundred historic lures, plugs, and other tackle.

After viewing the exhibits and a short slide presentation in the auditorium, visitors are encouraged to wander through the hatchery itself to view millions of fish in the ponds. If you want to see something bigger, ask for some fish feed at the interpretive center and walk out on the small pier at the visitors' pond. The small lake was developed so that people, especially children, could actually see some large fish. Among the species in it are sturgeon, including one that is 5 feet long and weighs fifty-five pounds. Imagine that at the end of your line!

The center (616–668–2876) is open Monday through Saturday from 9:00 A.M. to 5:00 P.M. and also on Sunday from noon to 6:00 P.M. during the summer. There is no admission fee to visit Wolf Lake, which is reached from I–94 by heading north on US 131 for 4 miles and then west on M 43 for 6 miles.

Michigan has no short supply of vineyards and wine-tasting rooms to visit, but few have the Old World character of **Warner Vineyards** in Paw Paw. The building itself is a Michigan Historical Site, constructed in 1898 as the town's first waterworks station. The vineyard purchased it in 1967 and proceeded to renovate the structure using lumber from old wine casks to transform it into a wine haus and bistro.

Today the brick and stone building is reached by crossing a footbridge over the east branch of the Paw Paw River, which gurgles its way through the shaded grounds and around an outdoor deck. The whole setting is one of idyllic enjoyment. You can go on a wine tour or simply stop for a little wine tasting.

Warner Vineyards (616–657–3165) is reached from I–94 by taking exit 60 and heading north on M 40 into Paw Paw. The winery is at 706 South Kalamazoo and open from 10:00 A.M. to 5:00 P.M. Monday through Saturday and noon to 5:00 P.M. on Sunday.

Just down the road in Paw Paw is the **St. Julian Winery**, the state's oldest and largest vineyard. Founded in 1921, St. Julian (616–657–5568) produces forty types of wines and also offers tours and tasting as well.

Allegan County

On the map Saugatuck looks like just the next beachfront community along the lake, but in reality it is a trendy resort whose streets are lined with fine restaurants, quaint shops, and lots of tourists. Perhaps the most striking sight in Saugatuck is the docks along the Kalamazoo River, where moored at the edge of the shopping district is an armada of cabin cruisers and sailboats 30, 40, or 50 feet in length or even longer. You can pick up the boardwalk that winds past the boats anywhere along Water Street, and if you follow it north, eventually you'll come to the most-unusual vessel afloat, the ***Saugatuck Chain Ferry***. It's the only chain-powered ferry in the state and has been carrying passengers across the Kalamazoo River since 1838. An operator hand-cranks a 380-foot chain attached at each shore, pulling the small white ferry through the water.

It's only $1.00 for the five-minute ride, and it is your escape from the bustling downtown shopping district to one of the most beautiful beaches on the lake. Once on the other side, you walk north for a few hundred yards until you reach ***Mount Baldhead Park***, with tables, shelter, and a dock on the river. There is also a stairway that takes you (after a little huffing and puffing) to the top of the 200-foot dune, where you are greeted with a glorious panorama of Saugatuck, Kalamazoo Lake to the southeast, and Lake Michigan to the west. On the other side you have a choice. You can descend to ***Oval Beach*** along the Northwoods Trail, an easy walk that includes a view of the lake and beach along the way. Or you can dash madly down the steep and sandy Beach Trail, right off the towering dune, across the beach, and into the lake for a cool dip.

Moving inland, another interesting attraction is the old Allegan County Jail in Allegan. Seriously. The imposing red brick building was built in 1906 and features Greek Revival architecture with a peaked roof and columns along the porch. There are bars on the windows, a hexagonal turret in the corner, and a three-story grandeur that is lacking in its newer counterpart across the street.

But most unusual is the small red sign on Walnut

The Saugatuck Chain Ferry

Street that says **Allegan County Historical Museum**. Go to jail and get a history lesson in penitentiary punishment. Within the museum are a variety of exhibits, including a country store loaded with nineteenth-century merchandise, a display devoted to Allegan's General Benjamin Pritchard, whose men captured Confederate President Jefferson Davis during the Civil War, and a historical laundry room.

But coat hangers and wringers are not what draw more than 1,000 visitors to the museum every year. It's a macabre fascination with slammers and pokeys. To that end, a guide leads you through the sheriff's living quarters and the large kitchen, where his wife would prepare meals for up to thirty prisoners a night and then pass plates through a small door in the wall. On the second floor are rows of 6-by-8-foot cells, complete with the graffiti that disheartened convicts scratched on the walls in the 1930s. You can even walk through the maximum-security cells, now filled with a historical toy collection, view the old padded cell, and examine the holding pen for "ladies."

The jail is open on Friday 2:00 to 5:00 P.M. from June through Labor Day or by appointment by calling Marguerite Miller at (616) 673–4853. To reach the museum, take M 222 (exit 55) off / and head west into Allegan. The Old Jail is at 113 Walnut Street, between Hubbard and Trowbridge.

Ottawa County

every spring Holland bursts into a rainbow of colors thanks to the millions of tulips that residents plant seemingly everywhere. The event climaxes during the Tulip Time Festival in mid-May, when the flowers are in full bloom and the Dutch-founded city hosts more than a half-million visitors, who book hotel rooms months in advance.

But historical Holland can be an interesting trip the rest of the year as well. Found in 1847 by Dutch religious dissenters, Holland celebrated its sesquicentennial in 1997 and today is the undisputed center of Dutch culture in Michigan. For a dose of old Holland, visit **Dutch Village**. This fifteen-acre theme park is a recreated nineteenth-century Dutch Village complete with canals, tulip gardens, and historical displays along with some kitschy attractions like a wooden-shoe slide to keep the kids happy. Among the many buildings are a wooden-shoe factory and Queen's Inn, Holland's only restaurant serving Dutch food.

Dutch Village (616–396–1475) is along US 31, 2 miles northeast of downtown Holland. From April through mid-October the grounds are open from 9:00 A.M. to 6:00 P.M. Admission is $5.00 for adults.

Windmill Island is a city park that features De Zwaan, the only working Dutch windmill allowed to be shipped out of the Netherlands. The five-story-high windmill is still operating as it grinds whole wheat flour that is sold in shops nearby. Also at Windmill Island is the Posthouse Museum, Little Netherlands Museum, and an 1895 carousel. The park (616–396–5433) is just northeast of downtown Holland at Seventh and Lincoln Streets and open in the summer from 9:00 A.M. to 6:00 P.M. Monday through Saturday, 11:30 A.M. to 6:00 P.M. on Sunday. There are reduced hours of operation in the spring and fall.

Holland also has two wooden-shoe factories where you can buy the oaken loafers or simply see a demonstration of how they are made. The best is the **Wooden Shoe Factory**, which also includes a display on the many kinds of wooden shoes worn in Europe. The Wooden Shoe Factory (616–396–6513) is off US 31 just south of Sixteenth Street. Hours are 8:00 A.M. to 6:00 P.M. daily.

Grand Haven has developed its waterfront along the Grand River and includes a riverwalk that extends several miles from downtown to the picturesque Grand Haven Lighthouse out in Lake Michigan. But by far the most noted aspect of the river is the city's **Musical Fountain**, the world's largest, which performs nightly during the summer with electronically controlled and synchronized music. Performances begin around dusk (9:00 to 9:30 P.M.), and most people enjoy the free concerts by assembling in the Waterfront Stadium.

Muskegon County

n the late 1800s this county was the heart of lumbering on Michigan's western side, and the city of Muskegon grew during the prosperous era to be known as the "Lumber Queen of the World." A drive down West Webster Avenue shows how much money was made and where much of it went: The Victorian mansions are fabulous. The most elaborate houses were built by the two men who prospered most of all from Michigan white pine, Charles H. Hackley and his partner, Thomas Hume. They built their homes next to each other, and it reportedly took 200 artisans and craftsmen two years to complete the houses. Behind the homes the men shared the same carriage house. The **Hackley House** and **Hume House** are listed on the National Register of Historic Places and have been called two of the nation's most outstanding examples of Victorian architecture.

Although restoration continues, the homes are open for tours. The Hackley House is especially impressive, a virtual museum of carved woodwork that strikes you from the moment you walk into the home and are greeted by unusual figures along the walls. Almost every aspect of the house is overwhelming, from its original furnishings and stained-glass windows to the hand-stenciled walls and the eleven fireplaces, each made unique with imported ceramic tiles. If you see only one restored home in Michigan, it should be the Hackley House, where it's hard to imagine living in such style.

> ## Strange As It Sounds
>
> *The world's largest weather vane is located in Montague. Erected in 1884 by the Whiteall Metal Studios across the street, the vane is 48 feet tall and weighs 3,500 pounds. It has a 26-foot-long arrow and directional letters that are 3 feet, 6 inches tall, and is topped off by a 14-foot-long schooner. The vane is right off Business US 31 in a park overlooking the town harbor.*

The Hackley and Hume Historic Site (231–722–7578) is at 484 West Webster Avenue. Tours are offered mid-May through September, Wednesday through Sunday from noon to 4:00 P.M. They are also offered the same hours on weekends in December There is a small admission fee.

The towering dunes along the eastern side of Lake Michigan are the world's largest accumulation of dunes bordering a body of freshwater and are renowned throughout the country. One of the best places for learning how dunes develop and change is the **Gillette Nature Center** within P. J. Hoffmaster State Park. The center is, in fact, overshadowed by a huge dune best viewed from the lobby's glass wall to the west. The center features an exhibit hall entitled "From a Grain of Sand," which guides you through the natural history of the dunes, and an eighty-two-seat theater that uses a nine-projector, multi-image slide show to further explain their delicate nature. On the ground floor is a gallery that offers hands-on exhibits to help children understand the environment of the park.

Most visitors view the exhibits and then hike up to the Dune Platform Overlook. The trail begins next to the center and includes a wooden

walkway of 165 steps. It puts you 190 feet above the lake, with spectacular views of the surrounding dune country. There is a vehicle permit fee
to enter the state park (231–798–3711), which is reached by heading
south of Muskegon on US 31 exiting at Pontaluna Road and heading
west. The Gillette Nature Center is open daily during summer from
10:00 A.M. to 5:00 P.M.; the rest of the year, hours are Tuesday through
Friday 1:00 TO 5:00 P.M. and weekends 10:00 A.M. to 5:00 P.M.

Newaygo County

The most distinctive structure in the southern Newaygo County
town of Grant is its wooden water tower. Built in 1891, it's the
classic "Petticoat Junction" water tower, the last one standing in the
state. Driving down Main Street, you half expect to see Uncle Joe and
the rest of the cast from that zany comedy.

Drive through the town to see the water tower, but stop because of its
train depot. Chuck Zobel has transformed the once-bustling passenger
station into the **Grant Depot Restaurant**, one of the county's best eater-
ies—unless you're a railroad enthusiast, then it's a fascinating train
museum that serves a very good Mile High Lemon (meringue) Pie.

After purchasing the empty depot in 1979, Zobel spent a year renovating it, and in the process of tearing down walls and replacing floors, he
turned up a variety of artifacts from the era of the iron horse: tickets
and train orders from 1903, bottles, telegrams, signs, even the remains
of a copper sulfate battery that powered the telegraph before the age of
electricity. Today you can sit at a table in what a century ago was the
passenger waiting room, or in a bay window overlooking the tracks,
where a station agent once worked a telegraph. What was the baggage
room is now the kitchen, and the dining room walls are covered with
memorabilia—from lanterns and oil cans to warning lights, tickets,
and an engineer's manual on how to operate a locomotive.

The Grant Depot Restaurant (231–834–7361) is open 7:30 A.M. to 8:00
P.M. Monday through Thursday, until 9:00 P.M. Friday and Saturday, and
from 11:30 A.M. to 3:00 P.M. Sunday. From I–96 in Grand Rapids, head
north on M 37 (exit 30). Grant is reached in 24 miles, and the Depot is
right off M 37.

Wildflower lovers ought to stay on M 37 in Newaygo County to reach the
Loda Lake Wildflower Sanctuary. In 1938, Forest Service rangers
invited the Federated Garden Clubs of Michigan to help them create a
sanctuary for native plants, including endangered and protected

species, to ensure their survival. Although part of the Manistee National Forest, the preserve is still managed by the Federated Garden Clubs, and over the years it has evolved into a unique haven for botanists, wildflower enthusiasts, and families who just want to know the difference between Michigan holly and Holly, Michigan.

The self-guiding trail is a mile loop of easy hiking where you encounter the first numbered post in less than 20 feet, and before you return to the picnic area, you'll pass thirty-eight others. The interpretive posts mark the locations of trillium, blueberries, swamp rose, insect-eating sundew plants, and fragrant water lily, among other plants, and they correspond to a trail guide available near the parking area.

From White Cloud head north on M 37 and then left on Five Mile Road, where the directional sign to Loda Lake is posted on the corner. Head a mile west and turn right on Fletcher Road. The entrance to the sanctuary is a mile to the north. For a trail guide, call or stop at the U.S. Forest Service Ranger Station (231–745–4631) at 650 North Michigan Avenue in Baldwin.

Lake County

When you look at a stump, what do you see? A stump? Is a tree root just a tree root? Not to Ray Overholzer. This hunting guide-turned-craftsman would stroll along the Père Marquette River, find a stump leftover from Michigan's logging era, and see a table or maybe a piece of a rocking chair. Then he would spend months fashioning it by hand until his unique vision became reality. This is woodworking as an art, and it's preserved today at the **Shrine of the Pines**, a small but—to those of us who struggled in shop class just to build that birdhouse—intriguing museum.

Overholzer constructed a rocking chair from roots that is so perfectly balanced it rocks fifty-five times with a single push. His gun rack holds twelve hunting rifles and rotates on hand-carved wooden balls like ball bearings—not a screw or a hinge in the elaborate cabinet. A stump became a bootlegger's table with a hidden compartment for the whiskey bottle and another for the shot glasses. Perhaps most amazing is the dining room table that began as a 700-pound stump of a giant white pine. By the time Overholzer was done working with the piece of discarded wood, it was a 300-pound table with roots carved into legs and storage bins hollowed out of the sides. In 1940 and 1941 Overholzer built a huge lodge on the banks of the Père Marquette and originally intended to operate it as a hunting lodge. But his furniture was too dear to him by then and, fearing it would get scratched, he changed his mind. The intended lodge became a museum of more than 200 pieces, the world's only collection of handcrafted white pine furniture.

The Shrine of the Pines (231–745–7892) is located on M 37, 2 miles south of Baldwin. The museum is open daily, May to October, 10:00 A.M. to 6:00 P.M. There is a small fee.

Oceana County

County Road B–15 turns off from US 31 north of Whitehall and swings west toward Lake Michigan before returning to the highway at Pentwater, the bustling resort community at the northwest corner of Oceana County. Along the way the county road passes Silver Lake, an impressive sight that slows most cars bearing sightseers to a crawl. The lake is bordered to the west by a huge dune that towers over it, and from the car window you see beach and sunbathers, crystal clear lake and sailboats, the mountain of sand and dune climbers. Much of what you see, including the strip of dunes between the inland lake and Lake Michigan, is part of *Silver Lake State Park*.

Blessing of the Bikes

One of the most unusual festivals in Michigan is the Blessing of the Bikes, which is held the third weekend in May in Baldwin. Hundreds of motorcyclists, many of them riding classic Harley-Davidsons, arrive in town for the weekend and gather on Sunday at the local airstrip to have their bikes blessed by a priest.

Silver Lake is different from other state parks along Lake Michigan because the dunes have been divided into three areas for three types of users. The section in the middle is the pedestrian area, where people scramble up the huge dunes and hike across them to Lake Michigan.

The region to the south is one of only two places in the state where dune rides are offered in large open-air jeeps that hold up to twelve passengers. *Mac Wood's Dune Rides* date back to the 1930s, and today thousands enjoy the popular rides every year from mid-May through mid-October. The scenic thirty-five minute ride takes passengers through the heart of the Silver Lake dune country from the top of the tallest dunes to the edge of Lake Michigan. It's a wild ride down sandy hills and through the surf of Lake Michigan but never too scary for small children to handle. The tour is even more spectacular near sunset on a clear summer evening.

Mac Wood's Dune Rides (231–873–2817) is on Sixteenth Avenue at

Scenic Drive just south of the state park campground. Hours are 9:30 A.M. to sunset daily from mid-May to mid-October. The cost is $11.00 for adults, $7.00 for children.

The northern area of the park is most unusual, as it is designated for off-road vehicles. This is the ORV capital of the Midwest, the only public dunes in Michigan where people can drive their three- and four-wheelers, dirt bikes, trail jeeps, or any other vehicle built for the soft sand and steep terrain. On almost any day of the summer, the ORV parking lot at the end of Hazel Road will be filled with a wide assortment of vehicles, their drivers, and the trailers and vans they arrived in. They come from Indiana, Illinois, Ohio, and Wisconsin to ride here, as well as from all over Michigan. Pedestrians don't venture into the motorized area, but there is a wooden viewing platform overlooking the ORV entry point. Here you can view all the daredevil drivers and their machines as they climb the first dune.

For the more adventurous, **Sandy Korners** offers guided drives through the area in dune buggies that hold three or four people. A guide then leads the caravan of open jeeps on a one- to two-hour run across the sandy hills. Sandy Korners (231–873–5048) is on Hazel Road before you enter the state park, and charges $65 an hour for the rides. All participants must have a driver's license. There is a vehicle fee to enter Silver Lake State Park (231–873–3083).

Nickerson Inn

*I*n northern Oceana County is the resort town of Pentwater, which was no more than a few settlers at the mouth of the Pentwater River until Charles Mears showed up in 1859. The timber magnate turned the town into a major shipping port by building mills, hotels, and docks. He even straightened out the end of the Pentwater River to assist ships carrying his lumber. Today there is a state park in the city named after Mears, while on a wooded dune overlooking the park's Lake Michigan beach is the Nickerson Inn, built in 1914.

The inn's trademark is its long veranda, where in the summer you can sit and watch families stream toward the beach. Upstairs are ten rooms, including two Jacuzzi suites with gas log fireplaces and balconies. The inn's restaurant is renowned. Its enclosed porch overlooking Lake Michigan is a stunning place to watch the sunset during dinner, and a favorite of former Governor James Blanchard.

Summer room rates begin on Memorial Day weekend and range from $100 to $185 for the suites including breakfast. Call (231) 869–6731 for reservations.

Mason County

Continue on South Lakeshore Drive, pass the huge Ludington Power Plant, and then after a few miles keep an eye on the east side of the road for **Bortell's Fisheries**. From the outside the fish market is not glamorous, but it has been in business since 1937 and gradually has evolved into western Michigan's finest shop for fish and seafood. It carries a variety of frozen seafood, makes delicious marinated herring in cream and wine, and smokes one of the best selections of fish in the state, including trout, chub, salmon, sturgeon, blind robin, and menominee. Want something fresher? When in season, its cases are filled with fresh perch, pike, walleye, trout, and even smelt in the spring, all half-buried in ice.

Still not fresh enough? Then you can wander around back with a pole and catch a rainbow trout out of one of its stocked ponds. Bortell's will cook any fresh fish right there in the market and serve it with french fries and homemade potato salad or coleslaw. You can enjoy your meal outside at one of a half-dozen picnic tables next to the market, or better yet, cross the street to Summit Park, where you have a view of Lake Michigan from your table. The freshest fish, good food, and beautiful scenery at a little out-of-the-way county park—it doesn't get much better than that.

Bortell's Fisheries (231–843–3337) is 7 miles south of Ludington on South Lakeshore Drive between Meisenhiemer and Deren Roads. From May through September the store is open daily from 11:00 A.M. until 8:00 P.M.

The first frame house in Mason County was built by Aaron Burr Caswell in 1849. Six years later the two-story home was still the only frame building in an area that was trying to organize itself into Michigan's newest county. So that year Caswell offered the front half of his home as the first courthouse and county seat of Mason. Today the preserved building is a

Death of Father Jacques Marquette

Located on Lakeshore Drive just north of White Pine Village is a memorial to Father Jacques Marquette, a 45-foot-tall metal cross set in stone. The seventeenth-century missionary explorer is famous for founding St. Ignace and Sault Ste. Marie and for joining Louis Jolliet on a 3,000-mile paddle in discovering the Mississippi River. Realizing he was losing his health, Marquette tried to return to his beloved St. Ignace mission in 1675 but never made it. Instead he died on the banks of Lake Michigan in Buttersville at the site of the cross. He was buried here but his remains were later exhumed and taken to St. Ignace for final burial.

state historic site and the centerpiece of **White Pine Village**, a museum complex operated by the Mason County Historical Society.

The village is composed of some twenty preserved buildings or replicas, all from the surrounding county and set up along streets on a bluff overlooking Lake Michigan. Each of the buildings, which range from an 1840s trapper's log cabin to a hardware store of the early 1900s, is completely renovated inside and can be viewed on a leisurely self-guided walk. Throughout the village people in traditional dress ply their trades, everything from a blacksmith to a turn-of-the-century housewife cooking on a wood stove to a violin maker.

What makes White Pine Village an enjoyable experience is the active visitor participation in the exhibits. A documented trial that was held in the Caswell home in the 1860s is reenacted today with visitors filling in as the jury, and nine out of ten times handing down the same verdict as the first time. A log chapel on the rise overlooking the area still holds a Sunday service, and afterward people are encouraged to help the village cooks and enjoy their fresh-baked treats.

White Pine Village (231–843–4808) is open from late April until mid-October Tuesday through Sunday from 11:00 A.M. to 5:00 P.M. The museum complex is located off US 31, 3 miles south of Ludington, and is reached by exiting west onto Iris Road and then turning north at South Lakeshore Drive for a quarter of a mile. There is a small admission fee.

Lake Michigan Carferry

*I*n 1897 the Père Marquette departed Ludington, offering the first ferry transportation across Lake Michigan between Michigan and Wisconsin. A century later you can still hop on a ferry for a trip to Manitowoc, Wisconsin, thanks to the S.S. Badger, the only steam-powered auto passenger ship on the Great Lakes.

Launched in 1952, the 410-foot ferry was extensively refurbished in 1991 and now includes staterooms, a maritime museum, food and beverage service, theater and bingo hall, an outdoor deck, and live entertainment.

The 60-mile crossing takes four hours but saves you the 450-mile drive around the lake between the two cities. The cruise, a throwback to when luxurious steamers sailed the Great Lakes in the 1920s, is so popular that the company offers a single-day ticket. The round-trip fare for an adult without a vehicle is $40, and $20 for children.

In the summer the ferry departs Ludington at 7:30 a.m. and 7:45 p.m. and Manitowoc at 1:00 p.m. and 12:30 a.m. For tickets or reservations call Lake Michigan Carferry at (800)

Trapper's Cabin in White Pine Village

From Ludington the famous dunes of Lake Michigan continue to the north, and the area immediately adjacent to the city has been preserved as *Ludington State Park*. It's a popular place where visitors enjoy miles of beach, rolling dunes, and modern campgrounds, or a hike to historic Point Sable Lighthouse. Along with a 300-site campground, the state park (231–843–8671) also features the Great Lakes Interpretive Center and an unusual nature trail in Hamlin Lake for canoers.

Where Ludington State Park ends, the *Nordhouse Dunes* begin, a 1,900-acre preserve in Manistee National Forest that is not as well known or as frequently visited as the state park but is equally beautiful.

A Michigan governor called the Nordhouse Dunes "one of the most outstanding scenic resources" in the state, and in 1987 they were given a federal wilderness designation. What makes these dunes unique is that the area is entirely undeveloped. Travel through the dunes is only on foot either along 10 miles of easy-to-follow trails or by simply making your way across the open hills of sand. The area is the only place in Michigan where you can hike in and camp among the dunes. Because of its inaccessibility to motorized traffic, the dunes area also offers those willing to hike in the opportunity of having a beach to themselves along its 4 miles of sandy lakeshore.

Access into Nordhouse Dunes is through the Lake Michigan Recreation Area, a semi-primitive campground on the northern end of the preserve that is maintained by the national forest's Manistee Ranger District (231–723–2211). Trails into the dunes begin from the recreation area, which also contains one hundred camping sites, a beach, and observation towers overlooking the lake. To reach the recreational area, take US 31 to Lake Michigan Road (also known as Forest Road 5629) located 10 miles south of Manistee. Follow Lake Michigan Road 8 miles west to the area. There is no fee for exploring the dunes or for day use of the recreational area. There is a nightly fee for camping.

Manistee County

Manistee is another lakeshore town that boomed during the lumbering era; at one time in the late 1800s, it boasted thirty-two sawmills and seventeen millionaire lumber barons among its residents. Almost the entire town was destroyed in the Great Fire of 1871 on the same day Chicago experienced its famous blaze. One of the first buildings erected after the fiery mishap was the **Lyman Building,** which was

Skyline Trail

Anyone who loves boardwalk paths with benches will savor the Skyline Trail, a short but spectacularly scenic hike in Ludington State Park. The path follows the crest of a wooded dune, and erosion of the original trail prompted the park staff to replace it with a boardwalk path in 1981. The two-year project included use of Air National Guard helicopters to airlift much of the lumber to the top of the dune.

The sweeping views of Lake Michigan and the park's open dune country are so good that numerous benches were built into the boardwalk. Sure, the trail is only a half-mile long, but if you sat on every bench and admired the scene, it would take you most of the after-noon to hike it. The view from the bench at Post Number 11 is especially scenic as you gaze south at the miles of open dunes stretched out to the Lake Michigan shoreline, the Ludington Harbor Lighthouse, and, on a clear day, even the Silver Lakes dunes 25 miles away.

Besides the benches are thirteen numbered posts along the boardwalk that correspond to information in a brochure available from map boxes at the foot of each staircase. They identify the three common evergreens in Michigan, explain dune country succession, and point out stumps and other remnants of the loggers who arrived in 1851 to cut down the white pine.

a place of business throughout its existence until the Manistee County Historical Society turned it into the only "storefront museum" in the state.

The Lyman Building Museum is not just another county museum displaying local artifacts. The many fixtures, walk-in vault, and wraparound balcony have been preserved, and part of the first floor has been restored as an early drugstore with brass apothecary scales, pill makers, an impressive selection of antique medicines and balms, and fading posters on the walls selling Pe-Ru-Na, which "cures catarrh." The other half of the first floor is set up as a general store, while in the back is an old newspaper office with original Linotype machines. Upstairs are ten more rooms, including a dentist's office, a bank, and the living room of an early 1900s home. The hallway between the rooms is filled with Victor talking machines and Victrolas. The Lyman Building Museum (231–723–5531), at 425 River Street in downtown Manistee, is open year-round from 10:00 A.M. to 5:00 P.M. Monday through Saturday from June through September, and Tuesday through Saturday the rest of the year. There is a small admission charge.

The Great Fire of 1871

A historical marker in Orchard Beach State Park 2 miles north of Manistee commemorates the Great Fire of 1871. On October 8, the day the famous Chicago fire began, fires also broke out in Michigan after an exceptionally long, hot summer. Most of Holland and Manistee was ruined within hours, with the flames sweeping east across the state and eventually reaching Port Huron.

Another impressive building left over from the town's golden lumbering era is the **Ramsdell Theatre**, built in 1903 by Thomas Jefferson Ramsdell and today listed on the National Register of Historic Places. Ramsdell, a local lawyer and later a state legislator, wanted to add some culture to the rough-and-tumble logging town and built one of the most elaborate opera houses in the state. It featured a double balcony upstairs and private viewing boxes along the main floor. It was proclaimed "acoustically perfect," and famed theatrical artist Walter Burridge painted the main curtain, which is still used today. Other paintings adorn the dome and archways of the lobby.

Local residents saved the theater from demolition in the 1920s, and the city finally purchased the structure in 1943. Today the Manistee Civic Players operates the facility and uses it to stage a summer series of plays. Stop in when the box office is open (a week before each show, Monday through Saturday from noon to 6:00 P.M.) and you can view the interior. Or call (231–723–9948) for a tour of the opera house. The Ramsdell Theatre is at First and Maple Streets.

Northern Michigan is famous for its trout streams, which attract fly fishers from around the country. In Manistee County you can either grab your fly rod and go fishing or go to school to learn how to fly fish. *The Michigan Academy of Fly Fishing* is part of the Wellston Inn and is located near some of the state's best blue-ribbon trout streams, in the small town of Wellston. Five times each summer the academy holds a two- or three-day class, with students staying at the historical Wellston Inn. Not only does the inn provide a comfortable room, but outside there also is a lighted fly-casting pond and a fly-tying hut.

Students divide their time between the inn's facilities and local rivers, learning how to work a fly rod, read trout waters, choose a fly, and even tie their own. The three-day sessions are $450 per person and include rooms. For reservations or dates write the Wellston Inn, P.O. Box 70, Wellston 49689, or call (231) 848–4163.

PLACES TO STAY IN THE LAKE MICHIGAN AREA

DOUGLAS
Sherwood Forest Bed & Breakfast,
99 Center Street,
(231) 857–1246

LUDINGTON
Daniel Goodenough House,
705 East Ludington Avenue,
(231) 843–3197

Pier House,
805 Ludington Avenue,
(800) 968–3677

MANISTEE
The Milwaukee House,
259 River Street,
(231) 723–7880

Riverside Motel,
520 Water Street,
(231) 723–3554

Lakeshore Motel,
101 South Lakeshore Drive,
(231) 723–2667

NEW BUFFALO
The Harbor Grand Hotel,
111 West Water Street,
(616) 469–7700

NILES
Ramada Inn,
930 South Eleventh Street,
(616) 684–3000

Yesterday's Inn,
518 North Fourth Street,
(616) 683–6079

ONEKAMA
Portage Point Inn,
8513 South Portage Point Drive,
(231) 889–4222

PENTWATER
Nickerson Inn,
262 West Lowell Street,
(231) 869–6731

Pentwater Inn Bed & Breakfast,
180 East Lowell Street,
(231) 869–5909

SAUGATUCK
Rosemont Inn,
83 Lakeshore Drive,
(800) 857–2637

The Maplewood Hotel,
428 Butler Street,
(800) 650–9790

Twin Gables Country Inn,
900 Lake Street,
(616) 857–4346

ST. JOSEPH
Boulevard Hotel,
521 Lake Boulevard,
(616) 983–6600

South Cliff Inn,
1900 Lakeshore Drive,
(616) 983–4881

SOUTH HAVEN
Old Harbor Inn,
515 Williams Street,
(616) 637–8480

Yelton Manor Bed
& Breakfast,
140 North Shore Drive,
(616) 637–5220

The Seymour House,
1248 Blue Star Highway,
(616) 227–3918

UNION PIER
Gordan Beach Inn,
16240 Lakeshore Road,
(616) 469–0800

Inn at Union Pier,
9708 Berrien Street,
(616) 469–4700

WHITE CLOUD
The Shack,
2263 West Fourteenth
Street,
(231) 924–6683

WHITEHALL
Michillinda Beach Lodge,
5207 Scenic Drive,
(231) 893–1895

**PLACES TO EAT IN THE
LAKE MICHIGAN AREA**

BRIDGMAN
Hyerdall's (American),
9673 Red Arrow Highway,
(616) 465–5546

BUCHANAN
Tabor Hill Winery (fine
dining),
185 Mt. Tabor Hill Road,
(800) 283–3363

B&W Olde Village Inn
(Greek and American),
116 Main Street,
(616) 695–5871

GRANT
Grant Depot Restaurant
(American),
22 West Main Street,
(231) 834–7361

HOLLAND
Queen's Inn (Dutch),
Dutch Village at US 31 and
James Street,
(616) 393–0310

Piper (American),
2225 South Shore Drive,
(616) 335–5866

Alpen Rose (pastry shop),
4 East Eighth Street,
(616) 393–2111

LUDINGTON
P.M. Steamers (American),
502 West Loomis,
(231) 843–9555

Gibbs Country House
(American),
3951 West US 10,
(231) 845–0311

Old Hamlin Restaurant
(American),
122 West Ludington Avenue,
(231) 843–4251

Selected Chambers of Commerce and Tourism Bureaus

Holland Area Convention and Visitors Bureau,
76 East Eighth Street, Holland 49423;
(800) 506–1299

Ludington Convention and Visitors Bureau,
5827 West US 10, Ludington 49431;
(800) 542–4600

Manistee Convention and Visitors Bureau,
P.O. Box 13, Manistee 49660;
(800) 288–2286

Muskegon Convention and Visitors Bureau,
690 West Webster Avenue, Muskegon 48161;
(231) 722–3751

South Haven Convention and Visitors Bureau,
415 Phoenix Street, South Haven 49090;
(800) SO–HAVEN

Southwestern Michigan Tourist Council,
2300 Pipestone Road, Benton Harbor 49022;
(616) 925–6301

Spring Lake Area Convention and Visitors Bureau,
One South Harbor Drive, Grand Haven 49417;
(800) 303–4094

MANISTEE
Four Forty West (waterfront dining),
440 River Street,
(231) 723–7902

NEW BUFFALO
Bilgewater Grill on the Lake
(outdoor dining),
244 North Whittaker,
(616) 469–5323

PENTWATER
Nickerson Inn (American),
262 West Lowell Street,
(231) 869–6731

SAUGATUCK
Billies Boathouse (American),
449 Water Street,
(616) 857–1188

SOUTH HAVEN
The Idler (Cajun),
Old Harbor Village on the
Black River,
(616) 637–8435

Three Pelicans
(Caribbean),
38 North Shore Drive,
(616) 637–5132

STEVENSVILLE
Tosi's (Italian),
4337 Ridge Road,
(616) 429–3689

ST. JOSEPH
The Mark III (Mexican),
4179 M 139,
(616) 429–2941

Lakeview Restaurant at the
Boulevard (fine dining),
521 Lake Boulevard,
(616) 983–0909

UNION PIER
Red Arrow Roadhouse
(American),
15710 Red Arrow Highway,
(616) 469–3939

Miller's Country House
(American),
16409 Red Arrow Highway,
(616) 469–5950

OTHER ATTRACTIONS

Curious Kids Museum,
St. Joseph

Southwestern Michigan
College Museum, Dowagiac

The Pearl Mill Museum,
Buchanan

S.S. Keewatin Museum,
Saugatuck

Manistee Fire Hall,
Manistee

Fernwood Botanic
Gardens, Buchanan

Trillium Ravine, Niles

The New Buffalo Railroad
Museum, New Buffalo

Northwest Michigan

n many ways Northwest Michigan is a continuation of the region stretching along Lake Michigan. It's accented by vast tracts of dunes, miles of beaches, and a handful of well-developed resort towns whose specialty shops bustle in the summer and winter. But it is also distinctly different.

This is "the land of many little bays," with scenic Grand Traverse Bay dominating the center of the region, Little Traverse Bay farther up the shoreline, and remote Sturgeon Bay at its northern tip. For many tourists this is Mackinaw City, a tour of Fort Michilimackinac, and a ferry ride to Mackinac Island, the summer resort island known throughout the country for its horse-and-carriage transportation and the Grand Hotel.

Most of all, this is Michigan's Cherry Country. Moderate weather from the Great Lakes and light soils help this region produce 80 to 85 percent of the state's total cherry crop. Drive along US 31 from Traverse City to Charlevoix in spring, and you'll pass rolling hills of trees in full bloom and air scented by cherry blossoms.

Arrive in July and you can enjoy the bountiful harvest these fruit farms produce. Along this 50-mile stretch of road, you'll pass dozens of farms and will undoubtedly see harvesting crews "shaking" one tree after another, with the cherries ending up in a large metal tank of water.

You'll also see numerous roadside fruit stands that will be hard to pass up, and you shouldn't even try. The most common sweet cherries sold are Bing and Schmidt; tourists often call them black cherries, though if they are, the fruit is overripe. Look for cherries that are firm and dark maroon, and be prepared when you bite into your first one. The juice will explode from the cherry, dribble down your chin, and send your taste buds into a state of ecstasy. There are few things as wonderful in this state as a northern Michigan cherry in July.

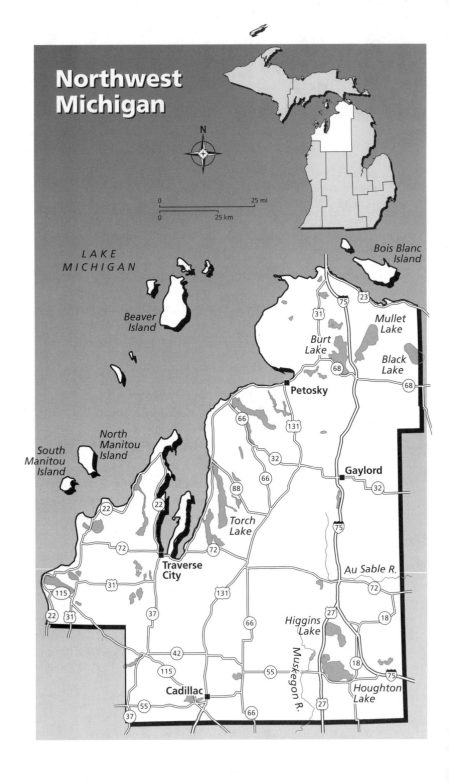

Benzie County

AUTHOR'S TOP TEN PICKS

South Manitou Island,
Leland; (231) 256–9061

*Tunnel of Trees Drive
and Legs Inn,* Cross Village;
(231) 526–2281

*Pierce Stocking
Scenic Drive,*
Empire; (231) 326–5134

Beaver Island,
Charlevoix; (888) 446–4095

Dennos Museum Center,
Traverse City;
(231) 922–1055

*The Michigan Forest
Visitor Center,*
Hartwick Pines State Park;
(231) 348–7068

Avalanche Peak,
Boyne City; (231) 582–6222

*Mill Creek Historical
State Park,*
Mackinaw City;
(231) 436–7301

Grass Lake Natural Area,
Bellaire; (616) 533–8576

Gwen Frostic Prints,
Frankfort; (231) 882–5505

One of the smallest counties in the state, Benzie is also one of the most scenic. It features rolling forested hills, spring-fed trout streams, towering sandy bluffs, and endless beaches along Lake Michigan and Crystal Lake, a body of water whose clarity lives up to its name. In the natural beauty of this northwoods setting, Gwen Frostic emerged as one of Michigan's most noted poets and publishers from her background as an artist and a conservationist. Her love of nature has always been with her, but she began writing and carving blocks for prints in the mid-1940s in the blue-collar community of Wyandotte, south of Detroit. In the early 1960s she moved to a wooded spot 2 miles west of Benzonia and set up **Gwen Frostic Prints** on a personal wildlife sanctuary of 285 acres.

Her large gallery is housed in a building of native stone, glass, and old wood, which seeks to "bring the outdoors in" while blending into the natural surroundings. She accomplished that surprisingly well. Inside you'll walk below rough-cut beams past huge stone fireplaces and view the tumbling water of natural fountains. You'll be surrounded by Frostic's woodblock prints, tables covered with books of her poetry, and bird carvings by some of the country's leading wildlife carvers. There is a small library overlooking a pond where waterfowl usually are feeding, and another room displays all the honors she has received, including a Michigan governor's proclamation of an official "Gwen Frostic Day."

Most impressive, perhaps, is the publishing aspect of the gallery. From a balcony above, visitors can view fifteen original Heidelberg presses clanking away as workers print a wide selection of cards, notepaper, wall prints, and books, all using block designs carved by Frostic, featuring natural subjects and sold in the gallery.

Gwen Frostic Prints (231–882–5505) is at 5140 River Road, 2 miles west of US 31 and 6 miles east of M 22 in Frankfort. The gallery is open daily from May to October from 9:00 A.M. until 5:30 P.M. and until 4:30

P.M. Monday through Saturday the rest of the year. The presses are in operation only Monday through Friday.

Back in the 1930s a small group of Frankfort residents discovered the thrill of soaring in gliders. They would take off from the high bluffs overlooking Lake Michigan and fly through the air, sometimes for hours, before landing on the beach. What emerged was the **Northwest Soaring Club of Frankfort**, which at one time hosted a national soaring championship in this small town.

The art of soaring has changed over the years, but the club is still around, offering lessons and, for visitors passing through on vacation, introductory rides. Passengers join a certified pilot in a two-seat glider 25 to 35 feet long, with a wingspan of about 50 feet. The glider is towed to a height of 2,000 to 3,000 feet by a small plane and then released. What follows is a spectacular ride along the Lake Michigan shoreline with extensive views of the lake, sand dunes, and beautiful Crystal Lake. The length of the ride depends on the wind and thermal conditions, but it ranges from thirty minutes to sometimes several hours.

Fun Facts

In 1873 a canal was built to Lake Michigan that drained the water out of inland Crystal Lake. The level of Crystal Lake dropped 25 feet, creating the beautiful beaches that make it such a popular resort area today. The canal, on the other hand, eventually became a swamp.

Introductory rides are offered from May through October and cost $40 per person for a 2,000-foot tow and $50 for a 3,000-foot tow. The higher the tow, the longer the flight. Interested persons should call ahead to the Northwest Soaring Club at (231) 352–9160. Club rides take off from Frankfort Airport, located on Airport Road south of M 115.

Of all the dunes along Lake Michigan, the best known are those in **Sleeping Bear National Lakeshore,** administered by the National Park Service. Thousands of people visit the area every year, and many head straight to the "**Dune Climb**," a 150-foot steep hill of sand located right off M 109 in Leelanau County. This is the park's most famous feature, a knee-bending climb up the towering dune and a wild run down through the soft sand. In addition, there are other aspects of the park, many having nothing to do with dunes and often overlooked by visitors who rush through the area in an afternoon.

The national lakeshore begins in Benzie County and includes one of the most scenic beaches on Lake Michigan. **Platte River Point** is a long, sandy spit divided from the mainland by the crystal-clear Platte River. It's pure sand, this narrow strip, with endless Lake Michigan on one side, the knee-deep salmon and trout river on the other, and panoramas of towering dunes off in the distance. To reach it, sunbathers turn west from M 22 onto the marked Lake Michigan Road and follow it to the end. Then it's a quick wade through the rippling waters of the Platte River with dad holding a young one or the picnic lunch high on his shoulder. There is no bridge.

People at Platte River Point swim, build sand castles, and beachcomb as on any other beach, but the favorite activity here is floating. They bring out an old inner tube or an air mattress, hike a few hundred yards up the point, and then let the Platte River give them a free ride right out to Lake Michigan if they wish. It's debatable who enjoys it more, the kids or the parents. If you don't have an inner tube, you can rent one from **Riverside Canoe Trips** (231–325–5622) located on M 22 right before you turn off for the beach. Tubes for one to four people can be rented, and there are dropoff and pickup services for those who want to spend an afternoon "tubing" the Platte River from the Platte Lake to the Great Lake. Rental rates depend on the length of your float and the size of your tube.

The sign out front says all you need to know about the **Homestead Sugar House**. It's attached to a wooden scaffold just below a large noose, and reads HANG THE DIET! Don't even think about "that four-letter word" when you stumble upon the maple bush (a farm on which sugar maples grow) of Jean and Russell Morstadt, home of Benzie County's oldest candymaking shop. Don't worry about counting calories or losing that 2-inch pinch at the waist. Just enjoy the aroma that greets you as soon as you pull in; let your eyes feast on the hand-dipped, long-stemmed chocolate cherries and maple creams displayed in the glass case inside; and when Jean Morstadt, dressed in a Grandma Moses style, offers you something sweet, don't be bashful.

The Morstadts were living in Chicago in 1948 when they decided they had had enough of city life, and they moved to northern Michigan.

Top Annual Events

Mesick Mushroom Festival,
Mesick, May; (231) 885–2679

National Morel Mushroom Hunting Festival,
Boyne City, May;
(231) 582–6222

National Cherry Festival,
Traverse City, July;
(231) 947–4230

Venetian Festival,
Charlevoix, July;
(800) 968–3302

Au Sable River Canoe Marathon and River Festival,
Grayling, July;
(800) 235–4625

Harbor Days,
Elk Rapids, August;
(231) 264–8202

Suttons Bay Art Fair,
Suttons Bay, August;
(231) 271–3050

Buckley Old Engine Show,
Buckley, August;
(231) 269–3750

Harbor Springs Cycling Classic,
Harbor Springs, September;
(800) 530–9955

Winter Fest,
Gaylord, February;
(800) 345–8621

North American Snowmobile Festival,
Cadillac, February;
(800) 22–LAKES

They bought a 300-acre maple bush in the rolling hills east of Beulah and began farming. After years of "harvesting nothing but bills," the couple began making candy in the shack outside their home in 1963. They recently celebrated their thirtieth anniversary as candymakers, and among their loyal customers is singer Linda Ronstadt.

From US 31 turn onto Homestead Road in downtown Benzonia and head east for 4.5 miles to the farm with a scaffold outside. The shop (231–882–7712) is open from 10:00 A.M. to 4:30 P.M. daily May through November.

Leelanau County

f it's March and you have a sweet tooth, head north to Maple City, where you'll find the **Sugar Shack**, a 200-acre, 900-tree sugar maple bush. In northern Michigan, the season can last up to six weeks and usually begins in mid-March, when the freezing and thawing cycle of spring causes the sap to flow. The season is a special time, and visitors can witness it by stopping in at this farm set in the rolling, wooded hills south of Glen Lake.

A visit to this bush is a view of a modern-day maple producer, and most people interested in the process begin with a walk into the bush to see a pumping station and the network of tubing. Others never leave the small store with its potbellied stove and rustic appearance. Shelves are stocked with maple sugar by the pound and by the piece, homemade maple pralines, maple-coated popcorn, and, of course, syrup.

The Sugar Shack (231–228–5835) is located just off M 72, 15 miles west of Traverse City. From M72 turn north on Fritz Road and in a quarter of a mile turn west on Baatz Road; the farm is 1.5 miles up on the left. During the syrup season and the summer, the store is open from 9:00 A.M. to 5:00 P.M. Monday through Friday and until noon on Saturday.

For a view of spectacular dune terrain, take a ride along the **Pierce Stocking Scenic Drive** at Sleeping Bear National Lakeshore. Often called "the slowest, shortest, but most scenic stretch of pavement in the state," the drive is only a 7.4-mile loop but passes three stunning overlooks of the national lakeshore's perched dunes. Pierce Stocking, the self-taught naturalist who built the road in the early 1960s and operated it until his death in 1976, charged each car $2.00. The next year the National Park Service took over the road and changed its name to honor the man who'd built it.

The speed limit is only 15 miles per hour, but even that seems fast at times. Along with the scenic viewing points of the dunes and the sweeping shoreline, there are also twelve interpretive stops that correspond with information in a brochure provided at the fee station. From the Dune Overlook you can also walk the Cottonwood Trail, a short nature trail that leads you to within view of the Dune Climb. Feel energetic? There is also a bicycle lane along the road, but keep in mind that it's a very hilly bike ride. Above all, pack a lunch and plan to picnic at the Lake Michigan Overlook.

The entrance to Pierce Stocking Scenic Drive is on M 109, 3 miles north of the Sleeping Bear National Lakeshore visitor center (231–326–5134) in Empire. A weekly or annual vehicle pass is required to enter the drive.

The dunes are one of the main attractions of the area today. At the turn of the century, however, the noted feature was the Manitou Passage, between the Manitou Islands and the mainland. During the heyday of Great Lakes shipping from the 1860s to 1920, when a hundred vessels might pass through on a single day, this was a shoal-lined shortcut they all took. The narrow Manitou

> ## Fun Facts
>
> *Michigan has a total of 275,000 acres of sand dune formations on three Great Lakes, with almost half of them in public ownership.*

Passage's shallow, reeflike shoals, and often-violent weather produced more than their share of shipwrecks, and eventually several lighthouses and lifesaving stations were built on the mainland and the islands.

One of them has been preserved by the National Park Service as **Sleeping Bear Point Coast Guard Station Maritime Museum**. The facility began its service in 1901 as a U.S. Life Saving Station and was actually situated on Sleeping Bear Point. When a migrating sand dune threatened to bury it in 1930, the U.S. Coast Guard (having replaced the U.S. Life Saving Service) moved the buildings 1.5 miles toward Glen Haven. The station ended its duty in 1942 and now is a well-restored museum that tells the story of the U.S. Life Saving Service, which manned the coastline all around the country.

Anywhere from six to ten men would live at the remote station, and their former living quarters, a huge two-story building, is now the main exhibit area. It allows visitors a glimpse of the regimented work they performed and the isolated life they lived. Nearby the boathouse contains the lifesaving boats, complete with tracks down to the beach for a quick launch, and other equipment, including the beachcart. When ships ran aground within 400 yards of shore, the lifesavers would pull out the beachcart and use the small cannon on it to shoot a guide line to the distressed vessel. That rope was used to string more lines across the water, and a breeches buoy was sent to the ship on a pulley. Then, one by one, sailors would step into the buoy's breeches and ride the line to the shore and safety.

Check with the park headquarters (231–326–5134) in Empire for time and day of the museum's "Heroes of the Storm" program, in which rangers demonstrate a turn-of-the-century shipwreck rescue using the beachcart, the breeches buoy, and volunteers from the audience who fill in for sailors and lifesavers. Only the cannon is missing.

The village of Leland's trademark is a row of weathered dockside shacks along the Leland River that at one time housed commercial fishermen and today is a historic district known as Fishtown. All the commercial fishermen except Carlson Fisheries have disappeared from the strip, but their buildings have been preserved and now house specialty shops and stores. With its unique setting and atmosphere, Fishtown is the proper place to begin a nautical adventure to **South Manitou Island**, a portion of the Sleeping Bear National Lakeshore located 17 miles from Leland in Lake Michigan.

Fun Facts

The Dune Climb in Sleeping Bear National Lakeshore is the most popular dune to climb in Michigan and possibly the country. Park officials estimate that more than 300,000 people climb it annually.

Island visitors board a ferry at the end of Fishtown and begin with a ninety-minute cruise to South Manitou that passes a lighthouse and the scenic shoreline of Sleeping Bear Dunes. The island, with its hardwood forests and natural harbor, attracted settlers, a lighthouse, and a lifesaving station as early as 1840, and it has an interesting history. The ferry has a four-hour layover at the national park dock, more than enough time to view the small museum at the visitor center, climb the 116 steps to the top of the lighthouse, and enjoy a lunch on a nearby beach.

For the more energetic, there are trails and old farm roads across the island, and it's possible to hike the 6-mile round trip to the **Francisco Morazan** and return to the mainland the same day. The Morazan was a Liberian freighter that ran aground in November 1960 at the southwest corner of the island, and a large portion of the battered vessel is still visible above the waterline today. For the best adventure on South Manitou, camp for a night or two at Weather Station Campground, a national park facility that is free. The campground is a 1.5-mile hike in from the dock, and you can explore the tract of sand dunes on the west side of the island. The dunes, perched on bluffs high above Lake Michigan, are probably the most remote and least visited ones in the state.

All visitors must bring their own food to South Manitou, and campers have to be self-sufficient with tent, sleeping bags, and other equipment. Contact Manitou Island Transit (231–256–9061 or 271–4217) about the ferry that sails to the island daily from June through August. The round-trip fare is $20 per adult.

The growing conditions in southwest Michigan that made Paw Paw the wine-producing center of the state are also found in Leelanau and Old Missionary, two peninsulas filled with fruit farms and a half-dozen vineyards of surprising quality. All the vineyards have a tasting room, and an interesting day can be had visiting each of them. The first bonded wine cellar in the area— and many think the most beautiful one in the state— is *Boskydel Vineyard*, a small winery on the shores of Lake Leelanau. There is no restaurant at Boskydel or even any picnic tables outside, but it is built on the side of a hill, and from the parking lot you have a view of the sloping vineyard leading down to the huge lake, framed by the rolling hills of the Leelanau Peninsula. All this prompted one wine critic to proclaim Boskydel the most beautiful site for a winery in the country.

It was within the family tradition that Bernie Rinke should plant a vineyard. He grew up on an Ohio farm, and his father bootlegged wine during Prohibition. Rinke began planting his vineyard in 1964 and now cultivates twenty-five acres of grapes, producing 6,000 gallons (2,500 cases) annually of several dry and semi-dry red and white table wines. The tasting room is open daily year-round from 1:00 to 6:00 P.M., and if you want a tour of the winery, Rinke will lead you through a ten-minute look at his facility.

Actually, Rinke would rather stay in the small tasting room, plop a large wine glass in front of you (no plastic cups here), and talk—about his

Leelanau Cheese

*I*n a converted gas station in the small town of Omena is Leelanau Cheese, the place to stop for delicious wedges of raclette cheese or containers of fromage blanc. Since 1995 husband-and-wife cheesemakers John and Anne Hoyt have been hand-crafting their product after learning the cheesemaking trade in Switzerland. Raclette is a semihard Swiss melting cheese made from whole cow's milk, with each eight-pound wheel aging ninety days before it is sold.

grapes, about wine tasting, about his days as Northwestern Michigan College's first librarian in nearby Traverse City. (Ask him where the name of the winery comes from.) A beautiful vineyard, a most delightful winemaker, and not a bad wine either, Boskydel (616-256-7272) is 3.5 miles southeast of the town of Lake Leelanau at County Road 641 and Otto Road.

Grand Traverse County

The most noted feature of the county is Grand Traverse Bay, a beautiful body of water with Traverse City at the south end and old Mission Peninsula splitting it up the middle. Its protected waters have become a haven for sailboats, catamarans, and sailboarders, but by far the most impressive vessel afloat during the summer is the *Malabar*, a replica of a two-masted, gaff-rigged, topsail 1850 schooner. The 105-foot, 100-ton ship was built in 1975 to look and sail like a traditional schooner, and it's that love for old wooden boats that draws most of its passengers on deck. From May to mid-October the Malabar offers three sailings daily, with two-hour cruises at noon and 3:00 P.M. and a two-and-a-half-hour sunset sail with picnic meal—the most popular trip, of course—at 7:00 P.M. Passengers who dream about a life on the high seas go a step further and book a cabin on the Malabar, which at night becomes Michigan's only floating bed-and-breakfast. The quarters are tiny, with bunks built into the curves and angles of the hull. The head is shared, and the showers are back on land. In the evening guests wander topside to take in Traverse City lights shimmering on the bay or snuggle up in their bunks to be put to sleep by the gentle swells and the creaking of the wooden hull.

The Malabar is operated by the Traverse Tall Ship Company (231–941–2000). Its office and dock are at 13390 Southwest Bay Shore Drive. Daily cruises range from $30 to $38 for adults, and overnight accommodations, which include a hearty breakfast with the crew in the galley, are $104 to $181 for singles or doubles.

You can also enjoy the water from above through *Grand Traverse Balloon*, which offers hot-air balloon rides across Grand Traverse Bay, often beginning at the Château Grand Traverse vineyards on Old Mission Peninsula. This may well be the most spectacular view from any hot-air balloon in Michigan, as below you lies the narrow peninsula, the rippling waters of the bay, Traverse City, and the endless rows of the cherry orchards to the northeast. The entire flight takes three hours, with an hour in the air, and flights are always at sunrise or sunset because there's less wind turbulence. They are priced at $185 per person. Jeff Geiger, the Traverse City balloonist who runs Grand Traverse Balloon (231–947–7433), recommends reservations but says he can usually fulfill last-minute urges to float above the bay.

For another unusual view of the bay, head to the highest ridge on the Mission Peninsula just before sunset. At this high point Robert Begin has built the state's newest vineyard, **Château Chantal**, and included a brick terrace that overlooks both the West Arm and East Arm of Grand Traverse Bay. With vineyards and cherry orchards at your feet, you settle back with a glass of Chardonnay or a semi-dry Riesling and some sharp cheeses or freshly cut fruit and watch the sky melt into a collage of oranges and reds over the bays of northern Michigan.

Begin, a former priest, and his wife have built the unique winery on a former ridge-top cherry farm and named it after their daughter. You can stop by for a tour or a sip in the vineyard's wine-tasting and sales area, a great room that features hardwood floors, a polished granite bar top, and a grand piano in front of a 20-foot-wide bay window overlooking Grand Traverse Bay. Or you can simply stop for the night and unwind. That's because this winery is also a bed-and-breakfast, featuring three rooms with sitting areas and private baths.

Château Chantal (231–223–4110) is located just off M 37 on Mission Peninsula, 12 miles north of Traverse City. Tours are offered daily during summer at 1:00, 2:00, and 3:00 P.M. The tasting room is open year-round from 11:00 A.M. to 6:00 P.M. Monday through Friday and noon to 5:00 P.M. on Sunday. Rooms range from $105 to $135 per night.

One of Michigan's newest art museums is no stuffy gallery with ancient masterpieces in gilded frames. Located on the campus of Northwestern Michigan College, the **Dennos Museum Center** opened in 1991 after more than a decade in the planning.

The jewel of the museum is its permanent Inuit Art Gallery, a collection that began in 1960 and was housed in

The *Malabar*

A "Chew-Chew" Train

Romance, adventure, and fine dining are all available with a trip on the Grand Traverse Dinner Train. The restored 1950s dining cars are used for a five-course gourmet dinner served during a three-hour ride along the Boardman River and deep into the Père Marquette State Forest. Entrees range from garlic prime rib to northern Michigan trout with peach salsa.

The trains depart from a depot at 642 Railroad Place in downtown Traverse City and run year-round, with the schedule depending on the season. Dinner is $55 per person. For reservations call Grand Traverse Dinner Train at (231) 933–3768.

the college library. Today there are 550 pieces of sculptured soapstone and colorful prints depicting the harsh life and fascinating culture of these Arctic people. Carvings and prints depict hunters pulling a walrus out of the ice with a rope, kayaking through the open seas, bedding down in an igloo, waiting patiently at a breathing hole in the frozen Arctic Ocean for a seal to surface.

But families and kids usually head for the Discovery Gallery, which combines art, science, and technology into an intriguing set of hands-on displays. One of the exhibits is the Recollections Piece. With the use of video cameras and computer-generated images, visitors can watch themselves "come alive in color" as they move in front of a room-size screen. The museum staff calls it "painting with your body."

From downtown Traverse City head north on US 31 to the Northwestern Michigan College campus. Dennos Museum Center (231–922–1055) is on the small campus. The center is open Monday through Saturday from 10:00 A.M. to 5:00 P.M. and Sunday 1:00 to 5:00 P.M. There is a small admission fee.

If you're traveling just north of Traverse City on US 31 and pass a place called **The Music House**, turn off the car stereo. Strip the headphones and Walkmans from your kids' ears and toss that huge boom box in the trunk. Then turn around and see how music used to be enjoyed. Housed in an old granary built in 1905, The Music House is a showcase for automatic musical instruments from the 1880s to the 1920s. Visitors are entertained rather than educated, as the hour-long tour is a musical journey with toe-tapping demonstrations ranging from small music boxes to one of the largest ballroom dance organs ever made.

Tours begin in the phonograph gallery, where a huge model of Nipper, the famous RCA Victor dog, greets you. There are rows of "talking machines" beginning from 1900 with their wax cylinders instead of records and colorful morning glory horns instead of speakers. In the main portion of the barn are larger musical machines set up in the environments in which they were enjoyed. The most impressive sight for many visitors is upstairs in the loft, which is home to the 30-foot facade of the Amaryllis dance organ. Built in 1922 for a palace ballroom in Belgium, the instrument plays a folded perforated cardboard book using hundreds of wooden and metal pipes along with percussion instruments.

The Music House (231–938–9300) is located on a 180-acre cherry farm off US 31, 1.5 miles north of the highway's junction with M 72 or 8 miles north of Traverse City. It is open daily from "cherry blossoms through fall colors," or, to be more exact, May 1 through October 30, 10:00 A.M. to 4:00 P.M. Monday through Saturday and 1:00 to 4:00 P.M. on Sunday. From mid-November through December, it is open Friday through Sunday. There is an admission fee.

Continue north on US 31 for a few more miles and you'll come to **Amon Orchards**, offering guided tours and the best view of a working cherry farm. Visitors ride in an open tractor trolley, and in July you can watch workers mechanically harvest cherries and even pick a few of your own. Tours at Amon Orchards (231–938–1644), beginning in July and continuing through September, are offered at 10:00 A.M. and 2:00 P.M. daily. There is a fee for the ninety-minute tour.

Antrim County

Speeding along US 131 in the middle of Antrim County, you pass one of the most spectacular inland viewing points in the Lower Peninsula, though you would never know it from this road. The side road to **Deadman's Hill** is 7 miles north of Mancelona, but there is little fanfare about the scenic overlook: Only a small brown sign points the

A Singer Named Jewel

In the mid-1990s, regulars at Ray's Coffeehouse in Traverse City remember, they would hear a young singer with a distinctly sweet and high voice. By 1997 they knew her well, though she had been gone for years. Her name—the only name she goes by—was Jewel. Now one of the hottest singers on the pop music scene, Jewel was a student at the Interlochen Fine Arts Camp that summer and playing for tips in local coffeehouses.

You can catch other possible future stars at the internationally acclaimed music camp that overlooks Green Lake near the town of Interlochen. The camp hosts more than 750 performances each year by faculty members, students, and big-name entertainers, with many of them taking place in its open-air pavilion overlooking Green Lake. For ticket information call (231) 276-6230.

way. Follow Deadman's Hill Road for 1.5 miles until it dead-ends at a pair of Department of Natural Resources pit toilets and a wood-chip path. Some 15 yards up the path is a spectacular panorama from a high point of more than 1,200 feet. You take in a 180-degree view of the Jordan River valley stretching 15 miles to rugged hills that fill the horizon. During October the view from this spot is priceless, as the entire valley with the river winding through it is on fire with autumn reds and oranges.

Deadman's Hill earned its name from the logging era at the turn of the century. The steep hills made the Jordan River valley a treacherous place to log, and numerous accidents occurred. But people grieved the most in 1910 when "Big Sam" Graczyk, twenty-one years old and soon to be married, was killed while driving a team of horses and a big wheel of logs. The name for the ridge stuck. You can admire the view and have a picnic while sitting on the edge, and the more adventurous can hike the Jordan River Pathway, which begins at this point. Part of the trail is a 3-mile loop down to the river and back, or it can be turned into an 18-mile overnight walk to a hike-in campground for backpackers.

Where there is a boardwalk or similar planking along a trail, there is usually a swamp, marsh, or bog surrounding it. At the **Grass River Natural Area**, there are an awful lot of boardwalks. Some trails are nothing but boardwalks, because a good slice of this 1,037-acre Antrim County park is sedge meadow, marsh, and cedar swamp.

Grass River itself is only 2.5 miles long and just chest deep. It's a crystal clear waterway that connects Lake Bellaire to Clam Lake as part of Antrim County's "Chain of Lakes." But the extensive floating sedge mats and other wetlands that surround the river are so intriguing that they prompted a fund-raising effort to buy the land and dedicate it as a natural area in 1976.

They've been building boardwalks ever since. Along with an interpretive center, which features several rooms of displays and a small bookstore, Grass River has a 5-mile trail system that is marked with interpretive posts and winds through a variety of habitats.

The Woodland/Wildfire Trail is the longest at 2.2 miles; the quarter-mile Tamarack Trail is designed to be handicapped-accessible. But to many the Sedge Meadow Trail is the most enjoyable. It's one long boardwalk—almost every step of it is on wood—that passes through a variety of wetlands where plants have been identified and numbered posts corresponded with information in a trail guide. Eventually the trail emerges at the edge of Grass Lake where observation platforms and towers have been built on the boardwalk along with a series of benches.

From US 131 in Mancelona head west on M 88 toward Bellaire and within 2 miles continue on Alden Highway (County Road 618). The entrance road to Grass River Natural Area (231–533–8576) is off CR 618 before you reach Alden. The trails are open from dawn to dusk. The interpretive center is open daily from 10:00 A.M. to 4:00 P.M. June through August.

Charlevoix County

South of Charlevoix off US 31 is yet another state park along Lake Michigan. *Fisherman's Island State Park* possesses many of the same features as the other parks: 3 miles of sandy shoreline, excellent swimming areas, scenic views of the Great Lake. But Fisherman's Island also has a couple of unique features. Not nearly as popular or crowded as some other locales, the park offers fifteen rustic campsites right on Lake Michigan. Each one is tucked away in the trees with a table and a spot to pitch a tent only a few feet from the lapping waters of the lake. These are some of the most beautiful campsites in the Lower Peninsula, and naturally they are the first to be chosen in the campground. Be prepared to camp at an inland site the first night and then claim a lakeside one first thing the next morning.

The other noted feature of the state park is the Petoskey stones. The state stone is actually petrified coral, a leftover fragment of the many coral reefs that existed in the warm-water seas from Charlevoix to Alpena some 300 million years ago. Today the stones are collected by rock hounds, and many of them end up polished and used in jewelry, paperweights, and other decorative items. Dry stones are silvery with no apparent markings to the untrained eye, but when the rocks are wet, it's easy to see the ringlike pattern that covers them. Rock hounds searching for the stones are usually seen closely inspecting the waterline or washing off handfuls of rocks in the lake.

The 2.5-mile park road begins at the ranger station and ends at the sandy beaches of the state park but along the way passes an extended rocky shoreline. Many gem enthusiasts say this is one of the best places in northern Michigan to find *Petoskey stones.* Stop at the ranger station for a park map and information on the famous stones. There is a vehicle fee to enter Fisherman's Island State Park (231–547–6641) and an additional charge to camp overnight.

The Great Lakes, which have blessed Michigan with miles of magnificent shoreline, also have given it many islands that have become unique destinations for visitors. The most popular is Mackinac Island, a non-motorized resort (no cars or buses) that tourists flock to each summer, taking ferries out of Mackinaw City on the Lower Peninsula or St. Ignace across the Mackinac Bridge on the Upper Peninsula. There are also many islands without the crowds, commercialization, and fudge shops of Mackinac that make for an interesting side trip. One of the largest is *Beaver Island*, reached by a ferry from Charlevoix.

Known as "Emerald Isle" for its strong Irish heritage, Beaver Island lies 32 miles northwest of Charlevoix and is fifty-five square miles of forests, inland lakes, and farms. Its recorded history dates to 1832, when Bishop Frederic Baraga, the "Snowshoe Priest," brought Christianity to a small Indian settlement here. The island's most bizarre period began in 1847 after James Jesse Strang arrived. Strang and his band of Mormon followers had just broken away from the leadership of Brigham Young and established St. James, the island's only village. Eventually Strang would crown himself "King of Beaver Island" and rule the island and its religious sect with an iron hand before being shot in 1856 by a disgruntled subject. Irish immigrants followed in the 1870s to fish the waters of northern Lake Michigan, and today many of the 350 people who live year-round in or near St. James have roots back in Ireland.

Beaver Island has an assortment of lodge and hotel accommodations and restaurants for overnight visitors, but on Saturdays in July and August, it also makes an ideal day trip. You can depart from Charlevoix at 8:00 A.M. on the ferry and reach the island by 10:30 A.M. for a seven-hour visit before catching the last ferry back to the mainland at 5:45 P.M. In St. James there are several museums, including the *Old Mormon Print Shop*, which was built by King Strang in 1850, and the *Marine and Harbor Museum*, a 1906 net shed dedicated to the time when the area bustled with fishermen.

The museums are open from June through August 11:00 A.M. to 5:00 P.M. Monday through Saturday and noon to 3:00 P.M. Sunday. There is a small admission charge.

Another interesting attraction in St. James is the *Toy Museum and Store* (231–448–2480). Once known as "the last nickel toy store in the U.S.," the Toy Museum is still affordable to anybody on a weekly allowance: Chinese fans three for a dollar, a disappearing dagger for 75 cents, and green army men at a nickel apiece. Suspended from the high-peaked ceiling is the "museum," an interesting collection of antique toys that range from foot-pedal Roadsters and "rocket cars" from the 1930s to clay marbles and dolls that precede the 1900s.

You can also rent a mountain bike or a jeep and tour the island, which has more than 100 miles of roads, most of them dirt and gravel. On a pleasant summer day, this is a most-delightful adventure and a great way to see the old farmhouses, inland lakes, remote shoreline, and lighthouse located outside St. James. Pack a picnic lunch and plan on driving three to four hours to circle Beaver Island.

The Beaver Island Boat Co. (888–446–4095) operates the ferry and charges $31 for a round-trip adult ticket. You can rent a vehicle for $55 a day from Gordon's Auto Clinic (231–448–2438) or a mountain bike from Lakesports Rentals (231–448–2166). For a complete list of island businesses, lodging, and sites, contact the Beaver Island Chamber of Commerce, P.O. Box 5, Beaver Island, St. James 49781, (231) 448–2505 or check out the Web site www.beaverisland.net.

A number of writers have ties to Northwest Michigan but none as famous as Ernest Hemingway, who spent the summers of his youth at his family's cottage on Walloon Lake. Hemingway buffs often tour the area to see artifacts and places that made their way into his writing. Most begin in Petoskey's Little Traverse Historical Museum (see Emmet County) and then head down US 141 past Walloon Lake. Some go to **Hemingway Point** on the south shore of Lake Charlevoix, to which the

The Escape from Rush-Hour Madness

*R*umbling along in his Suburban on Beaver Island, Keith Pintler slowed down when he approached East Side Drive, glanced up the dirt road for oncoming traffic, and then resumed his 30-mile-an-hour speed.

"I don't know why I bother to look," said the president of the Beaver Island Chamber of Commerce. *"In nine years of living here, I've never seen anybody come that way. Never, ever."*

Peaceful, tranquil, traffic-less Beaver Island, the true escape from the rush-hour madness of mainland Michigan.

If you've ever visited this 37,385-acre island in the summer and liked the

slow pace of life, you'll be enchanted with it in the fall. After Labor Day most of the 3,000 people who maintain summer cottages on the island are gone. So are their cars. So are the majority of the 30,000 visitors who step ashore at St. James annually.

What you'll find on the island in September and October are 488 year-round residents, stunning fall colors, and more than 50 miles of beaches where the only footprints in the sand are yours.

Sure, most of the shops and a few of the restaurants will be closed, but what price tranquillity?

young author once fled (it was owned by his uncle) when being pursued by a game warden.

Of course, almost all eventually stop at the **Horton Bay General Store**, located across the lake on Boyne City Road. Built in 1876 with a high false front, the store's most prominent feature is its large front porch with benches and stairs at either end. Hemingway idled away some youthful summers on that porch and fished nearby Horton Creek for rainbow and brook trout. He also celebrated his first marriage in Horton

An Anniversary on Avalanche Peak

*F*or a quick getaway to celebrate our anniversary, my wife and I spent a weekend near Boyne City, and on Saturday were blessed with one of those priceless Michigan autumn days. Set against a deep blue sky, the fall colors were more vivid than ever, and on such a clear, crisp afternoon, there is only one thing to do: "Overlooks," I announced.

We stopped at the Boyne City Brewing Company and picked up some sandwiches and a couple of bottles of its Lake Trout Stout. From there we drove to Avalanche Peak, a city park at the end of Lake Street, threw the lunch in a daypack and began hiking toward the base of this towering hill.

I don't think there's ever been an avalanche in Boyne City, but the hill is incredibly steep—so steep that in the 1950s, it was a downhill ski area with rope tows and even a chairlift. We had only reached the steps for the climb up when my wife said, "Okay, I'm tired, let's eat lunch."

"Um, honey, we have to climb to the top."

"Why?"

I turned to her and said what I'd been

waiting to say to somebody my entire life: "Because it's there." After a long pause, I added, "Besides, the view is nicer from the top."

Some 200 steps up I heard a familiar voice from behind say, "That view better be good." Another 100 steps and I had to retreat and use a chocolate chip cookie to coax her off a bench. At 400 steps I was sure that on the fifteenth anniversary of my marriage, I was headed for a divorce.

Finally, after 473 steps, we arrived at the top, where the city has thoughtfully built an observation deck with several benches. There isn't a better view below the Mackinac Bridge than what greets you from the top of Avalanche Peak. At your feet is Boyne City, while stretching out to the west is Lake Charlevoix dotted with sailboats.

We plopped down on a grassy knoll behind the observation deck and for more than an hour enjoyed our lunch while soaking in that view. Finally I said, in a romantic sort of way, "Think we should come back here for our twenty-fifth anniversary?"

"Only if they put back that chairlift."

You gotta love her.

Bay's Congregational Church, and eventually the general store, appeared in the opening of his short story "Up in Michigan." The Horton Bay General Store has had a string of owners, but remarkably little has changed about its appearance. It is still the classic general store; only the bright red benches outside receive a new coat of paint every now and then.

You enter through a flimsy screen door with a bell above it, and inside you find the worn wooden floors and shelves stacked with canned goods and other merchandise. There is an old wooden tub filled with ice and cold drinks, a small freezer that holds four or five flavors of ice cream, and the lunch counter where the morning coffee drinkers gather. Then as your eyes wander toward the ceiling, you realize this is more a preserved shrine to Hemingway than a store for the local residents. On one wall hang guns, old traps, mounted deer heads, and a panel of photographs of the author during his days in Northwest Michigan. Horton Bay General Store is open from 8:00 A.M. to 9:00 P.M. Monday through Saturday and until 5:00 P.M. on Sunday.

From Horton Bay you can continue around Lake Charlevoix in a scenic drive that will take you past Young State Park, through the historic downtown area of Boyne City, and near Hemingway Point, where Ferry Road abruptly ends at the South Arm of the lake. If you want to continue, you have to take passage on the *Ironton Ferry*, one of Michigan's most delightful boat rides even though it's only five minutes long.

Ferry service on the South Arm dates back to 1876, when the first barge was pulled back and forth by horses. It was apparently a money-maker right from the start, as the 1884 rates are still listed on the side of the ferry office. The present ferry was installed in 1926 and is guided by cables 35 feet down on the lake bottom, making it, say officials, one of two cabled-operated automobile ferries in the country.

That's only one of the Ironton Ferry's many little oddities, the reason it was once featured in "Ripley's Believe It or Not." Consider its size (so small it holds only four cars), the length of its trip (a mere 575 feet of water), and the fact that it doesn't have a rudder. Perhaps most unusual is that the Ironton Ferry doesn't make regularly scheduled crossings. It's operated on demand because the South Arm is so narrow that passengers can be seen waiting on the other side.

The ferry operates from mid-April to Thanksgiving Eve 6:30 A.M. to 10:30 P.M. daily. A trip across is $1.50 per vehicle or 50 cents for walkers.

On the shores where Hemingway's family had their cottage are a number

Passenger Pigeons

At one time Michigan was a favorite nesting ground for the passenger pigeon. Vast quantities of beech-nuts attracted them, and each spring immense flocks arrived, literally darkening the skies for hours at a time as they flew over.

At Crooked Lake in Emmet County, a nesting in 1878 covered ninety square miles, drawing the attention of thousands of hunters who quickly converged on the area. Millions of birds were killed, packed in barrels, and shipped to Petoskey. Such wanton slaughter led to the extinction of the passenger pigeon by 1914.

of historic buildings, including the Walloon Lake Inn. The century-old inn has a number of rooms upstairs, a fine lakeside restaurant downstairs, where you can arrive by car or boat, and, during the winter, the ***Fonds du Cuisine Cooking School.*** For four days small groups of students spend their mornings in the restaurant's kitchen working with chef David Beier and their afternoons in the dining room eating lunch. From Tuesday through Friday they are up to their elbows in sauces and batters at a school where textbooks are replaced by mixing bowls and wire whisks.

Classes are held between the countertop and the range, as the students receive their own ducks to truss and rainbow trout to fillet. Class ends with the midday meal, a lavish affair that may last two hours and usually involves a little wine tasting and comparing of each other's creations. Walloon Lake Inn (231–535–2999), in the heart of Walloon Lake Village, is 8 miles south of Petoskey and is reached from US 31 by heading west a quarter of a mile on M 75. The school is offered a dozen times from September through mid-March and costs $450 per person, including four nights of lodging, breakfast, and daily luncheon.

Emmet County

Housed in Petoskey's Chicago and West Michigan railroad depot, which was built in 1892, the ***Little Traverse Historical Museum*** is the first logical stop on any Hemingway tour. The display case is small but contains photographs, other memorabilia, and some rare first-edition books that Hemingway autographed for his friend Edwin Pailthrorp, whom he visited in Petoskey in 1947. There is also a display case devoted to another famous writer, Bruce Catton, who was born in the Emmet County town and grew up in nearby Benzonia. Later Catton would pen *A Stillness at Appomattox,* for which he won a Pulitzer Prize in 1953. The original manuscript of that book and other personal artifacts are in the museum.

The museum (231–347–2620) is on Dock Street on Petoskey's picturesque

Little Traverse Historical Museum

waterfront and is open May through October from 10:00 A.M. until 4:00 P.M. Monday through Saturday. There is a small admission fee.

From the well-developed resort town of Harbor Springs, M 119 heads north and hugs the coastline for 31 miles until it ends at Cross Village. The drive is often cited as a scenic one, but not for the views of Lake Michigan you might expect when tracing it on a map. This is the "*Tunnel of Trees*" Shore Drive, a narrow road that climbs, drops, and curves its way through the thick forests along the rugged coast. At times the branches from trees at each side of the road merge overhead to form a complete tunnel, shading travelers even when the sun is beaming down at midday. You finally emerge from the thick forest at Cross Village, a small hamlet and home of *Legs Inn*.

The inn is the creation of one man, Stanley Smolak, a Polish immigrant who fell in love with this part of Michigan and moved here from Chicago in 1921. Smolak quickly made friends with the local Ottawa Indians, who inducted him into their tribe as "Chief White Cloud." Then in 1930, with a Polish past, a love for northern Michigan, and his new Indian heritage, Smolak began building the inn. He combined the driftwood and stones he found along the shoreline to construct an unusual building on a bluff overlooking Lake Michigan. From the outside the architecture of the Legs Inn is bizarre at best, but the interior is even more fascinating, for Smolak loved to carve the driftwood. He would take a piece, see something in it, and then whittle away. The inn has several rooms, all filled with Smolak's driftwood sculpture.

Naturally, the menu reflects Smolak's homeland and includes entrees of pirogi, gotabki, and bigos, a hearty Polish stew. The restaurant even serves a beer imported from Poland. The Legs Inn (231–526–2281) is located in the heart of Cross Village (you'll know it when you see it) and is open May through October from 11:00 A.M. until 10:00 P.M. and even later on Friday and Saturday. Dinner entrees on the menu range from $9.00 to $15.00.

Cheboygan County

The residents are certainly friendly in Cheboygan. Arrive in this Lake Huron town of 5,100 from June to September, and the first place people want you to go is the jail. Stay as long as you like, they say. Plan to spend a few minutes in each cell, because that's where you'll find the pride and heritage that is Cheboygan—in the *Cheboygan County Historical Museum* located in the old county jail. At this museum you not only get to view the history of the area in an interesting series of displays and exhibits, you also have the opportunity to wander through a nineteenth-century jail. It's debatable which is more fascinating.

Built in 1890, the facility served as the area jail until 1970, when the county board of commissioners gave the building to the historical society. You enter the attached brick home where the county sheriff and his family lived, and the first room you walk into is a huge kitchen, where his wife cooked not only for him and his family but for all the prisoners as well. From the home you pass through a metal door, entering the jail. Little has changed about the facility except that the historical society has filled each cell with a display, ranging from the town's first hardware stores to its maritime history to an exhibit on logging. Call it "history behind bars."

The museum is at Huron and Court Streets. From US 23 within town, head south on M 27 and then west on Court Street for 3 blocks. The jail is open from June through Labor Day 1:00 to 3:00 P.M. Monday through Friday.

Another intriguing historical spot in Cheboygan County is just a few miles north on US 23. *Historical Mill Creek* was opened in 1984 after the site was "rediscovered" in 1972 by a local archaeologist. It dates to the 1780s, when a Scottish trader named Robert Campbell obtained a 640-acre tract of land around the only stream in the area with enough power to operate a mill, making the creek one of the oldest industrial centers in the Midwest. There was a great demand for lumber at the time, since the British were moving their military post from Fort Michilimackinac at the tip of the Lower Peninsula to Mackinac Island. The island's high limestone bluffs made it easier to defend against the Americans, who were thought to be on their way.

Visitors enter the area through an orientation center that houses a museum and a small auditorium, where a slide show on the mill's history is presented. From the center, trails lead through the 625-acre park to exhibits that include a working reconstructed mill as well as other buildings, nature trails, and scenic overlooks where the straits and Mackinac Island can be viewed through telescopes. The park is reached from I–75 by taking exit 338 and heading south on US 23 for 4 miles. Mill Creek (231–436–7301) is open from mid-May to mid-October from 10:00 A.M. to 4:00 P.M. daily with extended hours from 9:00 A.M. to 6:00 P.M. from mid-June through August. Admission is $5.00 per adult or $14.00 per family.

Otsego County

The eastern elk, once a common sight to Indians in the Lower Peninsula, disappeared from Michigan around 1877. After several unsuccessful attempts to reintroduce the animal in the early 1900s, seven Rocky Mountain elk were released in Cheboygan County in 1918, and today biologists believe Michigan's herd of 1,400 elk descended from those animals. The herd ranges over 600 square miles in Cheybogan, Montmorency, Otsego, and Presque Isle Counties, but its heaviest concentration is in the wilderness areas of the **Pigeon River Country State Forest.**

The 95,000-acre state forest features rustic campgrounds, miles of hiking trails, and fishing opportunities, but come fall most visitors have their hearts set on seeing the elk. As big as the adults are (ranging from 700 to 900 pounds), they're tough to spot during the summer, for they

Strange As It Sounds

You can only drive north on I–75 so many times before the billboard about a "man-eating clam" entices you off the highway at exit 326 and into the parking lot of Sea Shell City.

Inside this huge gift shop, between the rows of rubber tomahawks and other tacky souvenirs for tourists, is a 505-pound Giant Clam (Tridacna gigas) from the Philippines. This is reputed to be the largest mollusk in the world and "has the capacity to snuff out a man's life with one sharp snap of its shells." Reality is that the clam is a vegetarian that feasts on algae.

break up into small groups or are solitary and lie low in the thick forest. But in September the bulls begin the "bugling season," when they move into open areas and form harems of fifteen to twenty cows by calling out to them with.a high-pitched whistlelike sound. Watchers will see from thirty to a hundred elk gathered in an open field and then hear the most amazing sound—the huge bull making his high-pitched mating call.

To witness one of Michigan's great wildlife scenes, head to the Pigeon River forestry field office, 13 miles east of Vanderbilt, just off Sturgeon River Road. The office is open from 8:00 A.M. to 4:30 P.M. Monday through Friday, and workers can provide maps and suggest open areas to view the elk. The rule of thumb is that two weeks on either side of September 20 is the best time to catch the bugling, or rutting, season. Plan to be at an open area just before dawn or dusk, and sit quietly to await the movement of the herd. One traditional spot to see elk is off Ossmun Road near Clark Bridge Road northeast of the forestry office. Here you will find a large open field, a small parking lot off the road, and a few elk viewers waiting patiently during September.

Crawford County

The best-known attraction in this county is **Hartwick Pines State Park** and its **Michigan Forest Visitor Center**, the new interpretive center dedicated to Michigan's lumber era at the turn of the century. On the outside the building, decks, and wooden walkways blend naturally into a grove of pines. Inside there are sitting areas with glass walls looking out over the ancient trees, the reason the state park was created.

The hands-on displays, dedicated to Michigan's vast forests, are excellent. There is a mounted wolf that looks so real a sign was needed saying PLEASE DON'T PET THE WOLF. Instead you touch a piece of fur and immediately a pack of wolves begins to howl all around you. The "Living Giant" is a white pine that talks to you, explaining what heartwood is or how its needles produce food. But the most captivating display is "Reading The Rings." The computerized program displays a cross section of a white pine. Touch one of its rings and the screen flashes to what happened that year, including 1994 when the tree was blown down in a windstorm and cut up for firewood.

From the interpretive center you can walk the Virgin Pines Trail which loops through a forty-nine-acre stand of 300-year-old virgin white pine. Along the way you will pass through a reconstructed loggers' camp with various lumber machines on display, including "Big Wheels" that were used to haul giant logs out of the woods.

The state park (517–348–7068) is north of Grayling and can be reached by exiting I–75 at M 93 and following the park signs. The Michigan Forest Visitor Center is open 8:00 A.M. to 7:00 P.M. daily except Monday from June through September. After Labor Day the center switches to winter hours: 9:00 A.M. to 4:00 P.M. A vehicle permit is required to enter the park.

By the time the logging of the late nineteenth century was finished, much of the state had been reduced to a stump-ridden wasteland. The Civilian Conservation Corps (CCC) replanted the forests, and its story is also told in Crawford County. The *Civilian Conservation Corps Museum* is located in North Higgins Lake State Park and is dedicated to the program created during President Franklin Roosevelt's administration to help the vast numbers of unemployed people during the Great Depression. It was signed into law as the Emergency Conservation Work Act on March 31, 1933, and by July of that year Michigan had forty-two CCC camps employing 18,400 men. In all, more than 102,000 Michigan men were enrolled in CCC work projects that involved constructing

The Holy Waters

*T*he most revered trout stream east of the Mississippi River is an 8-mile stretch of the Au Sable River east of Grayling that is known among fly fishers as the Holy Waters. It was on the banks of the Holy Waters that Trout Unlimited was founded in the 1950s.

Ironically trout are not native to the river but were introduced. The original fish of the Au Sable was grayling, the troutlike fish with the distinctively high dorsal fin. These were first classified by biologists in 1864, and within a decade, after railroads had penetrated northern Michigan, anglers from all over the country were arriving in Grayling to fish for grayling.

The fishing was so easy that anglers could often catch three or four grayling at time by tying multiple hooks to their line. Such heavy fishing pressure and the deforestation caused by the lumber industry made the Michigan grayling rare by the turn of the century and extinct by 1930.

The Battle of Sherman

The first settlement and first county seat in Wexford County was Sherman, which was settled in 1863. Several years later Cadillac was founded and immediately wanted to be the seat of government, setting off a ten-year struggle between the two logging towns that became known as "the Battle of Sherman."

In 1881 the seat was moved to Manton, but later that year Cadillac residents arrived and took the county records by force. The next year Cadillac was officially designated the county seat while Sherman eventually became a ghost town.

dams, building hiking trails, stocking lakes, and putting up fire towers. They are best known for planting trees—during the CCC era Michigan led the nation in planting 485 million trees.

The museum consists of several buildings, including an original cone barn, where workers extracted the seeds from pine cones to be planted later. There is also a replica of a CCC barracks with displays inside that examine the spartan camp life of the men and the duties they performed for $30 a month, of which $22 had to be sent home to their families.

North Higgins Lake State Park (517–821–6125) is reached from US 27 by exiting east on Military Road and from I-75 by heading west at exit 244. There is no admission fee for the CCC museum, but there is a vehicle entry fee for the rest of the park. The museum is open from 10:00 A.M. to 6:00 P.M. daily from mid-June to Labor Day.

Wexford County

Hunting and fishing have a long tradition in Michigan. How long? In 1994 the state celebrated the one hundredth year in which deer licenses had been issued. There is no better place to see the history of hunters and anglers in Michigan than at the *Carl T. Johnson Hunting and Fishing Center*, a state interpretive site in Cadillac. Located adjacent to Mitchell State Park along M 115, the center features a variety of exhibits and hands-on displays, including a marsh diorama, a wall-size aquarium stocked with native fish, and a full-size stuffed elk, a species re-introduced to the state thanks to the efforts of sportsmen's groups. Push a button and you can hear the call of the elk along with the calls of many other Michigan species in the exhibit hall. From the center a trail leads north into the Heritage Nature Study Area, which includes observation platforms and marshes where you have a reasonably good chance of spotting many of Michigan's wild species.

The Carl T. Johnson Hunting and Fishing Center (231–779–1321) is open daily except Monday from 10:00 A.M. to 6:00 P.M. from April through November and the rest of the year from 1:00 to 5:00 P.M. on

Friday and 10:00 A.M. to 5:00 P.M. on Saturday and Sunday. A state park vehicle pass is required to enter.

PLACES TO STAY IN NORTHWEST MICHIGAN

BAY VIEW
Stafford's Bay View Inn,
US 31,
(800) 258–1886

Terrace Inn,
216 Fairview,
(800) 530–9898

BEAVER ISLAND
Beaver Island Lodge,
St. James,
(231) 448–2396

Laurain Lodge,
St. James,
(231) 448–2099

BELLAIRE
Grand Victorian Bed
& Breakfast,
402 North Bridge Street,
(800) 336–3860

CHARLEVOIX
Weathervane Terrace Hotel,
111 Pine River Lane,
(800) 552–0025

Edgewater Inn,
101 Michigan Avenue,
(231) 547–6044

Belvedere Inn Bed
& Breakfast,
306 Belvedere,
(800) 280–4667

ELK RAPIDS
Elk River Inn,
116 Ames,
(231) 264–8168

White Birch Lodge,
571 Meguzee Point Road,
(231) 264–8271

ELLSWORTH
The House on the Hill
Bed & Breakfast,
9661 Lake Street,
(231) 588–6304

EMPIRE
Maple Lane Resort,
8720 Dorsey Road,
(231) 334–3413

FRANKFORT
Chimney Corners Resort,
1602 Crystal Drive,
(231) 352–7522

GAYLORD
Marsh Ridge Resort,
4815 Old US27,
(800) 743–PLAY

Days Inn,
1201 West Main Street,
(517) 732–2200

HARBOR SPRINGS
Birchwood Inn,
7077 Lakeshore Drive,
(800) 530–9955

Harborside Inn,
266 East Main Street,
(800) 526–6238

LELAND
Falling Waters Lodge,
200 West Cedar,
(888) 908–2946

Whaleback Inn,
M 22,
(800) 942–5322

MAPLE CITY
Leelanau Country Inn,
149 East Harbor Highway,
(231) 228–5060

OMENA
Omena Shores Bed
& Breakfast,
13140 Isthmus Road,
(231) 386–7313

PETOSKEY
Apple Tree Inn,
915 Spring Street,
(800) 348–2901

Comfort Inn,
1314 US 31,
(231) 347–3220

Stafford's Perry Hotel,
Bay and Lewis Streets,
(800) 456–1917

TRAVERSE CITY
Grand Traverse Resort,
100 Grand Traverse Village
Boulevard (Acme),
(800) 748–0303

Beach Haus Resort,
1489 US 31,
(231) 947–3560

Comfort Inn,
1492 US 31 North,
(231) 929–4423

Grand Beach Resort Hotel,
1683 US 31 North,
(800) 968–1992

Budgetel Inn,
2326 US 31 South,
(231) 933–4454

Park Place Hotel,
300 East State Street,
(800) 748–0133

**PLACES TO EAT IN
NORTHWEST MICHIGAN**

ALDEN
Spencer Creek Cafe
(fine dining),
5260 Helena Road,
(231) 331–4171

BEAVER ISLAND
The Old Rectory
(American),
Grant's Road,
(231) 448–2318

Dalwhinnoe Bakery (deli),
St. James,
(231) 448–2736

BEULAH
Cherry Hut (American),
US 31,
(231) 882–4431

CHARLEVOIX
The Acorn Cafe
(American),
101 Park Avenue,
(231) 547–1835

The Gray Gables Inn
(fine dining),
308 Bevedere Avenue,
(231) 547–92619

Whitney's (seafood),
305 Bridge Street,
(231) 547–0818

ELLSWORTH
Tapawingo (fine dining),
9502 Lake Street,
(231) 588–7981

Rowe Inn (fine dining),
6303 East Jordan Road,
(231) 588–7351

FRANKFORT
Chimney Corners Resort
(American),
1602 Crystal Drive,
(231) 352–7522

GAYLORD
Diana's Delights
(American),
143 West Main Street,
(517) 732–6564

Big Buck Brewery
(brewpub),
550 South Wisconsin,
(517) 732–5781

Mama Leone's (Italian),
2583 South Old US 27,
(517) 732–4431

GRAYLING
Albie's (pastries),
5604 M 72 West,
(517) 348–2240

HARBOR SPRINGS
Juilleret's (whitefish),
130 State Street,
(231) 526–2821

Selected Chambers of Commerce and Tourism Bureaus

Beaver Island Chamber of Commerce,
P.O. Box 5, Beaver Island 49782;
(231) 448–2505

Boyne Country Convention and Visitors Bureau,
401 East Mitchell Street, Petoskey 49770;
(800) 845–2828

Charlevoix Area Convention and Visitors Bureau,
408 Bridge Street, Charlevoix 49720;
(800) 367–8557

Gaylord Area Convention and Tourism Bureau,
P.O. Box 3069, Gaylord 49735;
(800) 345–8621

Mackinaw Area Tourist Bureau,
708 South Huron Avenue, Mackinaw City 49701;
(800) 666–0160

Sleeping Bear Dunes Visitors Bureau,
P.O. Box 517, Glen Arbor 49636;
(231) 334–2000

Traverse City Convention and Visitors Bureau,
101 West Grandview Parkway, Traverse City 49684;
(800) 872–8377

New York Restaurant
(American),
101 State Street,
(231) 526–1904

LAKE LEELANAU
Key to the County
(fine dining),
104 Main Street,
(231) 256–5397

LELAND
Bluebird (fish),
102 East River,
(231) 256–4030

The Cove (outdoor dining),
111 River Street,
(231) 256–9834

MISSION PENINSULA
Bowers Harbor Inn
(fine dining),
13512 Peninsula Drive,
(231) 223–4222

Old Mission Tavern
(American),
17015 Center Road,
(231) 223–7280

PETOSKEY
Jesperson's (American),
312 Howard Street,
(231) 347–3601

Bear River Brewing
Company (brewpub),
317 East Lake Street,
(231) 348–8466

City Park Grill (pasta),
432 East Lake Street,
(231) 347–0101

Roast & Toast (American),
309 Lake Street,
(231) 347–7767

Andante (fine dining),
321 Bay Street,
(231) 348–3321

TRAVERSE CITY
Poppycock's (vegetarian),
128 East Front Street,
(231) 941–7632

Blondie's (barbecue),
933 US 31 South,
(231) 943–8019

Don's Drive-In
(hamburgers),
2030 US 31 North,
(231) 938–1860

Omelette Shoppe & Bakery
(American),
1209 East Front Street,
(231) 946–0590

Mabel's (American),
US 31 North
and Eighth Street,
(231) 947–0252

Windows (French-
American),
7677 West Bay Shore Drive,
(231) 941–0100

OTHER ATTRACTIONS

Lighthouse Park,
Old Mission Peninsula

Clinch Park Zoo,
Traverse City

Benzie Area Historical
Museum, Benzonia

Empire Area Museum,
Empire

Sunset Park, Petoskey

Grand Traverse Lighthouse,
Leelanau State Park

Leelanau Historical
Museum, Leland

Gaslight Shopping District,
Petoskey

Colonial Michilimackinac,
Mackinaw City

Eastern Upper Peninsula

The "Mighty Mac" might sound like a hamburger with the works, but to most Michiganders it's the Mackinac Bridge, the only link between the Lower and Upper Peninsulas and the third-longest bridge in the country. Building a bridge was first considered in 1884, but the 5-mile span wasn't built until 1957, finally uniting a state that for its first 120 years was divided by a stretch of water known as the Straits of Mackinac.

Most travelers view the **Mackinac Bridge** as a very scenic drive. A trip across the Mighty Mac is a 360-degree panorama of shorelines, Great Lakes, and islands scattered everywhere, while below, the straits bustle with ferries, freighters, and fishing boats. The bridge is also the link between two worlds. Unlike industrialized southern Michigan, the Upper Peninsula's economy was based on lumbering and mining. After the majestic white pines were cut and the mines closed, this section of Michigan fell upon hard times, which in some ways continue today. Residents of the north, however, are quick to point out that the first permanent settlement in the state was not Detroit but Sault Ste. Marie and that their endurance proves their long history is not about to end anytime soon. Survival is a way of life in the U.P.

What travelers will quickly discover upon crossing the bridge is a place of remote beauty and unique character, where interstate highways are almost nonexistent, and motel chains and fast-food restaurants are few and far between. Almost every road in the U.P. is "off the beaten path," offering natural beauty, family-run inns and cafes, and outdoor opportunities that will satisfy any lover of pristine forests, lakes, and streams.

Mackinac County

The view from Mighty Mac is excellent, but the best view of the bridge itself is from the north shore at *Father Marquette National Memorial*, just outside St. Ignace. Father Marquette, a newly ordained Jesuit priest from France, paddled his way through the Great Lakes and founded Sault Ste. Marie in 1668, founded St. Ignace three years later, and

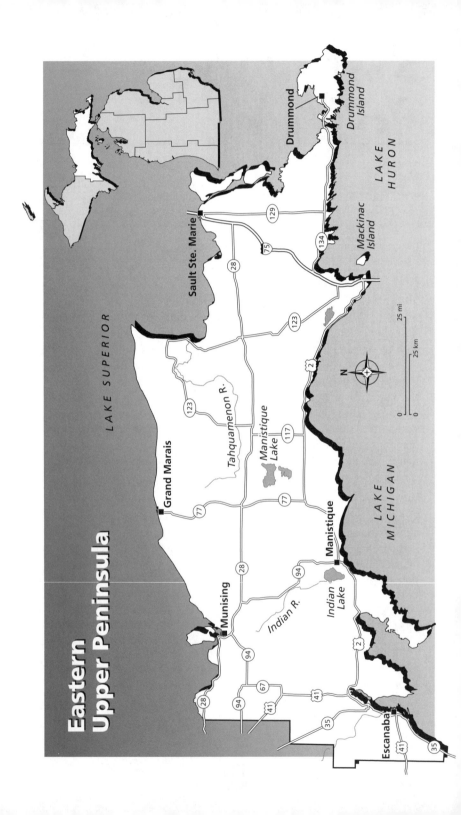

AUTHOR'S TOP TEN PICKS

Pictured Rock Boat Cruises,
Munising; (906) 387–2379

Fayette State Park,
Garden; (906) 644–2603

Fort Mackinac,
Mackinac Island;
(906) 847–3328

Great Lakes Shipwreck Museum,
Paradise; (906) 635–1742

Seney National Wildlife Refuge,
Germfask; (906) 586–9851

Kitch-Iti-Kipi,
Manistique; (906) 341–2355

Tahquamenon Falls,
Paradise; (906) 492–3415

Soo Locks Park;
Sault Ste. Marie;
(906) 632–3311

Father Marquette National Memorial,
St. Ignace; (906) 643–8620

Peninsula Point Lighthouse,
Stonington; (906) 474–6442

then joined Louis Jolliet on a 3,000-mile paddle discovering the Mississippi River. He did this—along with converting thousands of Indians to Christianity—in only nine years, dying on the banks of Lake Michigan in 1675.

To celebrate the tricentennial of Marquette's discovery of the Mississippi, a presidential committee chose St. Ignace as the site of a permanent memorial. Also on the grounds is a museum (open 8:00 A.M. to 8:00 P.M. daily June 1 through Labor Day) that includes displays on Marquette and the Indian tribes he encountered, an auditorium with a sixteen-minute film on the life of the priest, and, perhaps most intriguing, a replica of the explorer's Mississippi journal in both the original French and an English translation. Here you can flip through the pages and read segments of this man's incredible odyssey. Outside the museum is an overlook with a public telescope that gives you a sweeping view of the Mackinac Bridge. There are posted exits to the park from both I–75 and US 2.

A portion of US 2 west of St. Ignace is gradually becoming a row of motels, convenience stores, and cafes—one business little different from the next—but one notable establishment is worth a stop. Some 8 miles west of town is **Lehto's Pasties**, the first of many pasties shops you are bound to see in the U.P. The Cornish pasty, an Upper Peninsula specialty, looks like a king-size apple turnover crust, but it is filled with meat, potatoes, onion, and a little rutabaga for flavor. Pasties were supper for the miners, who could take them down the shafts and at mealtime heat them on their shovels with the candles on their helmets. Although many believe they originated in the U.P. copper mines in the mid-1800s, they actually date back much earlier, to mining days in Cornwall, England.

The lunch counter run by John and Katherine Lehto doesn't look like much, but they have been making pasties since 1947, when John arrived at St. Ignace to take a job on the Straits of Mackinac ferry and his wife opened up the "pasty drive-in." Business was so good that John quit his state job three years later and built the small eatery. Nothing has changed since then—certainly not their pasties, which are hard to

Labor Day Bridge Walk

Labor Day is the only time of the year that people are allowed to walk across the Mackinac Bridge. More than 70,000 people trek across the 5-mile-long bridge that day, including the governor of Michigan and, in 1992, President George Bush. Walkers begin on the north side of the bridge and jump on free shuttle buses to return to their cars afterward.

beat anywhere in the north. Pasties to go are $3.75 each, and it's an extra dollar if you want to occupy one of the eight seats at the lunch counter. Lehto's Pasties is open May through November from 8:30 A.M. until 6:00 P.M., or whenever John and Katherine run out of pasties.

Scenic shoreline drives abound in Michigan, but it's hard to argue when someone says the most-spectacular of all is the stretch of US 2 from St. Ignace to the hamlet of Naubinway. The views of Lake Michigan, beaches, dunes, and offshore island are rarely interrupted along this 42-mile segment. One of the places to spot for a panoramic view on this drive is *Cut River Gorge Roadside Park* on US 2, 26 miles west of St. Ignace.

Actually there are three parks on both sides of this stunning gorge that are connected by the impressive Cut River Bridge, a steel arch cantilever structure that was built in 1948 and stands 147 feet above the river. You can walk across the bridge for an impressive view of Lake Michigan or follow one of three foot trails that wind down to the Cut River and then out to a beautiful beach on the Great Lake. By combining the two trails with a walk across the bridge itself, you'll enjoy an interesting loop of between 1 and 1.3 miles.

Sometimes in our rush to see one place, we overlook another. Such is often the case of a place like St. Ignace. This historical town, the second-oldest settlement in Michigan, has a scenic harbor and a main street full of shops and restaurants. Only who takes the time to look around when we're all racing through to catch the next boat to Mackinac Island?

Slow down. St. Ignace is an intriguing city, and you don't have to go any farther than *Marquette Mission Park and Huron Boardwalk* to discover why. The boardwalk winds 2 miles from near the historical park, and together they take you back more than 300 years into the life of this town.

Marquette Mission Park features Father Marquette's grave and several outdoor exhibits that retrace the significance of this little plot of land. From the park you then cross the street to Huron Boardwalk, which winds south along the St. Ignace waterfront. The boardwalk features its own series of historical displays, which cover everything from "Nineteenth-Century St. Ignace" to the "Legacy of White Pine" in text and photos. Between the displays are benches, each with a million-dollar view of Mackinac Island, the ferries making high-speed runs to the resort island and the rest of the bustling waterfront. To reach Marquette Mission Park and Huron Boardwalk from I–75 on the north side of the Mackinac Bridge, take exit 344A and follow Business Loop I–75 to State Street, which parallels the boardwalk.

There are numerous forts to visit in Michigan, but without a doubt the most famous and probably the most beloved is **Fort Mackinac** on Mackinac Island. Built and first occupied by the British in 1779, the fort is part of Mackinac Island State Park and is the scene of cannon firings and other living-history demonstrations throughout the summer. The Officer's Stone Quarters, constructed of limestone in 1781, is the oldest building in Michigan. The scene of the white stockade looming above the island's downtown area is probably one of the most photographed in the state.

The fort is open daily 9:00 A.M. to 6:00 P.M. from mid-June through August and 10:00 A.M. to 4:00 P.M. from mid-May and after Labor Day through mid-October. Admission is $6.75 per adult, $4.00 per child, or $20.00 per family but includes six other interesting museums in the downtown area of Mackinac Island including Mission Church, the oldest church in Michigan; Indian Dormitory, with displays and craft demonstrations on Native American cooking and weaving; and Beaumont Memorial.

Mackinac Island State Park actually covers 1,800 acres, or 83 percent of the island, and offers much more than just cannon demonstrations twice a day. There are 140 miles of roads and trails, open to use by hikers, cyclists, and equestrians but not cars, which are not allowed on the island. The roads and trails loop through a surprisingly rugged and wooded terrain, past some of the most interesting natural formations in Michigan, including **Arch Rock**, the almost-perfect 50-foot-wide limestone arch. The vast majority of visitors reach these attractions on a bicycle, which can either be brought to the island on the ferry or rented in the downtown area.

For more information on Mackinac Island State Park, call (906) 847–3328, beginning in mid-May. For information on the three ferry companies that provide transportation to the island, call Arnold Transit

TOP ANNUAL EVENTS

Straits Area Antique Auto Show,
St. Ignace, June;
(800) 338–6660

Lilac Festival,
Mackinac Island, June;
(800) 4–LILACS

International Bridge Walk,
Sault Ste. Marie, June;
(800) 647–2858

Les Cheneaux Antique Wooden Boat Show,
Hessel, August;
(888) 364–4726

Upper Peninsula State Fair,
Escanaba, August;
(800) 437–7496

Labor Day Bridge Walk,
St. Ignace, September;
(800) 338–6660

A Battle Without a Shot

Mackinac Island was the site of one of the most celebrated moments in Michigan's history. After Americans took over Fort Mackinac diplomatically, the British recaptured it during the War of 1812 by secretly landing in the middle of the night and dragging a cannon up a bluff overlooking the fort. When the American garrison woke up the next morning and saw what was aimed at them, they gave up without firing a single shot.

(906–847–3351), Shepler's Mackinac Island Ferry (231–436–5023), or Star Line (906–643–7635).

A much less traveled but equally scenic route is east of the Mackinac Bridge on M 134. The road follows the U.P. shoreline along northern Lake Huron, passing the intriguing Les Cheneaux Islands and ending at De Tour, the departure point for remote Drummond Island, a haven of fishing resorts. The best stretch is the 24 miles from Cedarville in Mackinac County to De Tour in Chippewa County. This segment is one continuous view of the lake, the islands, and long stretches of sand where there are more than a dozen turnoffs and roadside parks, allowing everybody an uncrowded beach for a lazy afternoon in the sun.

Chippewa County

Sault Ste. Marie is synonymous with the Soo Locks, the world's largest and busiest locking system, the crucial link for freighters passing between Lake Superior and Lake Huron. The city of 15,000 is Michigan's oldest and has been an important center since the French Canadian voyagers in the 1700s portaged their long canoes and bales of furs around St. Mary's Rapids.

Most of this colorful history of shipping can be appreciated by walking along Water Street, beginning at its east end, where the **SS Valley Camp** is docked next to the Chamber of Commerce Information Center. The 550-foot freighter was once owned and used by the Republic Steel Corporation and frequently passed through the locks. Today it has been turned into one of the largest Great Lakes marine museums and is listed as a National Historic Site. From the pilothouse and the 1,800-horsepower steam engine to the captain's quarters and the galley, visitors are free to roam the ship for a close-up look at life aboard an ore carrier, where a crew of almost thirty worked, slept, and ate. Down below, in its massive cargo holds, are models and displays of Great Lakes vessels, aquariums of the freshwater fish that abound nearby, and a room devoted to wreckage of the

Fun Facts

The only Michigan highway not used by cars or trucks is M 185, the 8-mile black-topped road that circles Mackinac Island. Except for emergency vehicles—fire trucks and ambulances—travel on M 185 is restricted to pedestrians, bicyclists, and horses.

Edmund Fitzgerald, the ore carrier that sank in raging Lake Superior in 1975, taking its captain and crew of twenty-eight with it.

The SS *Valley Camp* (906–632–3658) is open daily from 10:00 A.M. to 6:00 P.M. mid-May through June, 9:00 A.M. to 9:00 P.M. in July and August, and 10:00 A.M. to 6:00 P.M. September to October 16. There is an admission fee.

The newest stop in any tour of the city is the ***River of History Museum,*** which opened in 1993. Through the use of eight exhibit galleries and a state-of-the-art audio system, the museum takes you on an 8,000-year journey along the shores of St. Mary's River. You begin with the sounds of ice melting and the rapids roaring as a glacier carves out the river valley. You move on to the sprawling Indian camp that was once here and then see the first French explorers paddling ashore in 1662.

The River of History Museum (906–632–1999) is at 209 East Portage Avenue. It's open mid-May to mid-October from 10:00 A.M. to 5:00 P.M. Monday through Saturday and noon to 5:00 P.M. Sunday. There is an admission fee.

To reach the locks to the north, return to and follow Water Street, which in 1982 was renovated into the ***Locks Park Walkway,*** providing an excellent overview of the city's 350-year past. The walkway is marked by blue symbols of freighters, and interpretive plaques explain the history of various areas and renovated buildings. Along the way you'll pass the Baraga House, the 1864 home of Bishop Frederic Baraga, a missionary and historian known as the "Snowshoe Saint" who was the first bishop of the U.P. Nearby is the Johnston House, which was constructed in 1794 for an Irish fur trader, making it the oldest surviving home in Michigan. The walkway also passes the site of Fort Brady, built by the Americans in 1823, and the spot where in 1820 General Lewis Cass lowered and removed the last British flag to fly over U.S. soil.

Water Street ends at ***Soo Lock Park*** in the heart of downtown Sault Ste. Marie. The U.S. Army Corps of Engineers maintains the park and visitor center, and next to the locks it has built a raised viewing platform that provides an excellent view of ships being raised and lowered to the different lake levels. Your chances of seeing this take place are quite good; some 12,000 vessels pass through the locks annually. During the summer an average of 30 freighters pass through each day.

The interesting visitor center was doubled in size in 1995 and tells the history of the locks, beginning with the construction of the first American lock in 1853. Exhibits include a short video and a working model of

Feasting on Mackinac Island

*D*inner began downtown, near Huron Street, where daytime visitors, with a rubber tomahawk under one arm and a one-pound box of fudge under the other, were scurrying toward the ferries to get off this historical island before dark. We went in the other direction.

We signaled for a horse-drawn taxi and then settled back in the cushioned carriage seats as it clip-clopped its way past the Grand Hotel, up a steep hill, and finally into the island's wooded interior. Some fifteen minutes later we emerged from the trees at the impressive Stonecliffe Mansion.

Built in 1905 it was once the site of several religious and educational institutions and today houses the Woods Restaurant. The interior is a cross between a hunting lodge and a Bavarian mountain retreat with clunky wooden chairs, a huge stone fireplace, and enough stuffed animals on the walls to make any hunter feel at home.

We feasted on Mackinac whitefish baked in parchment, grilled venison chops with red current glace, and wild mushroom stew, and then enjoyed a second bottle of wine, not worrying about drinking and driving because, as our waiter pointed out, "there are no cars on the island to drive." We topped off the evening with another carriage ride back to our hotel.

And you thought the only thing to eat on Mackinac Island was fudge.

There is more to dining at this summer retreat than its legendary candy shops. Dozens of restaurants, cafes, and pubs cater to thousands of tourists each summer, satisfying even those with the most finicky taste buds. But the key to a memorable dining experience is to stick around after the last ferry has pulled out, to book a room in a hotel or a bed-and-breakfast, and then indulge in that time-honored tradition of a late and leisurely dinner, enjoyed long after the daytime crowds have vanished.

Reserve a room by first calling the Mackinac Island Chamber of Commerce at (906) 847–6418 for a list of accommodations. Then hop on the first ferry leaving the mainland and take a gastronomic romp around the island:

Horn's Gaslight Bar: *In the 1920s, Ed Horn was working for the Life Saving Service at the Round Island Lighthouse when he and his wife opened up a pool hall and snack shop on Huron Street. After Prohibition, Horn acquired one of Michigan's first liquor licenses, and his pool hall became Horn's Gaslight Bar in 1933. It still is, and the interior includes the original tin roof, historical photos on the walls, a long polished bar, and, of course, a honky-tonk piano player. Try the tequila prawns, oversized shrimp sauteed in tequila, lime, and garlic.*

Grand Hotel Main Dining Room: *Everybody knows there is a $5.00 fee during the day to stroll along the world's longest porch if you're not a guest. Few people realize you can have dinner at the hotel's main dining room without either booking a room or paying that fee. And everybody should, at least once. Dinner at the Grand Hotel is an experience, not a meal. You begin*

Feasting on Mackinac Island (cont.)

by strolling through the middle of the huge, 760-seat dining room along the carpeted runway affectionally known as "Peacock Alley." Go ahead, strut a little on the way to your table.

An army of fifty-five Jamaican waiters will tend to your needs as you indulge in such entrees as broiled whitefish and trout scaloppine, sliced veal loin with sweetbreads, or herb-roasted prime rib of beef. Afterward you can enjoy a fine cigar and a snifter of brandy on the porch.

Fort Mackinac Tea Room: There's more to this fort than just the musket and cannon demonstrations. The Tea Room Restaurant in the Officer's Stone Quarters is a string of yellow-canopy tables overlooking the island's bustling harbor, the Mackinac Bridge, the two Great Lakes that meet there, and so on.

Thus at the fort they boast that you can enjoy sandwiches, soups, and salads in the oldest building on Mackinac Island (1781) with the best view in the state.

a lock. The Soo Locks Information Center (906–632–3311) is open mid-May through mid-November 8:00 A.M. to 10:00 P.M. There is no admission fee.

You can experience the locks directly through *Soo Locks Boat Tours*. For an admission fee, people take a two-hour cruise up and down St. Mary's River, first passing through an American lock and then returning through the Canadian one. Boats depart daily from May 15 through October 15, beginning at 9:00 A.M. and ending with the last cruise at 5:30 P.M. Soo Locks Boat Tours (800–432–6301) maintains two docks, both on Portage Avenue south of the SS *Valley Camp*. Tickets are $13 for an adult.

As well known to locals as the locks is *The Antlers*, an Irish bar and restaurant on Portage Avenue. The exterior of the simple stone building that houses the seventy-five-year-old eatery is misleading. Inside, the decor is a museum of collectibles (or, some say, junk) including hundreds of mounted animals on the walls, a birch-bark canoe hanging from the ceiling, and a 15-foot boa constrictor overlooking the bar. No wall is left bare. Hockey great Gordie Howe (whose picture also adorns the walls) was a frequent patron of the restaurant, which is known for its steaks and "Paul Bunyan" hamburgers. The Antlers (906–632–3571) is open daily from 11:00 A.M. to 9:00 P.M., and dinner prices range from $6.00 to $15.00.

Fun Facts

More than eighty-two million tons of cargo pass through the Soo Locks annually, with more than half of it iron ore from mines in the Upper Peninsula and Minnesota. Coal being shipped north accounts for fifteen million tons, and Minnesota wheat being shipped east nine million tons.

Fun Facts

One of the more-interesting drives in the U.P. follows Whitefish Bay, beginning at Brimley (reached from M 28) and ending at desolate Whitefish Point. At Brimley follow Lake Shore Drive to the west as it hugs the shoreline, with frequent views of beaches and Lake Superior. In 7.5 miles, you'll come to the ***Point Iroquois Lightstation.*** The classic lighthouse was built in 1870 and operated until 1963, when sophisticated radar made it obsolete. The Coast Guard turned it over to the U.S. Forestry Service, which worked with local historical societies to open it to the public in 1984. It has since been added to the National Register of Historic Places and features a few displays and artifacts in three rooms of the lightkeeper's house. This lighthouse is mainly popular for its curved staircase of seventy steps that leads to the top of the tower and a view of the surrounding area. The panorama, needless to say, is impressive, as you can see almost the entire coastline of Whitefish Bay and miles out into Lake Superior, including any freighter that happens to be passing by. The lightstation is open Memorial Day through Labor Day 9:00 A.M. to 7:00 P.M. daily.

Lake Shore Drive, with its numerous pulloffs and scenic beaches, ends at M 123. The state road is well traveled as it first heads north along Whitefish Bay and then swings west at Paradise to head inland to Tahquamenon Falls. Though the popular falls, second in size only to Niagara Falls east of the Mississippi River, is the destination for most travelers, there is a good reason to continue heading north on Whitefish Point Road. At the very end, at the very tip of the remote peninsula that juts out into Lake Superior, is the ***Great Lakes Shipwreck Museum.*** Whitefish Point is a combination of sandy beach, small dunes, and thunderous Lake Superior waves crashing along the shoreline. It also marks the eastern end of an 80-mile stretch that sailors knew as the "Graveyard of the Great Lakes." Raging northwest storms, built up over 200 miles of open water, have caused 300 recorded shipwrecks in which 320 seamen have died along this section of shoreline.

The Great Lakes Shipwreck Historical Society, a group of divers researching the wrecks, opened the museum in 1986 in abandoned buildings of the Coast Guard station, whose light, beaming since 1849, is the oldest active one on Lake Superior. In the main museum, each display is devoted to a different shipwreck. Visitors see a drawing or photograph of the vessel and artifacts that divers have collected, and read the story of its fatal voyage. The ships range from sailing schooners of the early 1800s to the *Edmund Fitzgerald,* the latest and largest shipwreck, which continues to fascinate residents of the U.P. A darkened interior with theatrical lights, soft music, and special sound effects of sea gulls and fog horns sends tingles down the spines of most people.

Another building has been turned into a theater where underwater films of the wrecks are shown, and the lightkeeper's house has been recently restored. The museum (906–635–1742) is open from mid-May until mid-October daily from 10:00 A.M. to 6:00 P.M. Admission is $6.00 for adults.

Most of the point is a state wildlife sanctuary, renowned for the variety of birds that pass through. The Michigan Audubon Society has established the ***Whitefish Point Bird Observatory***, across from the lightstation, where a small information room tells birders the species to be watching for as they hike along the point's network of trails. The point is best known for hawks, as up 25,000 have been sighted in a season, while in April and May, as many as 7,000 loons will pass by. Other

Point Iroquois Lightstation

species seen include bald eagles, peregrine falcons, and a variety of songbirds. The observatory is open from 9:00 A.M. to 4:30 P.M. mid-April through mid-October.

Luce County

The county that lies between Chippewa and Alger is probably best known for the Two Hearted River, used by Ernest Hemingway as the setting for one of his stories. Today it remains a favorite for anglers and canoers, who enjoy the solitude of this remote wilderness river that empties into Lake Superior.

The best place to soak in this wilderness setting is Tahquamenon Falls State Park, the second-largest state park in the Upper Peninsula. Split between Luce and Chippewa Counties, the 38,496-acre park includes *Upper Tahquamenon Falls*, which spans 200 feet across the Tahquamenon River and descends 50 feet into a sea of mist and foam. You can hear the thunder of the falls the minute you step out of the car.

East of the Mississippi River, only Niagara Falls in New York and Cumberland Falls in Kentucky have longer drops than Tahquamenon.

The falls is a day-use area 21 miles from Newberry on M 123. From the parking lot, it's a quarter-mile walk to bluffs overlooking the Upper Falls. The best views, however are obtained by descending the long staircase into the gorge.

Four miles downriver is *Lower Tahquamenon Falls*. While not as impressive as the Upper Falls, this series of cascades is much more fun because it is best viewed by combining a short paddle across the river with a walk around a small island.

The adventure begins by renting a rowboat from the park concession and then shoving off into the brown waters, which are stained by tamarack trees, of the Tahquamenon River. At the island there is a large dock at which to tie up your boat while a wooden stairway leads to the start of the trail. Step-for-step this is one of the most beautiful footpaths in the state, only there are not a lot of steps. It's a loop of less than a mile that skirts the outside of the island, passing one display of tumbling water after another. Along the way parents and kids kick their shoes off, wade out onto the ledge of one of the many drops, and let the river cascade across their legs.

Lower Tahquamenon Falls (906–492–3415) is on M 123, 12 miles west of Paradise and 23 miles northeast of Newberry. A vehicle entry permit is required to enter the state park, and there is a small fee to rent the rowboats.

For travelers in Luce County who want to spend their nights in comfort at an inn or hotel, two interesting places are located on the northeast corner of Manistique Lake near the Mackinac County line. The first is the **Helmer House Inn**, reached by heading north from US 2 on County Road H 33 and then onto County Road 417. The inn was built in 1881 by a minister as a mission for early settlers; Gale Helmer turned it into a general store and resort six years later. The area thrived as a summer getaway, so the federal government set up a post office in the inn, appointed Helmer postmaster, and named the spot, for lack of a better name, Helmer.

The post office lasted only nineteen years, and eventually the building was abandoned. Rob Goldthorpe and his wife renovated the lodge and reopened it in 1982. Today the inn is a state historic site and offers five guest rooms, all furnished with antiques. The lodge is probably better known, however, for its wraparound porch that has been glassed in and turned into a delightful little restaurant. Every table has a view of the

Frozen Falls

*T*he Upper Tahquamenon Falls, a stunning sight in the summer, is equally beautiful in the winter when the Upper Peninsula's frigid tempera-tures turn the tumbling water into sculptured ice. There is no need to pack snowshoes. The falls is such a popular sight with snowmobilers that the park staff plows the parking lot and keeps the short path and stairs to the viewing decks open.

During most winters the river above the falls remains open and flows to the brink of the cascade where the water in the middle tumbles down across large ice formations. Downriver every-thing is frozen white, and along the rocky bluffs that enclose the falls are gigantic stalactites and stalagmites, some of them 10 to 15 feet long.

The walk in is short. Within a quarter-mile from the parking lot, you're standing at the first overlook, viewing the falls from a distance. The best view, however, is reached by descending the ninety-four steps into the gorge to a platform right above the cascade where you can lean against the railing for a close-up of the ice formations that grow larger with every splash of water heading downstream.

The formations are so varied and intriguing that you could study them for hours. But most winter visitors are scurrying back up the stairs after ten or fifteen minutes before their toes and fingers turn into stalagmites and stalactites, too.

rural setting outside, and the menu includes steaks, fish, and, occasionally, stuffed trout.

Overnight guests are treated to a full breakfast in the morning as well as a soft bed at night. Rooms, with shared bathrooms, range from $40 to $60 for singles or doubles. The restaurant is open 3:00 to 9:00 P.M. daily from May to mid-October and noon to 9:00 P.M. daily in July and August. For room reservations write to the Helmer House Inn at McMillan 49853, or call (906) 586–3204.

The other interesting place to stay is **Chamberlin's Ole Forest Inn** right on H 33, a mile north of the blinker light to Curtis. Built in the late 1800s, it was originally a railroad hotel near the Curtis depot. The railroad stopped service in 1909, and fifteen years later the building was moved to its present location on a high bluff overlooking Manistique Lake.

The classic nineteenth-century hotel features a wraparound veranda overlooking the lake; a sprawling lobby complete with wicker chairs, deep sofas, and a 6-foot stone fireplace; and ten rooms with a unique turn-of-the-century decor. Room rates for the Ole Forest Inn (800–292–0440) range from $65 to $75 per night and include a full breakfast in the morning.

Another pleasant spot in Luce County to spend a night is **Muskallonge Lake State Park** at the north end of County Road H 37 in the northwest corner of the county. The park is actually a strip of land between Muskallonge Lake, known for its pike, perch, and smallmouth bass fishing, and Lake Superior. You can camp on a site overlooking the small lake and then wander over to Lake Superior to enjoy its seemingly endless sandy shoreline. There is a vehicle fee to enter Muskallonge Lake State Park (906–658–3338) and an overnight fee of $14 for one of its 179 campsites.

Alger County

rand Marais, a booming lumbertown of 2,500 at the turn of the century, is a sleepy hamlet of 400 today and the gateway for the eastern half of Pictured Rocks National Lakeshore. The National Park Service maintains the **Grand Marais Ranger Station and Maritime Museum** near the harbor. It provides maps and information on the park along with a sailor's history of the area. Displays range from a breeches buoy used in this former Coast Guard station to photos of the station when it was part of the U.S. Lifesaving Service. It was from this building that a Coast Guard radioman made the last contract with the *Edmund Fitzgerald* before it sank in 1973.

To reach the museum (906–494–2669) follow M 77 through town toward Lake Superior and then turn right on County Road 702. There is no admission charge.

One spot to see within the national lakeshore is the **Grand Sable Banks and Dunes.** To reach the sandy hills, follow County Road H 58 west of town, first passing the parking lot and short side trail to Sable Falls and then the Grand Sable Visitor Center. From both places there are half-mile trails that lead to the Grand Sable Dunes. Or you can continue following the county road a mile past the visitor center. On one side of the road is the picnic area and beach of Grand Sable Lake, and on the other side is a huge dune. There are no more than 50 yards between the lake and this mountain of sand. Visitors first tackle the heart-pounding scramble up the dune, where the top offers a magnificent view of the windswept sand, Grand Sable Lake, and Lake Superior off in the distance. Then it's a mad dash down the steep bank of sand and usually right into the lake to cool off.

The dunes are a four-square-mile area of sandy hills about half as high as Sleeping Bear Dunes in the Lower Peninsula, but no less impressive. They end with the Grand Sable Banks, steep sandy bluffs some 300 feet tall that tower right above the Lake Superior shoreline. The best view is obtained by turning off H 58 onto a marked side road for the **Log Slide** located 8 miles west of Grand Marais. A short boardwalk leads to a breathtaking overlook 300 feet above Lake Superior, where Au Sable Point Lighthouse to the west is silhouetted against the water and the banks to the east curve 5 miles back toward Grand Marais. Down below is the 500-foot wooden slide that loggers used in the 1800s to send trees into Lake Superior on their way to town.

To see shipwrecks without swimming in frigid Lake Superior, continue along County Road H 58 to Hurricane River Campground. East of the campground, Lakeshore Trail becomes an old access road to **Au Sable Lightstation,** and near its trailhead is a SHIPWRECKS sign pointing down to the beach. These ruins lie in the water and are hard to spot when the lake is choppy. But walk another mile and a half up the trail, and you'll see a second shipwreck sign that directs you to three sets of ruins half-buried in the sandy beach.

The lighthouse, which was built in 1874, has been renovated by the National Park Service and makes a perfect place to lunch before heading back to the campground.

You could continue along H 58, although only about half of it is paved, and end up in Munising. The scenic town is the gateway to the Pictured

Rocks, sandstone cliffs that rise 50 to 200 feet above Lake Superior and stretch for 15 miles to the east. They are one of the top attractions in the U.P., and a **Pictured Rock Boat Cruise** is the best way to view them.

The three-hour cruises depart from Munising City Harbor, swing past Grand Island, and then skirt the most impressive stretch of Pictured Rocks. Along the way you view such noted formations as Miner's Castle, Battleship Rock, Indian Head, Rainbow Cave, and the Colors Caves, along with waterfalls that leap into Lake Superior and kayakers bobbing in and out of sea arches.

Pictured Rock Boat Cruises (906–387–2379) offers daily trips at 10:00 A.M. and 2:00 P.M. Memorial Day through June and September through mid-October, and daily trips at 9:00 A.M., 11:00 A.M., 1:00 P.M., 3:00 P.M., and 5:00 P.M. from July through August. The best trips to take are in late afternoon when the sun setting in the west makes the cliffs even more colorful. The cost is $21.00 per adult, $7.00 for children six to 12 years old.

Waterfalls abound in the Munising area, some right on the edge of town. One of them is **Munising Falls**. From H 58 head up Sand Point Road a short way to the National Park Visitor Center, where a quarter-mile path takes you into the woods and up a shaded sandstone canyon. The first viewing platform provides a fine overview of the 50-foot cascade that tumbles straight down a sandstone cliff; a nearby stairway lets you walk up to the falls for a most unusual view of the falling water.

Munising is also on the edge of another park, the Alger Underwater Preserve, a graveyard of shipwrecks that date to the 1800s and early 1900s. The preserve and especially the waters around Grand Island are a haven for scuba divers, who view the wrecks that lie 10 to 100 feet below the surface.

But nondivers can also enjoy the treasures of Lake Superior through **Grand Island Shipwreck Tours**. The company uses a 42-foot vessel with

Michigan's Smallest State Park

*T*he smallest unit of the Michigan State Park system is Wagner Falls Scenic Site. The day-use park is only twenty-two acres and consists of a small parking area along M 94, 2 miles south of Munising, and a 200-yard trail that ends at an observation deck. The park is small but beautiful as the deck overlooks Wagner Falls, a 20-foot cascade that splashes down several rock ledges.

a specially designed hull glass viewing area to let passengers see wrecks in Lake Superior. The two-hour tours depart from Munising daily during the summer and glide over three wrecks as well as sail past the historic lighthouse and the intriguing rock formations of Grand Island.

The most intriguing wreck is the *Bermuda*. The wooden schooner was loaded with 488 tons of iron ore when it left Marquette in 1870 and sank in Grand Harbor during a fierce storm. In 1884, a Canadian salvage company raised the ship, removed its cargo, and resank it in Grand Island's Murray Bay. The *Bermuda* lies only 10 feet below the surface, and in the clear, protective waters of the bay, you can glide right over it and view an entire nineteenth-century ship.

"Everything is still there," says one guide, "everything except the sails and the crew."

Grand Island Shipwreck Tours (906–387–4477) departs from the Munising Dock 1.5 miles west of downtown off M 28. Tours are offered at 10:00 A.M., 1:00 and 3:30 P.M. daily from mid-June through September, weather permitting. The cost is $18 per adult.

Schoolcraft County

B*laney Park* is the town that refuses to die. It's been foreclosed on, boarded up, even auctioned off building by building, but today the village is surging back as a quiet resort with an ideal location for touring the Upper Peninsula. No more than ninety minutes from this one-road hamlet are the U.P.'s most popular attractions: Tahquamenon Falls, Pictured Rocks, the historic town site of Fayette, and miles of Lake Michigan's sandy shoreline.

Snorkeling for Shipwrecks

C*aptain Peter Lindquist of Grand Island Charters, a diver's charter service out of Munising, will also take snorkelers, who can view a number of wrecks, including a three-masted schooner that lies off Grand Island only 10 feet below the surface. Other wrecks lie 20 to 30 feet below the surface, but in Lake Superior's crystal-clear water, even snorkelers can get a good view of them.*

The cost is $25 per person for each wreck; a two-wreck trip lasts two and a half hours. You can write to Grand Island Charters at 1204 Commercial Street, Munising 49862, or call (906) 387–4477.

Originally a logging camp, Blaney and the area around it were logged out by 1926, so its owners searched for another endeavor for the town's residents. With all the lakes and sandy beach nearby, recreation was the answer, and soon Blaney became Blaney Park. Tourists began arriving from all over the Midwest to spend their vacations on the Upper Peninsula. The resort featured a nine-hole golf course, tennis courts, riding stables, daily excursions to Lake Michigan beaches, and a lighted swimming pool for those who preferred to stay close to their cottages. A lumber baron's mansion was renamed Celibeth and was described in one brochure as "a beautiful club-type hotel." The boardinghouse where loggers had lived was turned into a twenty-one-room lodge, and in 1934 the Blaney Inn was built, a huge dining facility that featured stone fireplaces, walls paneled in knotty pine, and seating for 400.

Improved roads in the Upper Peninsula were Blaney Park's downfall. The family that owned the town tried twice to sell it, only to end up with it again when the buyers defaulted on their payments. The last tourist season was in 1972, after which many of the buildings were boarded up, and Blaney Park finally was auctioned off in 1985. Celibeth was purchased by Elisa Strom, who had once worked as a waitress there. After spending more than a year restoring the mansion, she reopened it in 1987 as a bed-and-breakfast.

The twenty-two-room *Celibeth* has nine bedrooms decorated with antiques and furnishings from the Blaney Park resort period. There is an enclosed porch that overlooks the front lawn and features a row of rocking chairs and a 1913 hand-cranked phonograph, a reading room stocked with issues of *Life* magazine from the 1950s, and a sunroom where a leisurely breakfast is served. Down the street the rest of the resort town is slowly coming alive. You can once again enjoy dinner at the Blaney Inn, browse through a woodcarving-gift shop, or stop at the old school, now a grocery whose front walls are covered with fading photographs of Blaney Park in the 1940s.

From the Mackinac Bridge follow US 2 west for 66 miles and then turn north on M 77 for a mile to reach the town. The bed-and-breakfast (906–283–3409) is open from May through October, and the rooms range from $50 to $55 per night.

The heart of Schoolcraft County, some 96,000 acres, has been preserved as the largest wildlife refuge east of the Mississippi River. The *Seney National Wildlife Refuge* was established in 1935 by the U.S. Fish and Wildlife Service to provide a habitat for wildlife, primarily waterfowl migrating to nesting grounds in Canada. The refuge surrounds the

Great Manistique Swamp, which endured rough treatment beginning in the 1870s when loggers were intent on stripping every tree from the area. Fires were then set deliberately to clear away the debris of the lumbering operation, preventing new forests from taking root. Finally a land development company came through, drained acre after acre of the swamp, and sold the land to farmers for agriculture in 1911. The farmers lasted about a year before discovering they had been swindled—the soil would grow little.

Seney was a wasteland that nobody wanted. The state ended up with it and during the Great Depression deeded it to the federal government with the recommendation that it be turned into a refuge. Civilian Conservation Corps workers came in and built dikes, dug ditches, and used other water-control devices to impound 7,000 acres of water in twenty-one major ponds, almost miraculously restoring the marsh. Seney again became a habitat for waterfowl when 332 Canada geese were released in 1936 and established its present nesting flocks. Still more geese and other species of birds depend on the area as an important rest stop on their long migration to and from nesting sites in Canada.

Other wildlife—timber wolves, deer, black bears, moose, and coyotes—live in the refuge, but the Canada goose has clearly become the symbol of Seney's return to wilderness. You will see the "honkers" the minute you drive into the parking lot of the visitor center, as a few tame ones are always around looking for a handout from soft-hearted tourists. The center overlooks one of the many ponds in the refuge, and a telescope at its large viewing window lets you search the marsh area for some of the more than 200 species of birds that can be found here. The center has displays, a children's touch table, and an auditorium that hosts nature movies and slide programs each hour. It is open from mid-May through mid-October from 9:00 A.M. until 5:00 P.M. daily.

The best way to view the wildlife is to follow the 7-mile *Marshland Wildlife Drive* in your car as it winds its way among the ponds, starting near the center and ending at M 77 just south of the refuge entrance. Pick up a free guide that points out items of interest at a number of marked stops, including an active bald eagle nest that can be seen clearly from the drive. Timing is important for spotting wildlife, and it is best to follow the drive either in early morning or at dusk when the animals are most active. Often during the peak of the tourist season, the refuge will stage guided evening tours that depart around 6:00 P.M. and last for almost two hours. Call the visitor center (906–586–9851) for information about the auto tours.

Another unique way to view more remote areas of the refuge is to paddle the handful of rivers that flow through it. **Northland Outfitters** (906–586–9801), located in nearby Germfask, offers canoe rentals for the area. It will supply canoes, paddles, life jackets, and transportation to the Manistique River, which runs through the southeast corner of Seney. The trips are self-guided, last either two or four hours, and offer the possibility of spotting beavers, deer, otters, and a variety of birds or of fishing for walleye or pike in the river.

Strange As It Sounds

Manistique boasts a bridge "below the level of the river." Built in 1919, the 300-foot-long Siphon Bridge crosses the Manistique River and is actually below the river because water is atmospherically forced under it. The bridge became famous when it was featured in the "Ripley's Believe It or Not" newspaper series. The bridge is on M 94 at the north end of the downtown area.

Next to the outfitters is **Eagle's Nest Inn**, a restaurant housed in one of the original refuge buildings constructed in the late 1930s. The inn (906–586–6444) now looks like a Cape Cod–style eatery and specializes in whitefish, perch, and trout from the Great Lakes. Hours are 8:00 A.M. until 9:00 P.M. daily except Monday from mid-April through November. Dinners range from $10 to $18.

On the opposite scale of parks is Palms Brook, a state park of only 388 acres located 12 miles northwest of Manistique on M 149. The park may be small, but it's equally intriguing because of **Kitch-Iti-Kipi**, Michigan's largest spring. The natural spring pours out more than 10,000 gallons of water per minute from fissures in the underlying limestone, and has created a crystal-clear pool 200 feet wide and 40 feet deep. Visitors board a wooden raft with observation holes in the middle and pull themselves across the spring to get a good view of the fantasy world below. Between the swirls of sand and ghostly bubbles rising up, you can view ancient trees with branches encrusted in limestone, huge brown trout slipping silently by, and colors and shapes that challenge the imagination. The spring is especially enchanting in the early morning, when a mist lies over the water and the trout rise to the surface. Palms Brook has a picnic area but no campsites, and there is a vehicle fee to enter. The raft is free.

Delta County

In the mid-1800s iron ore was shipped from the Upper Peninsula mines to foundries in the lower Great Lakes area at a tremendous cost to companies. The high price of shipping was due to the inefficient method of transportation coupled with the nearly 40 percent waste the ore contained. Fayette Brown, general manager of the Jackson Iron

Company, studied the problem and decided the solution was to build a company-owned furnace not far from the mine, where the ore could be smelted into pig iron before it was shipped to the steel-making centers. The town he planned to build at the smelter had to be a reasonable distance from the Escanaba ore docks, possess a natural harbor, and be near large amounts of limestone and hardwood forests to smelt the iron ore. In 1866 Brown chose a spot on the Garden Peninsula overlooking Big Bay de Noc, and the town of Fayette was born.

A year later work began on the furnace and charcoal kiln, and by Christmas the first iron from Fayette was cast. Quickly a town emerged. There was the superintendent's house on a bluff overlooking the harbor, a company office, nine frame dwellings for the engineers and skilled workers, and forty log cabins for the laborers. Eventually Fayette featured a machine shop, a small railroad, barns, a blacksmith shop, a hotel, and even an opera house. It was a total community that in 1884 had a population of almost 1,000 and turned out 16,875 tons of iron. Toward the

A Hemlock Cathedral

*W*hen we entered the cathedral it was quiet, a little dark, and almost spiritual. It was a place to ponder, maybe even meditate, but this was no church. It was a stand of hemlocks that somehow survived the logging era Michigan experienced at the turn of the century.

Today the Hemlock Cathedral is part of the Little Bay de Noc Recreation Area, and it's where you go to see what a 300-year-old tree looks like. Trees that old are so tall you can't see the tops of them, so big that two people can't link arms around them, so rare that all that's left are pockets scattered across a state that was once blanketed by them.

In Escanaba residents could see the giant hemlocks on the other side of Little Bay de Noc, and by the late 1800s the spot was a popular weekend retreat known as Maywood. When a small resort hotel was built there in 1904, this pocket of old growth was preserved from the loggers advancing down the Stonington Peninsula.

Today the Hemlock Cathedral in the Little Bay de Noc Recreation Area is as quiet and impressive as it was a century ago. The virgin hemlocks are seen by hiking the Maywood History Trail, an easy half-mile loop that includes almost a dozen interpretive plaques.

The recreation area also includes a sandy beach, picnic area, thirty-six rustic campsites and two other trails. The Hiawatha National Forest facility is on County Road 513, 7 miles south of US 2 on the Stonington Peninsula. There is a vehicle entry fee and a nightly fee for camping. For more information call the Rapid River Ranger Station at (906) 474–6442.

end of that decade, however, Fayette's fate was sealed. The price of pig iron fell, and newly developed coke blast furnaces produced a higher-quality iron at a much cheaper cost. In 1891 the company closed down the furnaces, and within a few years Fayette became a ghost town.

Fayette changed hands several times; at last the state of Michigan obtained the area in 1959 and turned it into *Fayette State Park*. The town booms again now as a scenic ghost town overlooking Snail Shell Harbor, with its towering white cliffs. The 365-acre park is reached from US 2 on County Road 483 and contains an interpretive museum with information, guide maps, and a scale model of Fayette during its heyday. From there you leisurely wander among twenty-two existing buildings, of which nine are open. The renovated structures, which are furnished, include the company office, the hotel, the opera house, and a home of one of the skilled employees. More will be opened up in the future.

Fayette State Park (906–644–2603) also has eighty campsites, a beach and picnic area, and boat-launching facilities. The museum is open daily mid-May to mid-October from 9:00 A.M. to 5:00 P.M. and until 9:00 P.M. in July and August. There is a vehicle fee to enter the park and a per-night fee to camp.

Another spot worth searching out on the Garden Peninsula is *Portage Bay State Campground*, which is reached from County Road 483 (before

Charcoal Kiln in Fayette State Park

the state park) by turning off on County Road 08 and carefully following the signs. Getting to the rustic campground (no electricity, pit toilets) is a bumpy 5-mile ride along dirt roads, but the camping area is worth it: You pitch your tent or park your trailer among the pine trees that border the sandy beach of the bay. You can stroll along the beach, follow the hiking trails in the area, or take a dip in the clear water of Lake Michigan.

A delightful picnic area in Delta County is **Peninsula Point Lighthouse,** the guiding light at the very tip of the Stonington Peninsula that was built in 1865. Congress authorized the funds the year before, because the wooden sailing ships hauling lumber, iron ore, and fish from Escanaba and Fayette were no match for the treacherous shoals and reefs that separated Big Bay de Noc from Little Bay de Noc. The light went out for the last time in 1936, and the house portion of the lighthouse burned to the ground in 1959. But the view from the point was so spectacular that the Forest Service made it into a public picnic area in 1937.

Climb the forty steps to the top of the square brick tower and you're greeted with a 360-degree panorama that includes the Escanaba waterfront to the west, the limestone bluffs of Fayette State Park to the east, and the length of Lake Michigan in front of you. You can either hike to it or drive in. The 1.5-mile hike is a scenic walk, while the final mile to the nineteenth-century light is a narrow, winding, and very bumpy one-lane road not recommended for vehicles more than 16 feet long or 8 feet high.

To reach the lighthouse from Rapid River, head east on US 2 to the Stonington exit. Go south 19 miles on County Road 513 to Stonington, and then take Forest Road 2204. The RV parking area and trailhead are reached before the forest road turns into a narrow, one-lane road in the final mile.

**PLACES TO STAY IN THE
EASTERN UPPER PENINSULA**

AU TRAIN
Pinewood Lodge Bed
and Breakfast,
M 28,
(906) 892–8300

BLANEY PARK
Celibeth House Bed
& Breakfast,
M 77,
(906) 283–3409

Blaney Cottages,
US 2,
(906) 283–3163

ESCANABA
Fishery Pointe
Beach Cottages,
E5041 M 35,
(906) 786–1852

Terrace Bay Resort,
US 2 and M 41,
(906) 786–7554

MACKINAC ISLAND
La Chance Cottage,
Huron Street,
(906) 847–3526

The Murray Hotel,
Main Street,
(800) 462–2546

Chippewa Hotel,
Main Street,
(800) 241–3341

Mission Point Resort,
Lakeshore Road,
(800) 833–7711

Grand Hotel,
West Bluff Road,
(906) 847–3331

MANISTIQUE
Northshore Motor Inn,
East US 2,
(906) 341–2420

Ho-Jo Inn,
726 East Lakeshore Drive,
(906) 341–6981

MUNISING
Best Western Munising,
M 28,
(906) 387–4864

Super 8 Motel,
M 28 and County Road
H 13,
(906) 387–2466

NEWBERRY
Comfort Inn,
M 123 and M 28,
(906) 293–3218

PARADISE
Birchwood Lodges,
M 123,
(906) 492–3320

ST. IGNACE
Aurora Borealis Motor Inn,
635 I–75 Business Loop,
(906) 643–7488

Days Inn,
1074 North State Street,
(800) 732–9746

SAULT STE. MARIE
Ojibway Hotel,
240 West Portage,
(800) 654–2929

Water Street Inn Bed
& Breakfast,
140 Water Street,
(906) 632–1900

Selected Chambers of Commerce and Tourism Bureaus

Delta County Tourism Bureau,
230 Ludington Street, Escanaba 49829;
(800) 437–7496

Mackinac Island Chamber of Commerce,
P.O. Box 451, Mackinac Island 49757;
(906) 847–6418

Newberry Area Tourism Association,
P.O. Box 308 Newberry 49868;
(800) 831–7292

St. Ignace Tourist Association,
560 South State Street, St. Ignace 49781;
(800) 338–6660

Sault Convention and Visitors Bureau.
2581 I–75 Business Spur, Sault Ste. Marie 49783;
(800) 647–2858

Comfort Inn,
4404 I-75 Business Loop,
(906) 635-1118

**PLACES TO EAT IN THE
EASTERN UPPER PENINSULA**

AU TRAIN
Brownstone Inn
(American),
M 28,
(906) 892-8332

BRIMLEY
Wilcox's Fish House (fish),
Lakeshore Drive,
(906) 437-5407

ESCANABA
Hereford & Hops
(brewpub),
624 Ludington Avenue,
(906) 789-1945

Delona (American),
7132 US 2,
(906) 786-6400

GERMFASK
Eagle's Nest Inn
(American),
M 77,
(906) 586-6444

GRAND MARAIS
Lake Superior Brewing
Company (brewpub),
M 77,
(906) 494-BEER

MACKINAC ISLAND
French Outpost
(outdoor dining),
Cadotte Avenue,
(906) 847-3772

The Governor's Dining
Room (fine dining),
The Island House Hotel,
(906) 847-3347

The Pilot House
Restaurant,
Lake View Hotel,
(906) 847-3384

MANISTIQUE
Sunny Shores (American),
US 2,
(906) 341-5582

MUNISING
The Navigator (American),
101 East Munising Street,
(906) 387-4423

The Camel Riders,
Star Route (Wetmore),
(906) 573-2319

NEWBERRY
Pickelman's Pantry
(American),
M 123 and M 28,
(906) 293-3777

PARADISE
Tahquamenon Falls
Brewery (brewpub),
Tahquamenon
Falls State Park,
(906) 492-3300

ST. IGNACE
Galley Restaurant
(American),
241 North State Street,
(906) 643-7960

SAULT STE. MARIE
The Antlers (American),
804 East Portage,
(906) 632-3571

Studebaker's (American),
3583 I-75 Business Spur,
(906) 632-4262

Freighters (fine dining),
Ojibway Hotel,
240 West Portage
(906) 632-4100

OTHER ATTRACTIONS

Mackinac Island Carriage
Tours, Mackinac Island

Tahquamenon Logging
Museum, Newberry

Sand Point Lighthouse,
Escanaba

Grand Island Recreation
Area, Munising

Paulson House Museum,
Au Train

Western Upper Peninsula

Michigan's most remote and rustic region is the rugged western Upper Peninsula. Two small ranges located here constitute the only true mountains in any of the Great Lakes states; between Baraga and Marquette lie the Huron Mountains, and along the Lake Superior shoreline, from west of Ontonagon to Copper Harbor, is the Copper Range. Within these rugged hills are Mount Arvon, the highest point in Michigan at 1,979 feet above sea level, and the Porcupine Mountains, between whose ridges and peaks lies the stunning Lake of the Clouds.

It was in these hills of the western U.P. that the great iron and copper mines flourished from the 1800s to the 1940s, bringing boatloads of immigrants from Norway, Finland, and Italy to work in the shafts. Today the remnants of the mining era are ghost towns, abandoned mines, and communities with strong ethnic heritage and pride.

For most Michigan residents, this region of the state is a remote, distant place; driving to Copper Harbor from Detroit is the same distance as traveling to Washington, D.C. But once it is "discovered," travelers marvel at the western U.P.'s natural wonders. More than for its mines, pasty shops, and historical museums, you come to this region of Michigan for the beauty of nature's handiwork: cascading waterfalls, panoramas of forested wilderness, a lake set in a sea of reds, yellows, and oranges painted by autumn leaves.

Marquette County

The largest county in Michigan consists of 1,873 square miles, 1,800 lakes, 73 miles of Lake Superior shoreline, and Marquette, the largest (and, some say, only) city in the Upper Peninsula. The city of 23,000 became a spot on the map with a post office in 1849, and it bloomed the following decade as the port and shipping center for the nearby iron mines and logging camps. The lumber and mining barons graced the streets of Marquette with mansions, many still standing today. From Front Street turn east onto Ridge Street and you'll head

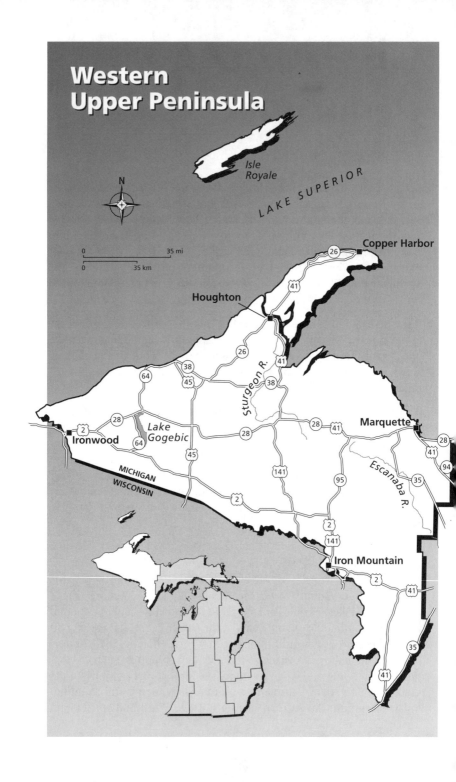

Western
Upper Peninsula

*Isle
Royale*

LAKE SUPERIOR

N

0   35 mi
0   35 km

Copper Harbor

26

41

Houghton

26

38

41

45

64

38

Sturgeon R.

28

41

Marquette

28

28

41

28

Ironwood

28

*Lake
Gogebic*

64

45

141

95

Escanaba R.

35

94

MICHIGAN

WISCONSIN

2

35

141

Iron Mountain

2

2

141

2

41

35

41

toward Lake Superior, passing one late-Victorian home after another until you end up in the parking lot of the **Marquette Maritime Museum** on the waterfront.

The museum is housed in the red sandstone Old Water Works Building and features displays on shipwrecks, antique outboard motors and boats, commercial fishermen who worked the area, and other facets of the city's maritime days, which fed many and made some (from the look of their homes) incredibly wealthy. Open from Memorial Day until mid-September, the museum can be viewed from 10:00 A.M. until 5:00 P.M. daily. A small admission fee is charged.

The largest and most interesting structures on Marquette's waterfront are the iron ore docks that load the rock into Great Lakes freighters for a journey south. The Lake Superior and Ishpeming Railroad docks are still operating today, and the best vantage point is **Presque Isle Park**. The 328-acre city park is not an island but a peninsula that juts out into Lake Superior on the north side of Marquette. A road circles the park shoreline, beginning on the south side, where you can see the ore docks and, if your timing is right, watch a freighter take on its load (one to three times a week).

The drive continues and passes the steep red cliffs of Lookout Point and then the view at Sunset Point, where residents gather to watch the end of another day. The park also has an outdoor band shell with weekly events, a small zoo, a beach and bathhouse, picnic areas, and bicycle paths. Hiking trails crisscross the forested interior of Presque Isle and become a favorite spot for Nordic skiers during the winter. The park is open daily from 7:00 A.M. until 11:00 P.M., and perhaps the best time of year to visit it is the last weekend in July during its Art-on-the-Rocks Festival, when local artists gather to display and sell their work in this picturesque setting.

In Marquette's Lower Harbor are the Old Ore Docks, no longer operating, which have been designated a state historic site. An excellent place

---

Author's Top Ten Picks

Lake of the Clouds,
Silver City; (906) 885–5275

Black River Harbor Drive,
Bessemer; (906) 667–0261

Fort Wilkins,
Copper Harbor;
(906) 289–4215

Piers Gorge,
Norway; (906) 774–2002

Canyon Falls and Gorge,
L'Anse; (906) 524–7444

Michigan Iron
Industry Museum,
Negaunee; (906) 475–7857

Hanka Homestead,
L'Anse; (906) 353–7116

Iron County Museum,
Caspian; (906) 265–2617

Quincy Mine,
Hancock; (906) 482–3101

Sand Hills
Lighthouse Inn,
Eagle River; (906) 337–1744

Fun Facts

The Superior Dome on the Northern Michigan University campus is the largest wooden dome in the world. Dedicated in 1991, it is 150 feet high and covers 272,330 square feet. It contains more than 100 miles of Douglas fir tonque-in-groove decking.

to view the docks is from a table in **The Vierling Saloon** at Front and Main Streets. The saloon was opened in 1883 by Martin Vierling, an art lover and saloon keeper who headed north with his paintings after running an establishment in Detroit. Later the art lover's bar became just another cafe during Prohibition, but the present proprietors, Terry and Christi Doyle, have turned back the clock by renovating the interior and returning the building to its original function as a saloon, brewpub, and fine restaurant. The brick walls inside once again feature paintings and prints, as the owners exhibit the works of a different artist every month. There are also old photographs and artifacts of early Marquette, and the large windows in the rear of the restaurant overlook the iron ore docks. A pair of binoculars hangs on the back wall for anyone wanting a closer look at the massive structure.

The fare is "geared to healthy food," and the dinner menu features several shrimp and chicken entrees and Rogan Josh, an Indian spiced red stew served with yellow rice and chutney. The Vierling Saloon is open daily except Sunday from 11:00 A.M. to 11:00 P.M. Dinner is served after 4:00 P.M., and prices range from $9.00 to $12.00.

A Cabin in the Woods

*T*he newest lodging accommodations in Marquette County come without a flush toilet, a shower, or any plumbing, for that matter. There are no mattresses, telephones, or televisions with HBO. Heat is a stack of logs and a wood-burning stove. Hopefully you brought some matches.

But what a view!

From the porch of Cabin No. 3 in the Little Presque Isle State Forest Recreation Area, you can watch the rays of an early morning sun spread across Harlow Lake. In the background is the rocky crown of Hogsback Mountain, and when the rising sun paints it in a light shade of pink, it's the closest thing we have to alpenglow in Michigan.

Built in 1996, the six rustic cabins are scattered in Little Presque Isle, a 3,040-acre tract located 5 miles northwest of Marquette and split in the middle by County Road 550. You can't drive to them, but the walk in is not far. Cabins No. 1, 2, and 3 are a mere 200 yards from where you park the car. Cabin No. 5, the farthest from the trailhead, is only a half-mile away.

Yet for the price of a little boot leather and the $35-per-night rental fee, you're ensured of solitude and peace of mind in one of the most picturesque settings in the Upper Peninsula. To reserve the cabins or obtain a brochure on Little Presque Isle State Forest Recreation Area, call the Department of Natural Resources office in Ishpeming at (906) 485–1031.

WESTERN UPPER PENINSULA

For an excellent view of all of Marquette, head north of town on County Road 550 for a few miles and turn into the dirt parking lot marked by the large SUGAR LOAF sign. This is the start of the **Sugar Loaf Recreation Trail,** a wide and easy path that winds 0.6 mile up the peak of the same name. You actually climb 315 feet through forest and over granite ridges by a series of steps until you reach the rocky knob marked by a stone monument. The view is spectacular on a clear day, a 360-degree panorama that includes the city, Lake Superior, the rough coastline, and the many offshore islands.

By continuing north on County Road 550 for another 26 miles, you reach its end in the small village of Big Bay on the shores of Lake Independence. Big Bay is best known as a place where scenes for the film *Anatomy of a Murder,* starring Jimmy Stewart and Lee Remick, were shot. The story is true, though the murder really took place at the Lumberjack Tavern, a classic north woods bar that was used for one scene in the movie. Other footage was shot in the Big Bay Hotel, which is now the **Thunder Bay Inn.**

The large inn was built in 1911 as a company store and warehouse and then turned into a hotel. In 1943, Henry Ford purchased it along with the mill at the north end of the lake to produce the wooden parts for his cars. The industrialist extensively remodeled the hotel and reshaped the landscape in front of it. So obsessed was Ford with being able to see his factory from his hotel that he had the town's railroad depot moved and County Road 550 rerouted. It was in 1958, under different owners, that several short scenes of the famous murder mystery were filmed in the hotel's lobby, dining room, and bedrooms upstairs. Eventually the facility was abandoned and sat empty for ten years.

In 1985 Darryl Small bought the hotel, and he opened the first of twelve rooms two years later. Today the large inn is an interesting place to stay or have dinner. All the rooms have been renovated. (You can even stay in Ford's Room.) Guests begin their day with coffee and rolls served on the second-floor balcony, which is furnished with wicker and overlooks the lake and, yes, Ford's old factory. Room rates for double occupancy range

Noquemenon Ski Marathon,
Marquette, January;
(800) 544-4321

Hiawatha Music Festival,
Marquette, July;
(800) 637-7813

U.P. Championship Rodeo,
Iron River, July;
(906) 265-3822

Winter Carnival,
Houghton, January;
(800) 338-7982

U.P. 200 Sled Dog Championship,
Marquette, February;
(800) 544-4321

Pine Mountain Classic,
Iron Mountain, February;
(800) 562-7134

North American Ski-Jumping Tournament,
Ishpeming, February;
(906) 485-6323

Snowburst,
Porcupine Mountains Wilderness State Park,
February; (906) 885-5275

from $50 to $125. For reservations call (906) 345–9376 or write Thunder Bay Inn, P.O. Box 286, Big Bay 49808.

An equally interesting place to stay in the area is the **Big Bay Point Lighthouse,** the secluded retreat 3.5 miles north of town on Lighthouse Road. The light at Big Bay was built and put into service in 1896, and included a two-story, red brick dwelling with eighteen rooms. The house was divided in half, with the lightkeeper living in one half and his assistant in the other. The Coast Guard automated the light in 1941 and then sold the structure in 1961 after building a new steel tower nearby.

In 1986 the lighthouse became a unique bed-and-breakfast offering guests the rare opportunity to stay overnight in one of its six bedrooms. The lights stand high above Lake Superior on a rocky point in the middle of forty wooded acres that include 2 miles of trails. You can climb the narrow staircase to the top of the tower for a splendid view of the area, catching a sunrise over Lake Superior at daybreak, a sunset over the Huron Mountains at dusk, or possibly the Northern Lights at night. The interior has been completely renovated and refinished, showing its natural wood and brick, and the various rooms include a delightful sauna.

The lighthouse (906–345–9957) is open year-round, with special rates for the off-season, weekdays, and package stays. The basic rate for the

Mountain Biking in the Huron Mountains

T here is some great mountain biking in the Big Bay area along old logging roads and two-tracks into the foothills of the Huron Mountains. Bisected by County Roads 550 and 510, this scenic area is a rugged forest laced with trout streams, waterfalls, and miles of old logging roads and obscured two-tracks.

Unlike most southern Michigan trails, there are no directional arrows, mileage markers, or cute names for technical sections in the woods north of Marquette. Before heading out purchase the most detailed topographical maps the U.S. Geological Survey produces on the area, the 7.5-minute

quadrangle series of Silver Lake Basin, Negaunee NW, and Buckroe. Then pack a compass, a few pieces of survival gear in case you get totally lost and have to spend the night in the woods, and head down County Road 510 from Big Bay, stopping at the first two-track that looks inviting.

Mountain bikes can also be rented in Big Bay for $25 a day at North Country Outfitters (906–345–9504). Great Northern Adventures offers both day trips for mountain bikers out of Big Bay and multi-day packages with accommodations at the Thunder Bay Inn. Call the tour company at (906) 225–8687 for a brochure.

summer ranges from $85 to $175 for rooms that sleep from two to four people. For reservations write Lighthouse, P.O. Box 3, Big Bay 49808.

The railroad depot that Henry Ford moved in Big Bay is yet another addition to the unusual lodgings found in this small town. After being salvaged in 1988, the **Big Bay Depot** is now offering history, natural beauty, and a comfortable bed.

The depot has five large rooms available, featuring private baths, kitchens, and sitting areas. Best of all, every room on the second floor leads out to another deck with a panorama of the lake, anglers jigging for perch, and Ford's old mill.

From Marquette, head north on County Road 550 for 25 miles to Big Bay. The driveway to the Big Bay Depot (906–345–9350) is across Country Road 550 from the Lumberjack Tavern. Rooms are $55 a night.

The newest Michigan historical museum is tucked away in the woods near Negaunee and is probably passed up by many visitors. That's a shame. **The Michigan Iron Industry Museum** is an interesting stop that lets you leisurely explore the history of the Upper Peninsula's iron industry. The museum lies in the forested ravines of the Marquette Iron Range and overlooks the Carp River, where the first iron forge in the Lake Superior region was built in 1848. The U.P.'s iron deposits had been discovered four years earlier when William Burt, leader of a U.S. Geological Survey party near the area, noticed the magnetic needle of his compass jumping wildly about. He instructed his men to search the ground, and they immediately turned up outcroppings of almost pure iron among the roots of pine trees. The iron era of the U.P. had begun, and in 1846 the Jackson Mine, the first operation in the U.P., was opened near Negaunee.

The museum does an excellent job of leading you through the history of iron, from its beginnings to its most robust era to the decline of the industry in the 1960s. Inside are several levels of displays, a recon-structed mine shaft to walk through, and an auditorium that presents a short introductory program. Outside are more artifacts, including a mine locomotive, and trails leading to the old forge site on the Carp River. The museum (906–475–7857) is reached from US 41 by turning onto County Road 492 about 3 miles east of Negaunee and is open daily from 9:30 A.M. until 4:30 P.M. from mid-May until mid-October. Admission is free.

Though it might surprise a few people, especially avid skiers, Ishpeming is home of the **U.S. National Ski Hall of Fame**. The hall was established here in 1954 because the Ishpeming Ski Club is "the oldest active ski club in the country."

Formed in 1887, the club was founded by Scandinavians who had emigrated to the U.P. to work the Marquette Range iron mines and brought their love of skiing with them. They were soon hosting ski jumping tournaments and in 1926 moved their ramps and competition site to a large bowl owned by Cleveland-Cliffs, Inc. When a skier badly injured himself in practice that first year, a local reporter dubbed the area "Suicide Hill" and the name stuck, much to the alarm of club officials who were trying to promote the new jumps.

In the early 1990s the Hall of Fame was relocated in a new building in Ishpeming that features an impressive roofline in the shape of a ski jump. Inside are exhibits and displays that detail the history of skiing from medieval times to the latest Winter Olympics. All three forms of skiing are included—Nordic, Alpine, and ski jumping—and many visitors are amazed to learn that Alpine skiing is a relatively new version of the sport.

The Ski Hall of Fame (906–485–6323) is on US 41 between Second and Third Streets and is open daily from 10:00 A.M. to 8:00 P.M. June through September and 10:00 A.M. to 5:00 P.M. the rest of the year. There is a small admission fee.

After visiting the hall, drive out to the ***Suicide Hill Ski Jumps***. There are three ski ramps built into the ridge, the largest being a 90-meter jump. It's an impressive sight any time of the year but especially in the winter when skiers are flying off the end of the ramp on their way to 200- or 300-foot jumps. From US 41 head south on Fourth Street and then east on Division Street. Call the Hall of Fame for the dates of competitions.

Baraga County

Most roadside rest areas in the Upper Peninsula consist of little more than picnic tables, a pair of pit toilets, and a hand pump for water. Then there is the one on US 41, 8 miles south of L'Anse. It consists of picnic tables, a pair of pit toilets, a hand pump for water, and one of the most beautiful canyons in Michigan. The state's Department of Transportation maintains the tables and the toilets, but it was forestry students from Michigan Technological University who built the wooden boardwalks and observation platforms that make ***Canyon Falls and Gorge*** such a pleasant stop.

From the large display map in the rest area, the path departs into the woods, crosses a bridge over Bacco Stream, and within a half-mile comes to the impressive Canyon Falls formed by the Sturgeon River. The falls mark the beginning of the canyon by thundering over a rock ledge to the river 30 feet below. Handrails have been erected here, and you can lean over the top of the cascade to listen to its roar or to feel the mist the falling water creates.

At this point there is a TRAIL ENDS sign, but the best part of the area, the gorge itself, can only be seen by following the original path, which snakes around a huge rock face. This path hugs the half-mile-long canyon and lets you view the Sturgeon River, a stretch of roiling white water that rushes through sheer rock walls 50 feet high. All visitors, especially families with young children, should be extremely careful if they choose to continue to the end of the old trail, a mile-long one-way hike. The original log handrails are still up, but they're flimsy and weak in places, and after they end there is nothing between you and the sharp edge of the gorge.

Strange As It Sounds

*H*ighpointers are a group of adventurers whose mission in life is to stand on the highest point in all 50 states. They used to come to L'Anse from every corner of the country looking for Mount Curwood, which for two decades was thought to be Michigan's highest point at 1,996.4 feet. They would fly to Marquette, drive to Baraga County, and then search out some local for detailed directions on how to follow a maze of logging roads to the top of the peak.

Imagine their shock when the Department of the Interior conducted a survey in 1982 and concluded that Mount Curwood is really only 1,978.34 feet in elevation and actually the second-highest spot in the state. Michigan's loftiest peak is nearby Mount Arvon, which at 1,979.238 feet above sea level is 11 inches higher than Curwood.

Many Highpointers, who had climbed Mount Curwood 15 or 20 years earlier, were forced to return to Michigan and climb Mount Arvon. And when they finally reached the peak, what did they see? Most of the time nothing more than the trees at the top. The exception is in late fall after the leaves have dropped and a view through the trees is possible.

What there is on the summit of Arvon is a USGS brass marker verifying the elevation. There is also a small yellow mailbox containing a log book so you can document your achievement of not getting lost as well as noting how many other high points you have reached.

To reach the roof of the state, you have to find **Mount Arvon** in the Upper Peninsula, which at 1,979 feet is 21 feet short of being a true "mountain" but still the highest point in Michigan. The outing involves following unmarked logging roads in a remote section of Baraga County and hoping you can find your way back. Once on top there is no majestic view, just a yellow box in a forest with a register book inside.

But enough people undertake this adventure that the Baraga County Tourism and Recreation Association (906–524–7444) publishes a set of detailed directions to the high point. The association visitor center is right off US 41 as you enter L'Anse from the east. It has irregular hours.

Although serious research on the subject has never been done, many say the largest and best sweet rolls in the state are found at the **Hilltop Restaurant**, on US 41 just south of L'Anse. One roll is an ample breakfast for most people since it measures more than 5 inches across and 3 inches thick and arrives filled with cinnamon and dripping in glaze. The restaurant is operated by Judy Jaeger and Vivian Delene, but its sweet-roll fame was already established when they bought the business in 1975. On a good weekend they will serve more than a thousand. The eatery also has other items on its menu (including good pasties), but who has room for anything else after devouring its sticky specialty with a cup of fresh-brewed coffee? The Hilltop is open from 6:00 A.M. to 8:00 P.M. daily.

One of Baraga County's most interesting attractions is the **Hanka Homestead,** a "living outdoor museum" where visitors learn about and see the lifestyle of the early Finnish farmers who immigrated to what was then a remote and isolated region of the state. The farm dates back to 1896, when the Hanka family applied for a homestead on two forty-acre parcels along the military road to Fort Wilkins at the tip of the Keweenaw Peninsula. The first thing Herman Hanka built was an 18-by-24-foot log house. But he was Finnish, so the second thing he constructed was his savu, or smoke sauna. Eventually he added barns, a self-cooling milk house that straddles a small spring, a horse stable, a blacksmith shop, and a granary.

The amazing thing about the farm is that it's never been wired for electricity, even though the youngest son, Jalmer Hanka, lived there until 1966. It was added to the National Register of Historic Places in 1984 and opened to the public the next year. Today there are ten buildings and a root cellar to explore, each filled with the Hanka possessions. From US 41 in L'Anse, head north toward Houghton, and in 12 miles turn west on Arnheim Road. Follow the small museum signs. If you pass Otter Lake, you've gone too far west. The homestead (906–353–7116) is open Tuesday, Thursday, Saturday and Sunday from noon to 4:00 P.M. from May through fall colors in October. There is a small admission fee.

Houghton County

One of the most spectacular areas of the U.P.'s interior is relatively unknown to travelers who are hesitant to leave paved roads. The **Sturgeon River Gorge Area** is located just inside Houghton County along its border with Baraga County south of M 3838. The wilderness area includes the gorge cut by the Sturgeon River, which in some places is more than 400 feet deep, making it the largest and deepest in the Great Lakes states. For the best view of it, follow M 3838 west of Baraga and turn south onto Prickett Dam Road (also called Forest Road 193), marked by a national forest sign. Within 11 miles the road merges into Sturgeon Gorge Road (Forest Road 191), and a few hundred yards to the right there is a sharp 90-degree curve. At this bend an extremely rough jeep trail leads west to the edge of the gorge. It is best to walk the quarter-mile that ends at one of the most beautiful panoramas in the U.P. You see the deep gorge below and miles of forested ridges and hills to the west.

Before reaching Sturgeon Gorge Road, you will pass a directional sign for **Silver Mountain**. Located on the edge of the Sturgeon River Gorge Wilderness in Houghton County, Silver Mountain is a 1,312-foot peak, once the site of a fire tower. At a small parking lot, you'll find a long stairway—long as in 250 steps—but once on top you'll see the foundation of the old fire tower, two USGS markers, and a view that includes miles of the rugged Sturgeon River Gorge Wilderness.

Toledo for the Upper Peninsula

By 1835 Michigan had grown sufficiently to qualify for statehood but Congress held it up because of a boundary controversy with Ohio over a sliver of land that included Toledo. The so-called "Toledo War" resulted in both states' calling out their militias but, fortunately, no bloodshed. When Michigan gave up claims to the city, it was awarded the Upper Peninsula and statehood, becoming the 26th state in 1837.

There are a handful of mine tours in the Upper Peninsula, but the best one is at the **Quincy Mine**. The Quincy Mining Company was organized in 1846 and for almost 100 years it mined the Pewabic copper lode located just north of Hancock. It was such a money-maker that the mine was nicknamed "Old Reliable," and today it is part of the new Keweenaw National Historical Park.

Fun Facts

In Laurium, where Tamarack Street joins M28, is the George Gipp Memorial. Better known as "the Gipper," Laurium's most famous son went on to become a football star at Notre Dame University. Legend has it that from his deathbed, he uttered the famous line to coach Knute Rockne, "Tell the boys to win one for the Gipper." The role of the Gipper and the deathbed scene gave Ronald Reagan his most memorable role.

The two-hour tour begins with the world's largest steam hoist, a giant spool that holds 13,200 feet of cable and lowered workers into Shaft No. 2 of the underground mine to a depth of 9,200 feet. You then board a cog tram for a journey down the steep Quincy Hill to the entrance of Shaft No. 5. Here tractor-drawn wagons take you a half-mile into a horizontal tunnel 400 feet below the surface.

Exhibits and videos in the hoist house round out a visit to the mine. The Quincy Mine (906–482–3101) is open from mid-May to mid-October, and full tours are $12.50 for adults and $7.00 for children. Summer hours are 9:30 A.M. to 6:00 P.M.

In nearby Lake Linden, right downtown on Calumet Avenue, is **Lindell's Chocolate Shop**. Joseph Bosch had the building erected in 1893 for his Bosch Brewing Company, but in 1918 it was refurbished with wooden ceiling fans, twenty high-backed oak booths, a nickelodeon, leaded-glass windows, and a 6-foot-long marble food preparation table that took four people to lift. It became the Chocolate Shop, and though the entire building was moved down the street in 1928, little of the interior has changed since then.

The menu has, however, as the shop no longer makes candy but specializes in homemade ice cream. The 1943 ice-cream maker is still proudly displayed in the front window. You can arise at 4:00 A.M. any day and watch the ice cream being made, or come by at a more reasonable hour and taste one of the four or five flavors.

Lindell's Chocolate Shop (906–296–0793) is also a restaurant and bar with a full menu, but unquestionably it is the ice cream and the malts, milk shakes, sundaes, and banana splits that are its most popular items. The shop is open Monday through Thursday and Saturday from 6:30 A.M. until 7:00 P.M. and on Friday until 8:00 P.M.

Keweenaw County

Under the forceful will of President Andrew Jackson, Michigan became a state in 1837, when it grudgingly accepted the entire U.P. in exchange for surrendering Toledo to Ohio. In only six years, this "worthless wilderness" became a land of incredible wealth after Douglas Houghton, the first state geologist, explored the Keweenaw Peninsula and reported finding chunks of pure copper. Miners began arriving by 1841, and within two years there was a lively copper rush to this small section of the U.P., forcing the U.S. Army to build Fort Wilkins in Copper Harbor (today a state historical park) to maintain law and order. As in all stampedes for a precious metal, many mines quickly died, and thousands went home disillusioned and broke. Nevertheless, substantial lodes of copper were uncovered, and by the 1860s this area was producing 15 million pounds annually or almost 90 percent of the national total. Two of the most profitable mines were Calumet and Hecla, and near them sprang up the town of Red Jacket. Later renamed Calumet, this city of 66,000 in 1898 had wealth, importance (it was considered as a new site for the state capital), and a peculiar problem.

Because of large contributions to the city budget from the mines, the council found itself with a surplus of funds. Already the community had paved streets, electric lights, and telephones, so the town decided to build an opera house, the grandest theater in the Midwest, one that would rival the stages of the East Coast. The *Calumet Opera House* was built in 1899 at Sixth and Elm Streets, and no expense was spared. It was designed in an Italian Renaissance style and inside featured two balconies, private viewing chambers along the walls, and rococo plaster ornamentation of gilt, cream, and crimson. The acoustics were nearly perfect: An actor could whisper on the stage and be heard in the last row of the top balcony.

On March 20, 1900, the first performance was given to a packed house of 1,100 and was described by the *Copper Country Evening News* as "the greatest social event ever known in the copperdome's metropolis." A string of legendary performers arrived at the famed opera house, including John Philip Sousa, Sarah Bernhardt, Douglas Fairbanks, and Lillian Russell. Eventually the theater, like the town, fell upon hard times. The local mines, the last to operate in the Keweenaw Peninsula, were closed for good because of a labor strike in 1968; by then Calumet's population had dwindled to 1,000.

The mines are still closed, but the opera house has reopened. Declared a National Historic Site in 1974, it was fully restored, and its opulence can

Calumet Opera House

be viewed on a guided tour from mid-June to mid-October. Tours are offered from 10:00 A.M. to 4:00 P.M. from Tuesday through Friday and 1:00 P.M. to 4:00 P.M. on Saturday and Sunday; it's $3.00 for a peek into Calumet's past. The building has also returned to live theater after a stint showing motion pictures of the 1920s and 1930s; major performances are scheduled from March through October. Call (906) 337–2610 for information

Next door to the opera house is **Shute's Bar**, which features what many say is the oldest wooden bar and back bar in the state. Both date to 1893 when Marco Curto, an immigrant miner who had saved his pay, opened up Curto's Saloon. One of forty-six in the area, it was a place where immigrant miners could always find somebody who spoke their native tongue. The bar is massive and polished to a gleam as is the back bar, which includes a huge mirror, wooden coolers, a metal cash resister, and two intriguingly carved liquor cabinets that are 10 feet tall. The whole unit is crowned by a spectacular colored glass canopy. The long narrow saloon also has the original booths and a ceiling and archway featuring classic trim and plaster work. Shute's is not just a place to have a beer; it's a proper complement to the historic opera house next door.

At one time or another in the late 1800s, there were fourteen active copper mines in the Keweenaw Peninsula, and today a number of them have been preserved, offering a glimpse of the underground world of the miners. The least promoted but perhaps the most intriguing is the **Delaware Mine** on US 41 between Calumet and Copper Harbor. To reach it you pass through Delaware, a ghost town of a half-dozen abandoned buildings and a sobering reminder that when the copper ran out, so did the lifeblood for boomtowns throughout the peninsula.

Interest in the copper at Delaware began in 1845 and involved one early investor by the name of Horace Greeley. The famous newspaper editor actually made a trip to the Keweenaw Peninsula but never traveled much farther than Eagle River. A mining company was organized in 1848, and actual mining began the following year. From 1849 to 1851 the mine produced 522,541 pounds of copper, but the Northwest Copper Mining Company lost almost $100,000 on the operation. The mine was sold again and again to new investors, with one company building a huge hoist house in 1870 to pull the cars out of the deep shafts that were being dug. Despite all efforts, the Delaware never really turned a profit, and the shafts were sealed for good in 1887. The town of Delaware, which in 1879 had 300 residents, also disappeared.

Now a tourist attraction, the Delaware offers two different tours during the summer. A forty-minute tour takes you down a 100-foot staircase into Shaft No. 1 to the first level. The top level is 900 feet of tunnel from which other passages, shafts, and a huge cavern can be viewed. The Rustic Lantern Tour goes deeper into Shaft. No. 3—without the aid of a staircase—and usually lasts ninety minutes. There is still plenty of copper lying around in this level, and in the information center visitors are told how to recognize and search for it in the mine. They are also given tips afterward on cleaning any metal they find.

You can explore the remains of the hoist house above ground on your own and get a good overview of the ghost town from the parking lot. The Delaware Mine (906–289–4688) is open from mid-May until mid-October from 10:00 A.M. until 6:00 P.M. daily. Admission is $7.00 per adult, $4.00 for children.

The men who actually worked the mines were often immigrants from the Cornwall area of England or from Finland or Norway, and they brought to Copper Country their strong ethnic heritages. Traces of that heritage can be seen in the Cornish pasties that are sold throughout the U.P. and in the popularity of Finnish saunas. For years the sauna took the place of bathtubs and showers in homes, as early settlers would build their sauna huts first and worry about their cabins later. A good sauna begins with a shower to open up the pores, followed by a stay in a cedar-paneled room where a small pile of rocks is heated. As water is tossed on the rocks, a dry heat emerges that makes the body perspire profusely, flushing out dirt and grime from the skin. The temperature ranges from 160 to 180 degrees, and the old miners used wicker sticks to beat their backs to get the blood moving. The entire ordeal ends with a cold shower to close the pores.

> **Fun Facts**
>
> *Lake Superior is the largest and deepest of the Great Lakes, and its 31,700 square miles is the largest surface area of any body of fresh water in the world. Measuring 383 miles long and 160 miles wide, Superior holds half of all the water in the Great Lakes.*

In Copper Harbor, you can experience this Finnish ritual at **Brockway Sauna,** operated by the Minnetonka Resort in the heart of town on US 41. The public sauna is across the street from the resort and consists of four private suites. Each is completely paneled in cedar and features a dressing area, shower, and sauna that will seat four to six people. The building is not that far from Lake Superior, and occasionally a local resident will finish the sauna with a mad dash into the chilly lake, a tradition most visitors pass up.

The Brockway Sauna (906–289–4449) is open daily May 15 to October 15 from 1:00 until 10:00 P.M. The price includes use of a room, towel, soap, and a wicker stick if you request it. Call for specific rates.

The Copper Rush of the Keweenaw Peninsula began in 1843, and Copper Harbor quickly became the center of exploration parties, newly formed mining companies, and a "rough population of enterprising prospectors, miners, and speculators." Because of the seedy nature of the miners and the constant threat of Chippewa Indians wanting to reclaim their lost land, Secretary of War William Wilkins dispatched two companies of infantry to the remote region of Michigan. They arrived in late May of 1844, and by November **Fort Wilkins** was built.

The threat of Indian hostilities never materialized, and the troops discovered the Upper Peninsula winters were long and cold. Isolated from the rest of the world with little more than duty and drill to occupy their time, the garrison of 105 men ran into problems of boredom, low morale, and illegal whiskey. The following year half the troops were transferred to Texas in preparation for the Mexican War, and in 1846, less than two years after it was built, Fort Wilkins was abandoned. In 1921 Fort Wilkins was recognized as a historic landmark by the state, and in 1923 it was designated a state park. Today the structure is noted for being one of the few surviving wooden forts east of the Mississippi River.

Although the fort was insignificant militarily, it's an outstanding example of a mid-nineteenth-century frontier outpost, with twelve of its sixteen buildings from the original structure. You can wander through the fort year-round, even ski through it in the winter, but the buildings are open mid-May through mid-October. Ranging from kitchen and mess room to the bakery, company barracks, and hospital, many contain restored furnishings and artifacts depicting the rough life troops endured here. From mid-June to Labor Day, interpreters in period dress give tours daily from 9:00 A.M. until 5:00 P.M., adding a touch of realism to the fort.

The main entrance to the park and the fort is a mile east of Copper Harbor on US 41. A vehicle pass is required to enter the park and the fort. For more information on Fort Wilkins or on camping in the state park, call (906) 289–4215.

Keweenaw is the smallest county in the U.P., but it has more than its share of scenic drives, where every curve reveals another striking view. The most famous is the **Brockway Mountain Drive**, a 10-mile stretch to Copper Harbor that is the highest above-sea-level drive between the Rockies and the Alleghenies. Less traveled but almost as scenic in its own way is the **Sand Dune Drive** between Eagle River and Eagle Harbor. From Eagle River this portion of M 26 heads west along the Lake Superior shoreline, climbing high above the water along sandy bluffs. The road provides sweeping views of the Great Lake on the horizon and the sandy shoreline below, and the best turnoff looms above Great Sand Bay. The road returns to the lake level at Cat Harbor, a delightful beach for sunning and swimming if you can handle Superior's chilly waters, and then swings through Eagle Harbor, passing the picturesque **Eagle Harbor Lightstation**, which is now a museum open to the public.

Built in 1871, the lighthouse and the lightkeeper's residence have been renovated and furnished to reflect an early-twentieth-century lightstation. Next door is a small museum that contains, among other things, a display on Keweenaw's prehistoric copper culture. Signs from M 26 lead

Sand Hills Lighthouse Inn

*B*uilt in 1919, Sand Hills Lighthouse is one of the largest along the Great Lakes and had enough rooms to house three lightkeepers and their families. The lighthouse was so big that the U.S. Coast Guard used it as a training base during World War II and housed 200 guardsmen on the grounds.

In 1954 Sand Hills' beacon was made obsolete by new navigational technology, and the building was abandoned. In 1961 Bill Frabotta purchased the three-story brick building and its seven-story beacon tower, and after 30 years of careful renovation opened it up as the Sand Hills Lighthouse Inn. The bed-and-breakfast offers eight guests rooms, a hearty breakfast in the morning, and more than 3,000 feet of Lake Superior shoreline from which to watch both sunrises and sunsets. Or you can climb the tower and enjoy the panoramic view from its walk-out roof.

Sand Hills Lighthouse Inn (906-337-1744) is 4 miles west of Eagle River at Five Mile Point. Rooms range from $125 to $175 per night. Make reservations well in advance if planning a trip from May through October.

you to the lighthouse, which is open daily from noon to 5:00 P.M. mid-June through September.

From Eagle Harbor M 26 continues east, first passing the junction to Brockway Mountain Drive and then returning to the edge of Lake Superior, whose shoreline becomes a rugged mass of red sandstone gracefully carved by the pounding waves. Along this segment you will pass *Devil's Wash Tub*, a huge depression in the shoreline that echoes the waves crashing in and out of it.

Ontonagon County

Three miles west of Silver City is *Porcupine Mountains Wilderness State Park,* a preserve of 58,000 acres of primitive forests, secluded lakes, and the rugged "Porkies." For most visitors, this state park is a quick drive to the end of M 107, where they follow a short wooded path to the escarpment overlooking "**Lake of the Clouds**," a watery gem between the peaks and ridges of the mountains. Those willing to don a pair of hiking boots can enjoy some of the most unusual accommodations found in the U.P. with a night in one of the park's rustic cabins.

Within the Porkies is a trail network of more than 85 miles, and scattered along the footpaths are sixteen wilderness cabins, each located in a scenic setting along a stream or lake or on the shore of Lake Superior. You can reach them only on foot, and some take an all-day hike while others lie only thirty or forty minutes from the nearest parking lot. The cabins have no electricity, running water, or toilets that flush. Modern conveniences are replaced by candles, wood stove, and an outhouse up the hill—ideal for anybody who wants to spend a night in the woods without having to "rough it" in a tent, sleeping on the ground.

Fun Facts

The Porcupine Mountains and the Huron Mountains to the east are the only ranges in Michigan formed by volcanic activity.

The cabins provide bunks, mattresses, cooking utensils, and for those on an inland lake, a small rowboat. You must provide sleeping bag, clothing, and food. The park rents the cabins, which hold from four to eight people, from April through November at $35 to $45 per night. Stop at the park visitor center just off South Boundary Road (open daily from 10:00 A.M. until 6:00 P.M. from mid-May to mid-October) for maps and a list of open cabins. Call (906) 885–5275 or write ahead for information and a cabin reservation to Porcupine Mountains Wilderness State Park, 412 South Boundary Road, Ontonagon 49953.

Thanks to a rich history of loggers and miners, Michigan is blessed (cursed?) with a scattering of ghost towns throughout the state. Fayette is the most famous and most visited, but **Old Victoria** can be an equally interesting stop. The Ontonagon County town was originally named Cushin and established in 1849 after the discovery of an ancient miner's pit that still contained a mass of copper. In 1858, a new group of investors came in, renamed the mine town Victoria, and the company town grew to more than 2,000 residents.

Victoria became a ghost town when the copper ran out. Most of the buildings date to the late nineteenth century. There are classic hand-hewn log cabins, ruins of a rock house, and mining equipment lying all over the place. Old Victoria is located 4 miles west of Rockland in Ontonagon County, with an entrance road that is clearly posted on US 45. Historical tours are given Memorial Day through fall colors in October daily from 11:00 A.M. to 5:30 P.M.

Upper Tahquamenon Falls in Luce County is the largest waterfall in the state, but many cascade connoisseurs think **Bond Falls** in southern Ontonagon County near Paulding is much more beautiful. The cascade is a drop of more than 50 feet where the Middle Branch of the Ontonagon River fans out and leaps down a series of steplike rocks and around a small island of large boulders in the middle. It's the constantly tumbling water that makes Bond Falls so alluring.

From US 45 in Paulding turn east onto Bond Falls Road and in 3.2 miles you'll come to the trailhead to the cascade and a small parking area. The falls are a half-mile hike that includes numerous stairways, some steep, and boardwalks. Nearby is a picnic area, beach, and campground.

Gogebic County

aterfalls of every type and description are the gems of the Upper Peninsula, and there are more than 150 of them scattered across this region of Michigan. For example, **Black River Harbor Drive** (also known as Black River Road and County Road 513) in Gogebic County is virtually a parkway of whitewater splendor. The 15-mile road departs from Bessemer on US 2 and enters Ottawa National Forest, ending at scenic Black River Recreation Area on Lake Superior. Heading north you first pass **Copper Peak Ski Flying Hill**, the largest artificial ski slide in the world and the site of 500-foot jumps during the winter. In the summer visitors take the chairlift and elevator to the top for a view of three states and Canada.

From Copper Peak, Black River Road enters the heart of the national forest and winds near five waterfalls, each lying at the end of a trail from a marked turnoff. Gorge and Potawatomi Falls are among the most spectacular and easiest to reach. The two falls are within 800 feet of each other and only a five-minute walk from the parking lot. Potawatomi is the larger, with a 130-foot-wide cascade that drops 30 feet into the Black River. Gorge, smaller with a 24-foot drop, is encased in a steep and narrow red rock canyon—a spectacular setting. A well-marked path with stairs and observation decks leads you past both falls.

At the end of the road, you can camp at Black River Harbor Recreation Area, or those who want a little more luxury can rent a log cabin at **Bear Track Inn** nearby. The small resort has been around since the 1930s, when it catered to lumbermen and commercial fishermen. Its name came from a hungry bear who wandered in one night while the main cabin was being built and walked in the wet cement of the front steps. The name stuck, and the tracks can still be seen today. The inn has only three cabins for rent, but two are authentic log structures, and all three feature natural wood interiors, wood stoves and stone fireplaces, and kitchen facilities. The large cabin can sleep ten, the others hold four people each, and during the summer the rates range from $50 to $60 per night for double occupancy. For reservations call the inn at (906) 932–2144 or write Bear Track Inn, 15325 Black River Road, Ironwood 49938.

Wolf Mountain

*T*his is a peak for those with short legs. The trek to the top of Wolf Mountain is only a half-mile from the trailhead. The trail, which is located southeast of Wakefield in the Ottawa National Forest can be reached by turning north onto Forest Road 9300 from US 2.

On Forest Road 9300 you cross Little Presque River and then see the mountain before reaching the trailhead at the end of the road. The hike is a stiff climb—no pain, no gain, right?—but within fifteen minutes or so, you're on a rocky knob looking at a 180-degree panorama.

The scenery is a rugged ridgeline to the west while to the south is an endless sea of pines that stretches into Wisconsin. It's such a great sunset-watching spot that some hikers have made a rustic "lounge chair" out of logs here. For more information on Wolf Mountain or a map, call the Ottawa National Forest Headquarters in Ironwood at (906) 932–1330.

Iron County

Perhaps the U.P.'s largest and least-known historical complex is the *Iron County Museum,* located in the village of Caspian on County Road 424, 2 miles south of US 2 at Iron River. The grounds include almost twenty buildings, many a century old, in a Greenfield Village–like setting that lacks some of the polish of the famous Dearborn attraction but is no less interesting. The park occupies the site of the Caspian Iron Mine, and the head frame that hoisted cars out of the mine in the 1920s still towers over the complex. The main museum is the former engine house, which has been considerably enlarged and today is a maze of displays and three-dimensional exhibits. The favorite is the iron ore mining model that, for a nickel, will automatically run through the process of the rocks being rinsed from the mine and loaded into railroad cars above-ground. Other interesting exhibits are the renovated saloon, blacksmith shop, and schoolroom, and a hand-carved model of a logging camp that fills an 80-foot display case with hundreds of figures and pieces.

Outside you can wander through one historic building after another: a logging camp bunkhouse with a table set for supper and mackinaw shirts (made of a heavy plaid wool) still hanging up near the door, a

Camping in Michigan

With more than 14,000 camp sites, the Michigan state park system ranks first in the country for total number of sites. Add almost 5,000 more sites in its national and state forests, and it's easy to understand why camping holidays are a time-honored tradition in Michigan, especially in the Upper Peninsula.

I prefer rustic campgrounds because they are smaller and more remote. For a list of and directions to all public campgrounds in the U.P., pick up a copy of the U.P. Travel and Recreation Association's Four Season Travel Planner. It's free and can be obtained by calling the association at (800) 562-7134. Here are my favorite rustic campgrounds in the U.P.:

Norway Lake National Forest Campground, Iron County

Gene's Pond State Forest Campground, Dickinson County

Big Knob State Forest Campground, Mackinac County

Big Eric's Bridge State Forest Campground, Baraga County

Mouth of Two-Hearted River State Forest Campground, Luce County

Bay View National Forest Campground, Chippewa County

barn filled with plows and threshers of the 1800s, a completely furnished homesteaders' cabin, and many other exhibits. You could easily spend an entire day exploring this fascinating folk-life complex. The Iron County Museum (906–265–2617) is open June through August from 9:00 A.M. to 5:00 P.M. Monday through Saturday and 1:00 to 5:00 P.M. Sunday. In May and September the museum is open 10:00 A.M. to 4:00 P.M. daily. There is a small admission fee.

Dickinson County

As in the copper fields, many workers in the iron mines were immigrants from Europe. At Iron Mountain, many Italians came to work the Chapin Mine, which opened in 1879 and went on to become the second-leading ore producer in the U.P. You can learn about the miners' life and work at the Menominee Range Historical Museum

Pine Mountain Ski Jump

Known as the "King of Hills," Pine Mountain Ski Jump is an awesome sight. Built in 1938 as a Works Progress Administration project and upgraded several times since, the 90-meter ski ramp features a 186-foot-high scaffold and a 381-foot slide. It sits majestically on top of a landing hill with a vertical drop of another 349 feet. Add it all up and you have a 1,440-foot run that sends skiers through the air at speeds of 55 to 65 miles an hour. In Iron Mountain they tell you it's like jumping off a twenty-nine-story building, of which there is none in the U.P.

Jumpers use skis that are wide, heavy, and often 265 centimeters or longer. Both their boots and bindings are much more closely related to Nordic skiing than Alpine, especially with the ability to lift the heels off the skis.

The jumpers are able to defy gravity by basically turning themselves into airplane wings when they lift out of the back of their bindings on takeoff and lean forward until their bodies are almost parallel to the skis. In 1994, an Austrian set a U.S. record at Pine Mountain when he leaped 400 feet.

If you're around Iron Mountain in mid-February, you can see the jumpers in action during the annual Pine Mountain Classic, which draws almost 20,000 spectators. In the summer you can climb the 280 steps to the top of the jump and be rewarded with a panoramic view that includes seven lakes.

To reach the ski jump from US 2, turn west on Kent Street and follow it past the Cornish Pump Engine and Mining Museum. Turn north on Upper Pine Mountain Road, which will wind to the ski ramp at the top of the hill.

and see the huge water pump that was built for the exceptionally wet mine at the **Cornish Pump Engine and Mining Museum**.

The pump engine was built for the Chapin Mine. Opened in 1879, the Chapin led iron ore production in the Menominee Range but was also one of the wettest mines ever worked. To dry things out, the E.P. Allis Company of Milwaukee was commissioned in 1889 to build a pumping system for the excess water. The centerpiece of the museum is the 725-ton steeple compound condensing engine that rises 54 feet from the floor and features a 40-foot flywheel. It has been documented as the largest steam-driven pumping engine in the U.S.

There are also photos and exhibits on the underground mining days of Iron Mountain and an intriguing exhibit on Henry Ford's World War II gliders, which were manufactured in the area and used to secretly deploy troops behind enemy lines. The museum (906–774–1086) is in downtown Iron Mountain, 1 block west of US 2 on Kent Street. Hours are 9:00 A.M. to 5:00 P.M. Monday through Saturday and noon to 4:00 P.M. Sunday from mid-May through mid-October. Admission is $4.00 for adults or $7.00 for a ticket that includes the Menominee Range Historical Museum.

The Menominee River forms almost half of the border between Wisconsin and Michigan's Upper Peninsula, beginning west of Iron Mountain and extending to its mouth on Green Bay. Two miles south of Norway, the river flows through Piers Gorge, a whitewater area of large falls, holes, and swirls as the river tumbles through a scenic forested canyon. The gorge picked up its name in the 1840s when loggers built piers along this section of the river to slow the current and prevent logs from jamming and splitting on the jagged rocks. You can view this spectacular stretch of wild water by heading south of Norway on US 8; just before its bridge across the Menominee, turn left onto Piers Gorge Road. The paved road quickly turns into a dirt one, and then after 0.6 mile it ends at **Piers Gorge Nature Trail**. The trail is a round-trip of 3 miles but swings past a series of viewing points above the falls.

During the summer you can also experience the gorge and what many rafters call the "Midwest's premier whitewater river" through **Argosy Rafting Adventures Inc.** The company offers a three-hour raft trip that takes you through Piers Gorge and over its falls. On Saturday and Sunday, the rafters meet nearby and then proceed to the river with their large inflated rafts. It's a wild ride, one that will leave you soaking wet but exhilarated. The company provides the rafts, guides, helmets, life jackets, and a paddle for each passenger.

Argosy Rafting Adventures (715–251–3886) is based in Wisconsin. The raft trips, which also can be set up during the week by advance reservation, cost around $30 per person.

Menominee County

One of the products of Michigan's white pine era was hardwood floors by the IXL Company of Hermansville. Established by C. J. Meyer in the 1870s as part of his Wisconsin Land and Lumber Company, IXL became world-renowned for its floors after machines were invented in Hermansville that could precision-manufacture tongue-and-groove hardwood flooring in one operation. By the early 1900s IXL had the largest such plant in the country, and its flooring could be seen (and walked on) in the main lodge at Yellowstone National Park and the Mormon Temple in Salt Lake City.

In 1881 Meyer erected a huge office building to manage his sprawling lumber operation, and today it's one of the most intriguing museums in the Upper Peninsula. The *IXL Office Museum* is literally a step into a nineteenth-century business office. On the first floor visitors wander through the payroll and accounting departments as well as the private offices of the company executives. All are fully furnished and appear as if the workers had just stepped out for lunch. In one room are dictaphones, mimeographs, typewriters, and other machines complete with instruction booklets, while across the hall beautiful rolltop desks and an ornate

IXL Office Museum

walk-in vault can be seen. On the second floor several rooms are devoted to the machinery and equipment used in the flooring industry, and on the third floor visitors can still flip through original payroll records and see what a worker earned each week (along with deductions) in the 1890s.

The museum is located in the heart of Hermansville, a small town on US 2, 26 miles west of Escanaba and 30 miles east of Iron Mountain. The museum (906–498–2498) is open June through Labor Day from 12:30 to 4:00 P.M. daily. There is a small admission fee.

PLACES TO STAY IN THE WESTERN UPPER PENINSULA

BIG BAY
Big Bay Pointe Lighthouse,
3 Lighthouse Road,
(906) 345–9957

Thunder Bay Inn,
County Road 550,
(906) 345–9376

BLACK HARBOR
Bear Track Inn,
15325 Black River Road,
(906) 932–2144

CALUMET/LAURIUM
Laurium Manor Inn Bed
and Breakfast,
320 Tamarack Street,
(906) 337–2549

Americinn,
5101 South Sixth Street,
(800) 634–3444

COPPER HARBOR
Lake Fanny Hooe Resort,
US 41,
(800) 426–4451

Keweenaw Mountain
Lodge,
US 41,
(906) 289–4403

EAGLE RIVER
Eagle River Inn,
M 26,
(800) 352–9228

Sand Hills Lighthouse Inn,
Five Mile Point,
(906) 337–1744

HOUGHTON
Charleston House Inn,
918 College Avenue,
(800) 482–7404

Franklin Square Inn,
820 Shelden Avenue,
(888) 487–1700

King's Inn,
215 Shelden Avenue,
(800) 528–1234

IRON MOUNTAIN
Edgewater Resort Cabins,
N4128 US 2,
(800) 236–6244

Woodlands Motel,
N3957 US 2,
(800) 394–5505

Comfort Inn,
1555 North Stephenson
Avenue,
(906) 774–5505

IRONWOOD
Sandpiper Motel,
1200 East US 2,
(906) 932–2000

Comfort Inn,
210 Cloverdale Drive,
(906) 932–2224

KEARSARGE
Belknap's Garnet House
Bed and Breakfast,
238 US 41,
(906) 337–5607

MARQUETTE
Landmark Inn,
230 North Front Street,
(800) 752–6362

Cedar Motor Inn,
2523 US 41,
(888) 551–7378

Tiroler Hof Inn,
1880 US 21,
(800) 892–9376

Super 8 Motel,
1275 US 41,
(906) 228–8100

SILVER CITY
Lake of the Clouds Lodging,
501 Lincoln Avenue,
(906) 885–5205

Mountain View Lodges,
M 107,
(906) 885–5256

**PLACES TO EAT IN THE
WESTERN UPPER PENINSULA**

BIG BAY
Thunder Bay Inn
(American),
County Road 550,
(906) 345–9376

CALUMET/LAURIUM
Toni's Country Kitchen
(American),
79 Third Street,
(906) 337–0611

COPPER HARBOR
Keweenaw Mountain Lodge
(fine dining),
US 41,
(906) 289–4403

Pines Restaurant
(American),
US 41,
(906) 289–4222

EAGLE RIVER
Fitzgerald's Restaurant
(lakeview dining),
M 26 in the
Eagle River Inn,
(906) 337–0666

HOUGHTON
Suomi Home Bakery
(Finnish),
54 North Huron Street,
(906) 482–3220

Marie's (deli),
519 Shelden Avenue,
(906) 482–8650

IRON MOUNTAIN
The Gathering Place
(bakery and cafe),
East A Street,
(906) 774–8757

Bruttomesso's (pizza),
305 North Stephenson
Avenue,
(906) 774–0801

IRON RIVER
Alice's (Italian),
420 West Adams Street,
(906) 265–4764

IRONWOOD
Mike's (American),
US 2 and Lowell Street,
(906) 932–0555

Manny's (Italian),
316 East Houk Street,
(906) 932–0999

L'ANSE
Hilltop Restaurant
(American),
US 41,
(906) 524–7858

MARQUETTE
Entre Amigos (Mexican),
124 West Washington
Boulevard,
(906) 228–4531

Sweet Water Cafe
(espresso and bakery),
517 North Third Street,
(906) 226–7009

Jean Kay's (pasties),
1639 Presque Isle,
(906) 228–5310

Landmark Inn
(fine dining),
230 North Front Street,
(800) 752–6362

Northwoods Supper Club
(fine dining),
260 Northwoods Road,
(906) 228–4343

Selected Chambers of Commerce and Tourism Bureaus

Tourist Association of Dickinson County,
P.O. Box 672, Iron Mountain 49801;
(800) 236–2447

Keweenaw Tourism Council,
1197 Calumet Avenue, Calumet 49913;
(800) 338–7982

Marquette Country Convention and Visitors Bureau,
2552 US 41 West Marquette 49855;
(800) 544–4321

Upper Peninsula Travel and Recreation Association,
P.O. Box 400, Iron Mountain 49801;
(800) 562–7134

Western U.P. Convention and Visitor's Bureau,
P.O. Box 706, Ironwood 49938;
(906) 932–4850

The Vierling Saloon
(brewpub),
119 South Front Street,
(906) 228–3533

MENOMINEE
Harbor House Gallery
(American),
1821 First Street,
(906) 863–7770

Iron Mountain Iron Mine,
Vulcan

Menominee Range
Historical Museum,
Iron Mountain

Open Pit Iron Mine,
Republic

Marquette County
Historical Museum,
Marquette

Coppertown USA,
Calumet

World's Tallest Indian,
Ironwood

Old Depot Park Museum,
Ironwood

Menominee County
Historical Museum,
Menominee

Indexes

Entries for Museums and Parks and Natural Areas appear in the special indexes beginning on page 213.

General

A

Abbott's Magic Manufacturing
   Company, 49
Ada Covered Bridge, 63
Allen, 48
Amon Orchards, 139
Antlers, The, 165
Arch Rock, 161
Argosy Rafting Adventures, Inc., 205
Au Sable Lightstation, 171

B

Backroads Bikeway, 102
Bank 1884 Restaurant, The, 37
Battle Alley, 15
Bavarian Inn, 79
Bay City City Hall, 84
Bay Port Fish Company, 39
Bay Port Fish Sandwich Day, 39
Bear Track Inn, 202
Beaver Island, 142
Bellaire Hotel, 32
Belle Isle Aquarium, 9
Big Bay Depot, 189
Big Bay Point Lighthouse, 188
Black River Harbor Drive, 201
Blaney Park, 173
Boat Night, 19
Bonnymill Inn, 78
Bortell's Fisheries, 118
Boskydel Vineyard, 135
Brenke River Sculpture and
   Fish Ladder, 60
Brockway Mountain Drive, 199
Brockway Sauna, 198
Bronner's Christmas Wonderland, 80

C

Calumet Opera House, 195
Canoe Race Monument, 86
Carl T. Johnson Hunting and
   Fishing Center, 152
Carry Nation Festival, 16
Cedar Brook Trout Farm, 86
Celibeth, 174
Chamberlin's Ole Forest Inn, 170
Charles H. Moore Public Library, 30
Château Chantal vineyard, 137
Chesaning Heritage House, 77
Chesaning Showboat Festival, 77
Cook Energy Information Center, 105
Copper Peak Ski Flying Hill, 201
Country Cupboard, The, 88
Croswell Berry Farm, 33

D

Delaware Mine, 196
Delta College Planetarium and Learn-
   ing Center, 84
Diamond Jack River Tours, 9
Dow Gardens, 83
Dow Visitors Center, 82
Dutch Village, 112

E

Eagle Harbor Lightstation, 199
Eagle's Nest Inn, 176
Eastern Market, 5
Edmund Fitzgerald, 167
Elk Viewing Sleigh Ride Dinner, 93

F

Fallasburg Covered Bridge, 63

Farm Tour, 39
Fireside Inn, 91
Fish Ladder Sculpture, 65
Fonds du Cuisine Cooking School, 146
Ford Wyoming Drive-in, 4
Francisco Morazan, 134
Frankenmuth Brewery, 79

G

Garfield Inn, 37
General Motors Lansing Car
    Assembly Plant, 62
GM Truck and Bus Assembly Plant, 74
Governor's Inn, 31
Grand Island Shipwreck Tours, 172
Grand Traverse Balloon, 136
Grant Depot Restaurant, 114
Greektown, 7
Greentop Country Village, 48
Gwen Frostic Prints, 129

H

Hathaway House, 47
Helmer House Inn, 169
Hemingway Point, 143
Hilltop Restaurant, 192
Historical Mill Creek, 148
Holly Hotel, 16
Homestead Sugar House, 131
Horton Bay General Store, 144
Hume House, 113
Huron City, 36

I

Idler, 107
Inn at Union Pier, 101
Ironton Ferry, 145

J

Japanese Cultural Center
    and Tea House, 82
John A. Lau Saloon, 90

K

Kellogg's Cereal City USA, 55
Kellogg Dairy Center, 58
Kirtland's Warbler Tour, 95
Kitch-Iti-Kipi, 176

L

Lafayette Coney Island, 7
Lake Michigan dunes, 130
LakeView Hills Country Inn, 94
Lapeer County Courthouse, 28
Legs Inn, 147
Lehto's Pasties, 159
Lindell's Chocolate Shop, 194
Lionel Train Company, 18
Litchfield Community Hand Tool
    Collection, 48
Log slide, 171

M

Mackinac Bridge, 157
Mac Wood's Dune Rides, 116
Magnolia Grille, 107
Malabar, 136
Metro Times, 8
Michigan Academy of
    Fly Fishing, 123
Michigan Library and Historical
    Center, 62
Michigan Space Center, 52
Midland Center for the Arts, 83
Miss Port Austin, 38
Mount Arvon, 192
Musical Fountain, 122

N

Nettie Bay Lodge, 92
New Hellas Cafe, 7
Northland Outfitters, 176
Northwest Soaring Club
    of Frankfort, 130

INDEXES

O

Old Home Shoppes, 77
Old Victoria, 201

P

Parlour, The, 51
Past Tense Country Store, 29
Peninsula Point Lighthouse, 179
Penny Whistle Place, 76
People Mover, 8
Petoskey stones, 141
Pictured Rocks, 172
Pictured Rock Boat Cruise, 172
Pierce Stocking Scenic Drive, 132
Point Iroquois Lightstation, 166
Polish Village Cafe, 7
Port Sanilac, 31
Port Sanilac Lighthouse, 31

Q

Quincy Mine, 194

R

Ramsdell Theatre, 122
Raymond House Inn, 32
R. Hirt Jr. Company, 6
Riverside Canoe Trips, 131
Roston Cabin, 15

S

St. Clair Art Fair, 19
St. Clair Inn, 19
St. Julian Winery, 109
Sand Dune Drive, 199
Sand Hills Lighthouse Inn, 199
Sandy Korners, 117
Shute's Bar, 196
Saugatuck Chain Ferry, 110
Sawmill Canoe Livery, 68
Soo Locks Boat Tours, 165
Squires Street Square, 67
SS *Valley Camp*, 162
Star Clipper Trains, 16

State Capitol Tour, 60
Steve's Soul Food, 7
Sugar Shack, 132
Suicide Hill Ski Jumps, 190

T

Tabor Hill Winery, 104
Thunder Bay Inn, 187
Tiffany Biergarten, 80
Townsend Hotel, 14
Toy Museum and Store, 142
"Tunnel of Trees," 147
Tridge, 83
Tristate Corner, 48
"Tunnel of Trees" Shore Drive, 147

U

Union Station, 74
University of Michigan–
    Dearborn Campus, 3
U.S. National Ski Hall of Fame, 189

V

Victorian Inn, The, 20
Vierling Saloon, The, 186

W

Warner Vineyards, 109
Whitefish Point Bird
    Observatory, 167
White Horse Inn, 27
White Pine Village, 119
White's Covered Bridge, 63
Wolf Lake State Fish Hatchery, 108
Wooden Shoe Factory, 112

Y

Yates Cider Mill, 17

Z

Zehnder's, 79

Museums

Allegan County Historical Museum, 111

Ann Arbor Hands-On Museum, 13

Cheboygan County Historical Museum, 148

Children's Museum, 75

Civilian Conservation Corps Museum, 151

Colon Community Museum, 50

Cornish Pump Engine and Mining Museum, 204

Croswell Museum, 34

Curwood Castle, 73

Dennos Museum Center, 137

Detroit Institute of Arts, 9

Dossin Great Lakes Museum, 9

1839 Courthouse, 106

Fairlane, 3

Father Marquette National Memorial, 157

Fort Mackinac, 161

Fort St. Joseph Museum, 105

Fort Wilkins, 198

Gilmore-Classic Car Club of America Museums, 58

Gerald R. Ford Museum, 63

Grand Marais Ranger Station and Maritime Museum, 170

Graystone Jazz Museum, 8

Great Lakes Shipwreck Museum, 166

Greenfield Village and Henry Ford Museum, 3

Grice Museum, 35

Hackley House, 113

Halls of Ideas, 82

Hanka Homestead, 192

H. H. Dow Museum, 82

Historical Museum of Bay County, 84

Homer Fire Museum, 53

Impression 5 Museum, 60

Iron County Museum, 203

IXL Office Museum, 206

Jesse Besser Museum, 90

Kalamazoo Aviation History Museum, 56

Kelsey Museum of Archaeology, 13

Lake Michigan Maritime Museum, 107

Lapeer Historical Society Museum, 28

Little Traverse Historical Museum, 146

Lumbermen's Monument, 85

Lyman Building, 121

Mann House, 52

Marine and Harbor Museum, 142

Marquette Maritime Museum, 185

Michigan Forest Visitor Center, 150

Michigan Iron Industry Museum, The, 189

Monroe County Historical Museum, 11

Motown Museum, 5

Murphy Museum, 35

Music House, The, 138

Old Mormon Print Shop, 142

Old Presque Isle Lighthouse, 91

Pioneer Log Cabin Village, 39

Plymouth Historical Museum, 10

Port Huron Museum of Arts and History, 20

R. E. Olds Transportation Museum, 60

River of History Museum, 163

River Raisin Battlefield Visitor Center, 12

Sanilac County Historical Museum, 31

Shrine of the Pines, 115

Sleeping Bear Point Coast Guard Station Maritime Museum, 133

Sloan Museum, 75

Sturgeon Point Lifesaving Station, 87

Three Oaks Spokes Bicycle Museum, 102

Travelers Club International Restaurant and Tuba Museum, 59

Van Andel Museum Center, 64

Walker Tavern, 45

Wright Museum of African American History, 10

Parks and Natural Places

Be Good to Your
Mother-in-Law Bridge, 34
Besser Natural Area, 90
Binder Park Zoo, 55
Bird Creek County Park, 37
Bond Falls, 201
Canyon Falls and Gorge, 190
Cascades, 50–52
Celery Flats Interpretive
Center, 57
Cut River Gorge State Park, 160
Deadman's Hill, 139
Devil's Washtub, 200
Dow Gardens, 83
"Dune Climb," 130
Fayette State Park, 178
Fisherman's Island State Park, 141
Frederik Meijer Gardens, 65
Gillette Nature Center, 113
Grand Sable Banks and Dunes, 171
Grass River Natural Area, 140
Hartwick Pines State Park, 150
Hidden Lake Gardens, 45
Huron Boardwalk, 160
Iargo Springs, 86
Lighthouse County Park, 35
Locks Park Walkway, 163
Loda Lake Wildflower Sanctuary, 114
Ludington State Park, 120
Marquette Mission Park and Huron
Boardwalk, 160
Marshland Wildlife Drive, 175
Maybury State Park, 10
Mill Creek Historical State Park, 149
Mount Baldhead Park, 110
Munising Falls, 172

Muskallonge Lake State Park, 170
Negwegon State Park, 89
New Presque Isle Lighthouse Park, 91
Nordhouse Dunes, 120
Oval Beach, 110
Palmer Park, 19
Père Marquette Rail-Trail, 81
Pierce Stocking Scenic Drive, 132
Piers Gorge, 205
Pigeon River Country State Forest, 149
Pinckney Recreation Area, 13
Platte River Point, 130
Porcupine Mountains
Wilderness State Park, 200
Portage Bay State
Campground, 178
Port Crescent State Park, 38
Presque Isle Park, 185
River Trail, 59
Roadside Table, The, 64
Sanilac Historical Site, 33
Seney National Wildlife Refuge, 174
Shiawassee National Wildlife
Refuge, 80
Silver Lake State Park, 116
Silver Mountain, 193
Sleeping Bear National
Lakeshore, 130
Soo Lock Park, 163
South Manitou Island, 134
Sturgeon River Gorge Area, 193
Sugar Loaf Recreational Trail, 187
Tahquamenon Falls, 168
Warren Dunes State Park, 103
Windmill Island, 112
Wolcott Mill Metropark, 18

Help Us Keep This Guide Up to Date

Every effort has been made by the author and editors to make this guide as accurate and useful as possible. However, many things can change after a guide is published—establishments close, phone numbers change, and facilities come under new management.

We would love to hear from you concerning your experiences with this guide and how you feel it could be improved and be kept up to date. While we may not be able to respond to all comments and suggestions, we'll take them to heart and we'll also make certain to share them with the author. Please send your comments and suggestions to the following address:

The Globe Pequot Press
Reader Response/Editorial Department
P.O. Box 480
Guilford, CT 06437

Or you may e-mail us at:
editorial@globe-pequot.com

Thanks for your input, and happy travels!

About the Author

Jim DuFresne is a Detroit-based travel and outdoor writer whose syndiated columns, "Travels in Michigan" and "Kidventures," appear in daily newspapers across the state. Formerly a sports and outdoors editor for the Juneau Empire in Alaska, DuFresne published his first travel book, *Tramping in New Zealand*, in 1982. His other books include *Isle Royale National Park; Voyageurs National Park; Alaska: A Travel Survival Kit; Glacier Bay National Park: A Backcountry Guide to the Glaciers and Beyond; Michigan State Parks;* and *Michigan's Best Outdoor Adventures with Children.*